PENGUIN BOOKS

Midnight in Peking

Born in London and educated there and in Glasgow, Paul French has lived and worked in Shanghai for many years. He is a widely published analyst and commentator on China and has written a number of books including a history of foreign correspondents in China and a biography of the legendary Shanghai adman, journalist, and adventurer Carl Crow. *Midnight in Peking* was a *New York Times* bestseller, BBC Radio 4 Book of the Week, an Edgar nominee, and will be made into an international miniseries by Kudos Film and Television.

Midnight in Peking

How the Murder of
a Young Englishwoman
Haunted the Last Days of Old China

PAUL FRENCH

PENGUIN BOOKS

PENGUIN BOOKS
Published by the Penguin Group
Penguin Group (USA) Inc., 375 Hudson Street,
New York, New York 10014, USA

USA | Canada | UK | Ireland | Australia | New Zealand | India | South Africa | China
Penguin Books Ltd, Registered Offices: 80 Strand, London WC2R 0RL, England
For more information about the Penguin Group visit penguin.com

First published in Australia by Viking, an imprint of Penguin Group (Australia) 2011
This revised edition published in Penguin Books 2012
Published in Penguin Books 2013

Map: National Library of Australia (MAP G7824.B4 1936)

THE LIBRARY OF CONGRESS HAS CATALOGED THE HARDCOVER EDITION AS FOLLOWS:
French, Paul, 1966–
Midnight in Peking : how the murder of a young Englishwoman
haunted the last days of old China / Paul French.
p. cm.
ISBN 978-0-14-312100-8 (hc.)
ISBN 978-0-14-312336-1 (pbk.)
1. Murder—China—Beijing—Case studies.   2. Beijing (China)—
History—20th century.   I. Title.
HV6535.C43F74 2012
364.152'3092—dc23   2012001874

Printed in the United States of America
1   3   5   7   9   10   8   6   4   2

Set in Bembo
Designed by Elke Sigal

For the innocent

For Pamela

The north wind came in the night, ice covers the waters:
Once our young sister has gone she will never return
   —TRADITIONAL SONG OF THE CANAL PEOPLE OF NORTHERN CHINA

Cut is the branch that might have grown full straight
   —CHRISTOPHER MARLOWE, *Doctor Faustus*

The belief in a supernatural source of evil is not necessary;
men alone are quite capable of every wickedness
   —JOSEPH CONRAD, *Under Western Eyes*

Contents

Contents

By day the fox spirits of Peking lie hidden and still. But at night they roam restlessly through the cemeteries and burial grounds of the long dead, exhuming bodies and balancing the skulls upon their heads. They must then bow reverentially to Tou Mu, the Goddess of the North Star, who controls the books of life and death that contain the ancient celestial mysteries of longevity and immortality. If the skulls do not topple and fall, then the fox spirits—or huli jing, 狐狸精*—will live for ten centuries and must seek victims to nourish themselves, replenishing their energy through trickery and connivance, preying upon innocent mortals. Having lured their chosen victims, they simply love them to death. They then strike their tails to the ground to produce fire and disappear, leaving only a corpse behind them . . .*

The Approaching Storm

*T*he eastern section of old Peking has been dominated since the fifteenth century by a looming watchtower, built as part of the Tartar Wall to protect the city from invaders. Known as the Fox Tower, it was believed to be haunted by fox spirits, a superstition that meant the place was deserted at night.

After dark the area became the preserve of thousands of bats, which lived in the eaves of the Fox Tower and flitted across the moonlight like giant shadows. The only other living presence was the wild dogs, whose howling kept the locals awake. On winter mornings the wind stung exposed hands and eyes, carrying dust from the nearby Gobi Desert. Few people ventured out early at this time of year, opting instead for the warmth of their beds.

But just before dawn on 8 January 1937, rickshaw pullers passing along the top of the Tartar Wall, which was wide enough to walk or cycle on, noticed lantern lights near the base of the Fox Tower, and indistinct figures moving about. With neither the time nor the inclination to stop, they went about their business, heads down, one foot in front of the other, avoiding the fox spirits.

When daylight broke on another freezing day, the tower was deserted once more. The colony of bats circled one last time before the creeping sun sent them back to their eaves. But in the icy wasteland between the road and the tower, the wild dogs—the *huang gou*—were prowling curiously, sniffing at something alongside a ditch.

It was the body of a young woman, lying at an odd angle and covered by a layer of frost. Her clothing was dishevelled, her body badly mutilated. On her wrist was an expensive watch that had stopped just after midnight.

It was the morning after the Russian Christmas, thirteen days after the Western Christmas by the old Julian calendar.

Peking at that time had a population of some one and a half million, of which only two thousand, perhaps three, were foreigners. They were a disparate group, ranging from stiff-backed consuls and their diplomatic staff to destitute White Russians. The latter, having fled their homeland to escape the Bolsheviks and revolution, were now officially stateless. In between were journalists, a few businessmen, some old China hands who'd lived in Peking since the days of the Qing dynasty and felt they could never leave. There was the odd world traveller taking a prolonged sojourn from a grand tour of the Orient, who'd come for a fortnight and lingered on for years, as well as refugees from the Great Depression in Europe and America, seeking opportunity and adventure. And there was no shortage of foreign criminals, dope fiends and prostitutes who'd somehow washed up in northern China.

Peking's foreigners clustered in and around a small enclave known as the Legation Quarter, where the great powers of Europe, America and Japan had their embassies and consulates—institutions that were always referred to as legations. Just two square acres in size, the strictly demarcated Legation Quarter was guarded by imposing gates and armed sentries, with signs ordering rickshaw pullers to slow down for inspection as they passed through. Inside was a haven of Western architecture, commerce and entertainment—a profusion of clubs, hotels and bars that could just as easily have been in London, Paris or Washington.

Both the Chinese and foreigners of Peking had been living with chaos and uncertainty for a long time. Ever since the downfall of the Qing dynasty in 1911, the city had been at the mercy of one marauding warlord after another. Nominally China was ruled by the Kuomintang, or Nationalist Party, under the leadership of Chiang Kai-shek, but the government competed for power with the warlords and their private armies, who controlled swathes of territory as large as western Europe. Peking and most of northern China was a region in flux.

Between 1916 and 1928 alone, no fewer than seven warlord rulers came and went in Peking. On conquering the city, each sought to outdo the last, with more elaborate uniforms, more ermine and braid. All fancied themselves emperors, founders of new dynasties, and all commanded substantial private armies. One of them, Cao Kun, had bribed his way to supremacy, paying officials large amounts in stolen silver dollars, since no official in China at that time trusted paper money. Another, Feng Kuo-chang, had been a violin player in brothels before illegally declaring himself president of all China. They and their ilk terrorised the city as they bled it dry.

Peking was certainly a prize. It was China's richest city after Shanghai and Tientsin. Unlike those two, however, Peking was not a treaty port—those places seized from the Qing dynasty by European powers in the nineteenth century. There foreigners governed themselves, and built trading empires backed by their own police forces, armies and navies. Peking was, at least for now, Chinese territory.

But it was no longer the capital, and had not been since 1927. In that year, Generalissimo Chiang Kai-shek, unable to pacify the northern warlords and struggling to cement his fragile leadership of the Kuomintang, had moved the seat of government to Nanking, some seven hundred miles south. From there he launched the Northern Expedition, a military campaign that attempted to wipe out both the warlords and the nascent but troublesome Communist Party, and unite China under his rule. He was only partially successful. Peking was run by the Hopei-Chahar Political Council, led by General Sung Cheh-yuan, commander of the Kuomintang's Twenty-Ninth Route Army. General Sung, who had a formidable reputation for soldiering, remained loyal to the Nanking government even after the arrival of a new player in the struggle to control China: Japan.

In 1931, under the guise of their long-dreamt-of Greater East Asia Co-Prosperity Sphere, the Japanese invaded Manchuria, in China's northeast. They then set about bolstering the region with troops in preparation for an advance south to capture the whole country. But there were constant skirmishes with Chinese peasants, who were resisting the theft of their lands. Even farther north, Japanese agents provocateurs were stirring up anti-Chinese feeling in Mongolia.

General Sung paid lip service to the Japanese while resisting their demands to cede the city, but his council was too weak and corrupt to stave off the encroachment of enemy troops. These steadily encircled Peking, and by the start of 1937 had established their base camp a matter of miles from the Forbidden City. Acts of provocation occurred daily, and the roads and train lines into and out of the city were disrupted. Japanese thugs for hire, known as *ronin,* openly brought opium and heroin into Peking through Manchuria. This was done with Tokyo's connivance and was part of an effort to sap Peking's will to fight. The *ronin,* their agents and Korean collaborators peddled the subsidized narcotics in Peking's Badlands, a cluster of dive bars, brothels and opium dens a stone's throw from the base of the foreign powers in the Legation Quarter.

Whatever the ferocity of the storm building outside—in Chinese Peking, in the Japanese-occupied north, across China and its 400 million people to the south—the privileged foreigners in the Legation Quarter sought to maintain their European face at all costs. Officially, Chinese could not take up residence in the Quarter, although in 1911 many rich eunuchs—former servants to the emperors and empresses who had been thrown out of the Forbidden City after the collapse of the Qing dynasty—had moved in. They were followed by warlords in the 1920s.

More than a few foreign residents of the Legation Quarter in its heyday described themselves as inmates, but if this gated and guarded section was indeed a cage, then it was a gilded one, with endless games of bridge to pass the time. Sandwiched between the legations were exclusive clubs, grand hotels and department stores. There was a French post office, and the great buildings of the Yokohama Specie Bank, the Banque de l'Indochine, the Russo-Asiatic Bank, and the Hong Kong and Shanghai Bank.

It was Europe in miniature, with European road names and electric streetlights. St Michael's Catholic Church dominated the corner of rue Marco Polo and Legation Street, and the latter was also home to the German hospital, where the nurses, Lazarene nuns, served *kaffee und kuchen* to their privileged patients. Residents of European-style apartment buildings went shopping at Kierulff's general store, which sold perfume, canned foods and coffee. Sennet Frères had a reputation as the best jewelers in northern China, and Hartung's was the leading photography studio and the first to have been established in Peking, while a Frenchman ran a bookshop and another a bakery. On Morrison Street (named after George Morrison—'Morrison of Peking,' the thundering voice of the *Times* of London in China) there was an English tailor and an Italian who sold wine and confectionery. White Russian beauticians staffed La Violette, the quarter's premier beauty parlour. There was also a foreign police force, and garrisons for the five hundred or so foreign troops stationed in Peking.

Eight gateways, each with massive iron gates, marked the entrances to the Quarter and were manned by armed guards day and night. Chinese needed a special pass or a letter of introduction to enter this inner sanctum. Rickshaw pullers had their license numbers taken and had to leave immediately after they'd dropped off their fare. At the first sign of trouble in Chinese Peking, the gates to the Quarter were slammed shut—there would be no repeat of the deadly siege that had occurred during the Boxer uprising.

The memory of the Boxers still loomed large over the Legation Quarter. In 1900 the Society of the Righteous and Harmonious Fists, dubbed the Boxers, had swarmed down on the Quarter, intending to massacre all the *yang guizi*—foreign devils—in the capital, and show that China could fight back against Western encroachment and gunships.

They had already beheaded missionaries working in remote outposts, and as they approached Peking, their numbers swelled, thanks in part to the rumours that they possessed magical fighting skills, and that bullets could not harm them.

The Boxers held the foreign community under siege within the Legation Quarter for fifty-five days. They lit fires around the outskirts, fired cannons into the legations and tried to starve the inhabitants into submission. Eventually the siege was lifted by a joint force of eight foreign armies, including those of Britain, America and Japan. After liberating the Quarter, these troops went on a horrific looting spree, rampaging throughout the city, terrorizing all Peking. With seized Chinese money, the Quarter was rebuilt grander than ever and was now far better protected.

Whereas to most Chinese the Quarter was a second Forbidden City, to the foreigners living there in the 1930s it was a sanctuary, even if in their claustrophobic confines they sometimes felt, as one visiting journalist remarked, like 'fish in an aquarium,' going 'round and round . . . serene and glassy-eyed.'

Rumour was the currency of the quarter. Conversations that started with who had the best chef and who was about to depart for home on a long-awaited furlough soon degenerated into who had commenced an affair with whom at the races, whose wife was a little too close to a guardsman at the legation. Sometimes darker things were hinted at, things beyond the normal indiscretions. Some people lost their moral compass in the East, or so the thinking went.

And there were plenty of places to spread rumours. The exclusive clubs and bars were hotbeds of intrigue and gossip. In the stuffy and very British Peking Club, it was black tie only. Whisky sodas were dispensed on trays by silent servants, the cacophony outside in Chinese Peking held at bay by windows covered with thick velvet curtains, and there were two-month-old copies of the *Times* and the *Pall Mall Gazette* on offer. In the swanky bar of the Grand Hôtel de Pékin, a respectable crowd sipped fancy drinks and twirled to an all-Italian band playing waltzes.

The more risqué Hôtel du Nord, on the edge of the Badlands, had a crowded bar that served draught beer, fashionable Horse's Neck cocktails and dry gin martinis. Here the patrons were more rambunctious—the polite word was 'mixed'—and they foxtrotted to jazz courtesy of a band of White Russians. And then there was the Grand Hôtel des Wagons Lits.

The Wagons Lits was a large, French-style hotel just inside the Quarter at the junction of Legation and Canal streets. Close to the city's main railway station, it was a popular meeting spot. The bar was famous for its diplomatic clientele during the day and bright young things later at night. A sprinkling of connected Chinese sometimes joined the crowd, as did the children of wealthy local businessmen who'd just returned from Paris or London. The Wagons Lits had always been a place to loosen tongues. There were tables to be had away from the dance floor, away from the band that strummed lightly for the mix of guests. This was the spot to meet the knowledgeable and opinionated old China hands.

But lately the once-packed hotels and clubs had been a little somber, and sometimes they were half empty. In truth, the Wagons Lits and other night spots were out of date. Shanghai had better bars, had much better everything. Peking was a relic, a onetime capital that was now far too close to the Japanese war machine. The city, its foreigners and their clubs were victims of history and geography.

These days, rickshaw pullers waited outside the exclusive Peking Club for well-heeled guests who never emerged, having never arrived. The diplomats and the old China hands stayed on, sticking their heads in the sand and hoping that both the Nationalist republic and the Japanese would go away, but the legations operated with reduced staff. Those foreigners who could were getting out: businessmen sent their wives and children home, or to the relative calm of Tientsin or Shanghai. Wealthy Chinese had their families go south to Canton or the British colony of Hong Kong. Peking was already lost ground; it was just that the Japanese hadn't got around to taking it yet.

To make matters worse, rumour had it that Chiang Kai-shek was about to cut a deal with Tokyo. Chiang had fought a long and bitter internecine battle to become leader of the Kuomintang, and his position was still precarious; he had political challengers to stave off as well as the Japanese, the warlords and the Communists. Many people believed he would sacrifice Peking in order to save his own skin: if the Japanese were to stop at the Yangtze River and leave him everything south as far as Hong Kong, Chiang could live with that. Chiang was finished with the north, the Chinese whispered—for you never knew who was listening—he would sell out Peking, and the Japs would massacre them all.

The city's inhabitants felt betrayed, expendable. The mood on the streets, of both foreign and Chinese Peking—in the crowded *hutong* (alleyways), in the teeming markets where prices were rising and supplies of essentials were dwindling—was one of fear mixed with resignation. People said that when the final push to conquer China came, the Japanese would starve the city into submission. The end was coming; it was just a question of when. The traditional trade routes into Peking from China's vast hinterlands were already being cut off. Chinese Peking was bursting with peasants who had crowded in from the surrounding provinces, fleeing the Japanese, the warlords, poverty and natural disasters. They wandered aimlessly, wondering what tomorrow would bring. They went to bed early in crammed houses to escape the dark and the biting cold, hoping to make it through another day.

When the catastrophe did finally hit, China would be thrown into a struggle for its very survival, in what would be the opening act of World War II. For now foreign Peking was in an uneasy lull, on the edge of panic at times, although an alcohol-assisted denial and the strength of the silver dollar made life more bearable for many. An American or a European could still live like a king in this city, with a life of servants, golf, races, champagne-fuelled weekend retreats in the Western Hills. The storm might be coming, but the last foreigners in Peking had battened down the hatches very comfortably.

The hunt for a young woman's killer was about to consume, and in some ways define, the cold and final days of old Peking.

The Body at the Fox Tower

$\mathcal{I}$t was an old man named Chang Pao-chen who reported the body. One of the *laobaixing*—literally, the 'old hundred names,' the working people of Peking—Chang was now retired and lived in a *hutong* not far from the Fox Tower. On that cold morning of Friday 8 January, he was taking his prized songbird for a walk along the Tartar Wall.

Caged songbirds were an ancient Peking tradition, and every morning old men like Chang could be seen carrying lacquered wooden cages draped with blue linen covers. All Pekingers, Chinese and foreign, recognized the distinctive sound of these swallows, which were let out of their cages with flutes attached to their tails to go whistling through the morning air, soaring across the Forbidden City and the Fox Tower before faithfully returning to their masters. Chang came to the Tartar Wall every day to smoke, drink tea and talk songbirds. The cold didn't deter him, nor the strong, bone-chilling winds. He was a Pekinger born and bred.

That morning, shortly after eight o'clock, he was following the Tartar Wall eastwards to the Fox Tower when he noticed two rickshaw pullers squatting below, pointing across the wasteland towards the rubbish-strewn moat at the base of the tower. The area was invariably quiet at that hour, and whatever was down there couldn't be seen by the traffic using the City Road, which ran parallel to the wall from the Fox Tower down to the Ch'ienmen Gate.

Chang drew closer, wary of the *huang gou*, but while the scabrous mutts had a fearsome reputation, the old man knew they rarely attacked humans. Like many a poor Pekinger, the dogs were hungry, homeless and desperate, as Tokyo increasingly choked off food supplies and commerce.

Later, what Chang saw was disputed as the local rumour mill swung into action, exaggerating the scene with each telling and re-telling. But there was no doubting that the woman he found at the base of the Fox Tower was dead, and not just any woman, but a foreigner. A *laowai*. Moreover she had been terribly mutilated. Even in the early-morning half-light Chang could see that the woman's body had been badly beaten. He could see cut marks on her pale, bare legs; her face appeared to have been stabbed repeatedly.

Old Chang was shocked, even though dead bodies in the open weren't rare that winter. Poverty was one cause, but suicide had become almost an epidemic, with slashed wrists or opium the most common routes. Every daybreak the city sent out carts to collect frozen corpses.

There'd also been a rise in politically motivated murders. The Kuomintang's enforcers and secret police clashed with turncoat Chinese, those who believed that Tokyo would inevitably crush Nanking as well as Peking, and were keen to be in a position to profit early from the occupation. There were also shootouts between rival factions, and outrages committed by Japanese *ronin* and their Korean allies from the north.

Old Chang hadn't come across such a corpse personally. As a younger man he'd seen the city ravaged and looted by the foreign armies that had come to rout the Boxer rebels, and then, in the 1920s, he'd seen the heads of warlords' victims on display. Now there was another war of sorts under way in Peking, between the Nationalists, the Communists and the Japanese agents—the papers were full of it every day. But a dead white woman, that was something else. Dead foreigners were altogether a rarer phenomenon.

Old Chang remembered that on a cold winter's night in 1935 a White Russian émigré had walked to the Fox Tower and taken from his threadbare coat an exquisite, ivory-handled cutthroat razor. He had rolled up his sleeves and slashed both his wrists, slumping to the ground by the tower wall as the life slowly drained out of him. He had been found in the morning by passing rickshaw pullers.

Was this another suicide? It didn't look like it, and whatever it was, it wasn't good. With his caged songbird, old Chang ran back along the Tartar Wall to the nearest police box, as fast as his aged legs would carry him.

The Police of Peking

*O*utside the foreign-controlled Legation Quarter, law and order was maintained through a series of manned police boxes at major intersections. The system was modeled on the one used in Japan, which itself had been borrowed from the Prussians. The police boxes, marked with an **X**, were equipped with telephones. In theory this meant that an officer was never far away.

On that cold January morning, the closest box to old Chang was near the Hatamen train station, about a quarter of a mile westward along the Tartar Wall. It was manned by young Corporal Kao Tao-hung, and an older veteran of the Peking force, Constable Hsu Teng-chen. They were nearing the end of their shift, and Constable Hsu was huddled by a charcoal brazier. When he saw the old man coming, he wondered what was about to disturb his morning, but he wasn't overly concerned; he knew old Chang and regularly saw him out walking with his birds.

But once a breathless Chang reported what he'd found, Constable Hsu donned his cap and greatcoat, got his bicycle and cycled quickly along the Tartar Wall to the Fox Tower. The two rickshaw pullers were still there, but as soon as they saw the police uniform they ran away, disappearing across the road and into the teeming alleys of the Tartar City.

Hsu knew immediately that the situation was more than he could cope with. He rode back to the police box, meeting Corporal Kao halfway along the Tartar Wall. Kao told him to return to the tower and stand guard over the body, chasing off any scavenging *huang gou*. He was not to let anyone touch the girl. Kao then went back to the police box to telephone for help. There he also told a third officer, a young constable, to find some bamboo matting to secure the crime scene and prevent any evidence being obscured by the churning of the muddy ground. Then Corporal Kao hurried once more to the Fox Tower, where he noted down everything he could see for the record.

Amid the horror of the scene—the mutilation, the torn clothing—Kao was intrigued for a moment by the woman's wristwatch. It was clearly a luxury item, and yet it hadn't been taken.

But he knew better than to disturb a murder scene any more than was necessary, and this clearly wasn't a simple robbery. Moreover this was no ordinary person; it was a *laowai*, which meant trouble, and a lot of paperwork. There would be pressure from above for results—failing to solve the crime would mean a massive loss of face before the foreigners.

狐 狸 精

Corporal Kao's request for assistance had been referred to the detective section of the Peking Bureau of Public Safety, South East Section, on Morrison Street. There Colonel Han Shih-ching was coming to the end of a long night shift and awaiting his replacement. Han was an experienced detective who'd trained at Peking's police academy, and who now commanded a sizeable portion of the city's ten thousand constables. He was not only the chief of the Morrison Street Detective Bureau, but also chief of police for the South East Section (First District) of Peking, and he'd had a busy night.

General Sung's political council had ordered a crackdown on

Japanese and Korean dope peddling, with an instant death penalty for dealers and either execution or life imprisonment for addicts. Han and his plainclothesmen had been out all night busting drug dens across the Tartar City and the Badlands. More than twenty dealers and addicts had been taken to the execution grounds on the edge of the city to be publicly shot alongside a burning pile of seized opium, in order to be made an example of.

After his hard night, Colonel Han was sipping cups of tea and smoking his strong local Hatamen brand cigarettes as he caught up on administrative matters. As of February, the Peking Bureau of Public Safety was to become the Peking Police Bureau, by official Nanking order. It was a simple enough name change, but it generated mountains of paperwork.

From time to time Han got up and wandered round the station, stretching his legs and seeing if any further word had come through about the night's catch of addicts and dealers. Since there'd been an outcry over the executions of Chinese, the word was that General Sung would carry on executing the Korean thugs, probably expel the Japanese *ronin* from the city so as not to antagonise Tokyo, and commute all sentences for the Chinese addicts to life imprisonment.

On one of his leg-stretching rounds, Han stopped to chat with the desk sergeant about the deteriorating political situation. It was all anyone talked about now. What would Chiang Kai-shek do about the increasingly belligerent Japanese? How would General Sung protect the city? What of all these assassinations and agents provocateurs? The Japanese tiger was waiting to pounce. Or perhaps the Japanese were more like hyenas: 'dwarf bandits' was the local slang for them.

Han was back in his office once more when the desk sergeant brought in Corporal Kao to present the case of the dead girl at the Fox Tower, a *laowai* with terrible injuries. As the senior detective at the station closest to the Legation Quarter, Han had dealt with dead foreigners before—brawling marines from the legation guards who'd ended up with a knife in their guts, or penniless White Russians who'd frozen to death in an alleyway, having nowhere to go. Foreign

Peking had been a safe place in the 1920s, but with the influx of the White Russians—well, things had deteriorated. Their skin-and-bone corpses, often dressed in nothing but rags and with not much to distinguish them from the impoverished rickshaw pullers, were sent to the now overcrowded Russian cemetery.

Han assumed this girl was another poor Russian, who had perhaps been cast out and decided that death was preferable to the shame of selling her body. Still, any dead foreigner was a difficult case. White skin meant questions—questions that would be asked by powerful people, and asked repeatedly until answers were provided. The Fox Tower was outside the Legation Quarter, but only just, and the body would need identifying as soon as possible. Sometimes relations between the Chinese police and the Legation Quarter police were fractious, but Han was a courteous man who did things by the book. Covering your back was an art you needed to master to survive in turbulent times.

Han ordered young Corporal Kao to take all the available men in the station back to the crime scene, and then he telephoned Commissioner W. P. Thomas of the Legation Quarter Administration and told him there was a dead foreigner at the base of the Fox Tower. It was outside legation territory, but perhaps the commissioner would like to attend and help identify the body? As a courtesy among officials? Thomas agreed to meet at the tower, bringing some of his men.

Colonel Han ground out his cigarette, put on his greatcoat, cap and gloves, and set off on the short walk to the Tower. He headed across Chang'an Avenue and through the imposing stone gates that marked the northern boundary of the Legation Quarter—these were in the style of a European castle but were manned by Chinese soldiers. He crossed the quarter to the Tartar Wall on the southern side, feeling like he was in foreign territory, and continued east. Where the ancient wall skirted the notorious Badlands it was poorly tended, but the sections that ran by the Quarter were in better condition, accessible from wide, street-level ramps and affording a good view across the low-level city.

Han passed through the wall at a small stone bridge and walked on to the Fox Tower. By the time he reached it a sizeable crowd of Chinese onlookers had gathered; the news had spread among the surrounding *hutong* as the city came to life. It didn't take much to get curious Pekingers to stop and watch something on the street, and a dead body certainly counted as a reason.

Corporal Kao and the men from Morrison Street had formed a ring around the corpse to stop the sticky-beaks getting too close. Some curious locals, taking up the traditional Peking pastime of poking fun at officialdom, jeered the police and had to be chased off.

Shortly afterwards, Commissioner Thomas and his Legation Quarter policemen arrived. Corporal Kao removed the straw matting used to keep the body from prying eyes, and Han and Thomas bent down to examine it.

The girl was lying by the ditch with her head to the west and her feet to the east, partially clothed in a tartan skirt and a bloodied woolen cardigan. Her shoes, into one of which a handkerchief had been stuffed, were lying some distance away.

Han pulled the skirt down to cover the girl's bare thighs. It was hard to tell from the features of her brutally stabbed and beaten face whether she was foreign or Chinese; instead, her fair hair and white skin identified her race. The two men lifted the body slightly, and Thomas pulled out a silk chemise from where it had been shoved beneath her. They could see that the girl had been cut and slashed everywhere. The knife cuts were deep, and Han and Thomas wondered whether some of the other marks were from *huang gou* tearing at her flesh during the night.

Colonel Han opened the cardigan and removed a piece of a woven cotton Aertex blouse to examine the cuts on the chest. As he did, both he and Thomas jumped to their feet in shock. The entire sternum of the corpse had been cut open and all the ribs broken, exposing the interior body cavity. The smell it gave off was strong, but the corpse was strangely bloodless. Nor was there blood on the ground, which was hard from the night's frost; the blood had to have drained away somewhere.

Both men had seen plenty of dead and mutilated bodies. Both had seen action in various wars—Han with the warlords of northern China and Thomas as a young student interpreter with the British Legation during the Boxers' murderous siege in 1900. But now they looked at each other with a realization too horrible to utter. Her heart was missing; it had been ripped out through her broken rib cage.

Han replaced the cotton material, covered the body again with the straw matting, and ordered his men to move the crowd farther back. This was not a sight for the public.

Next Han removed the expensive wristwatch: platinum with diamond settings. So this wasn't just another poor White Russian—but who was she? There were no other belongings, no purse; but, lying a short distance from the body, the men found a blood-spattered membership card for the French Club ice-skating rink. Han had it photographed before picking it up and slipping it into a manila envelope to enter as evidence.

Just then an elderly white man pushed his way through the crowd. He was wearing dark glasses, which he pulled off as he elbowed his way to the front. A crazed look came over his face and he screamed a single word, '*Pamela!*' Then he put his hand to his mouth and cried out, before collapsing in a heap on the ground.

狐狸精

At three o'clock the afternoon before, E. T. C. Werner had headed out for one of his walks across the city. He loved to stretch his legs after a morning spent on historical research and his routine correspondence.

His daughter was sitting at a desk by a window, writing letters. She told him she was going out shortly to meet an old school friend; they were taking tea together and then going ice-skating. She would be back home by seven thirty and would have dinner with her father as usual.

Werner returned from his walk before dark and finished some scholarly work. At seven thirty Pamela hadn't returned, but for a while he didn't worry. She was with friends, she knew Peking, and anyway the skating rink was barely a mile away, in the safety of the Legation Quarter. But when she still wasn't back an hour later, he started to fret. Why had she not telephoned to say she would be late?

By nine o'clock Werner was becoming seriously concerned, and then infuriated with Pamela for not calling to let him know where she was. His daughter wasn't always reliable, it was true, and her adolescence hadn't been easy, but going away to school in Tientsin seemed to have instilled some discipline in her. It was just a shame that things had gone wrong there as well, for different reasons. But she'd been enjoying herself back in Peking for the Christmas holidays, running around the city meeting old friends, dating and ice-skating, and spending time with her father. The two of them were preparing to leave for England in a few months, and so much still remained to be done before their departure.

At ten o'clock Werner could pace his study no longer. He wrapped himself up in his thick gabardine coat, grabbed a kerosene-fuelled storm lantern to light his way in the pitch-black night and headed out to look for her.

Peking was a city that retired early. In winter the streets of the Tartar City were virtually deserted by nine, the shops shut, the street hawkers gone and most sensible people home in bed. Outside the Legation Quarter, streetlights were infrequent, motorized taxis and rickshaws rare. Only the hardiest and most financially needy of the pullers were willing to ferry the night owls home from the bars and nightclubs, and the dens of the Badlands.

At seventy-two, Werner prided himself on his robust constitution. He walked briskly to the Legation Quarter, whose wide streets he knew well, found the house he was looking for, and banged on the door. Pamela's friend had returned home around eight o'clock, he learned from the girl's parents, who then tried to reassure him. Pamela must have bumped into an old acquaintance, got chatting and forgotten the time. He should just return home, and she'd surely be there waiting, sorry for the trouble she'd caused.

Werner did go home, but Pamela wasn't there, nor had she

telephoned. The cook, the amah, and the number-one boy were all waiting up, anxious themselves now. Werner sent the cook off to the skating rink, but it was closed, swathed in darkness for the night. He went back to Armour Factory Alley to tell Werner, who headed out to search again, this time taking an electric torch.

Around three a.m., he stopped at the office of Commissioner Thomas, an old acquaintance, but the bureaucrat was off duty and home asleep. Werner left him a note saying that Pamela hadn't returned home, that he was worried and had gone looking for her. Then he continued to tramp the streets of Peking, from the far east of the city to the far west. He went south as far as the Temple of Heaven, back through the Legation Quarter once more, then north to the Lama Temple, where monks from Tibet congregated. He passed the Confucian Hall of Examinations, where those hoping to enter the Imperial Civil Service had once anxiously awaited the results of their tests, and the Mohammedan Mosque on Cow Street, where Muslims from western China clustered in their communities. Then the Portuguese Church, from whose orphanage Pamela had been adopted. He walked for miles in the darkness.

In the silence, he could hear the kettledrum sound the hours at the Meridian Gate near the Forbidden City, as it had done for centuries. At the gates of courtyard houses, night watchmen struck clappers and cymbals to scare away evil spirits. They did this on the Chinese double hour, which was twice as long as a Western hour, and the cymbal clash lengthened as the hours passed to daylight. Finally Werner returned home, seeking news and needing rest.

As dawn broke, bringing the city slowly back to life on another cold January day, Werner left Armour Factory Alley once more. He was distraught by now, wandering helplessly through eastern Peking again, amid the heavy wooden carts that brought sacks of freshly ground flour to make *bing*, the city's traditional breakfast of unleavened wheaten cakes. He found himself back at the edge of the Legation Quarter, following the ancient Tartar Wall towards the looming fifty-foot walls of the Fox Tower.

As he neared the tower, thinking to skirt the railway arch where the train line began at its base and head to the Quarter to find Commissioner Thomas, he saw a crowd gathered. Werner rushed forward, propelled by instinct and a sense of doom.

He saw Colonel Han, whom he knew by reputation, and Commissioner Thomas, and the other policemen and photographers, all of them gathered around a corpse. He only needed to see the fair hair and clothing to know who it was.

狐 狸 精

Edward Theodore Chalmers Werner and his daughter lived in a traditional Chinese courtyard house on a *hutong* in Peking's Tartar City, just outside the Legation Quarter. No one watching them go about their lives at the start of 1937 would have gained the impression that China was tottering on the edge of a precipice. Their daily routine appeared comfortable and privileged, based more around English than Chinese traditions even though Werner, a widower, had chosen to avoid the overtly European world of the Legation Quarter.

In a city with plenty of old China hands, Werner was perhaps the most notable, having lived and worked in China since the 1880s. As a scholar and a former British consul, his life story was well known. His books were widely read and translated, his complex but highly regarded lectures to the Royal Asiatic Society and the Things Chinese Society well attended. He also wrote articles on Chinese culture, tradition and history for the local newspapers, and his experience and learning might have made him a much-sought-after dinner guest. But he rarely, if ever, accepted, preferring a solitary and scholarly life.

These days Werner had a post at Peking University, where he lectured occasionally, and he also sat as the only foreigner on the Chinese government's Historiographical Bureau. But mainly he worked from home, at his house at 1 Armour Factory Alley, in the shadow of the Fox Tower, from which it was separated only by an old canal and its population of noisy ducks. Once part of China's Grand Canal, it was now too silted up to allow the grain barges to transit, and had become a fetid rubbish dump.

Armour Factory Alley, known as Kuei Chia Chang by the Chinese, was close to the old imperial examination halls and a number of papermaking factories, small family businesses that had given the warren of lanes squeezed under the Tartar Wall the name of the Papermakers' District. The alley was lined with plane trees, and during the day it witnessed a constant procession, beginning with bird fanciers strolling with their covered cages, then street hawkers calling out their services, house staff carrying food back from the markets, people coming and going by taxi and rickshaw, and, finally, late-night sellers of snacks. It was a street that could have existed only in Peking, and one that dated back more than a thousand years.

It had become increasingly common for foreigners to reside outside the Legation Quarter. Landlords had fixed up premises to allow their tenants to live in the Chinese style but with modern conveniences. And a growing number simply couldn't afford to live in the Quarter, such as the White Russians who'd fled the Soviet Union and subsequently moved down from Harbin or other cities in northern China that had fallen under Japanese occupation. There'd also been a more recent influx of European Jews escaping persecution in Nazi Germany.

Though the bulk of these exiles headed for Shanghai, Peking was also seeing their numbers rise, and many were semi-destitute, forced to live in run-down lodging houses in the sprawling, often malodorous Tartar City, or around the fringes of the Badlands. They found work as doormen, barmen, croupiers, prostitutes and pimps, or survived by begging. The European community and the authorities in the Legation Quarter largely chose to ignore them; these low-life foreigners were considered a threat to white prestige in Peking, and it was hoped they'd move on to Shanghai.

Armour Factory Alley, although in the Tartar City, was certainly no place for poor foreigners. Grey courtyard residences, or *siheyuan*, sat behind ornate gates along both sides of the alley. Werner's house was built on a traditional north–south axis, with a raised step at the entrance to ward off ghosts. In the courtyard a century-old wisteria climbed the walls, and an ancient poplar tree stood amidst a small rockery. Werner rented the house from its Chinese owner, and although old it had been fitted out with electric lights, a palatial bathroom, steam heating and glass in the windows instead of paper.

The household had a cook, a housemaid who'd been Pamela's amah when she was younger, and Werner's number-one boy—a term used in the world of foreigners in China—who was actually a man in his forties. He'd been Werner's valet for many years and was the chief male servant in the household. There was also a gatekeeper who ensured the security and upkeep of the property, and he too had been with the family for a long time. Except for the cook, all the staff lived on the premises.

There were grander courtyard houses than Werner's along the alley. The best was owned by Dr E.T. Nystrom, a wealthy Swedish geologist who knew China's steel and coal reserves to the nearest ton. When he was in town, he was a fixture at the bar of the Peking Club, but he lived half the year in Sweden with his beautiful wife, who refused to move to Peking.

While he was away, Dr Nystrom rented out a portion of his vast courtyard house to two young Americans, the leftist journalist and author Edgar Snow and his fiery and attractive wife Helen Foster Snow, also a well-known journalist. The Snows were among the most notorious foreigners in Peking, and people either loved them or hated them, particularly Edgar, whose politics were anathema to the Establishment. Others viewed them dismissively as parlour pinks living high on the hog, professed revolutionaries who, thanks to the exchange rate of the mighty American dollar, were able to keep a racehorse at the Paomachang track four miles outside the city. The Snows were as likely to appear in the society pages as on the British Special Branch's Politically Suspect Persons list.

Werner loved the sprawling Tartar City and would regularly take long, invigorating walks through its hive of narrow *hutong*. This was an area of one-storey shacks, street markets with ramshackle restaurants, open-air butchers and hawkers. Winter in the Tartar City was the time for roasted chestnuts, cooked in braziers that were pungently fuelled by charcoal or animal dung. It was also the season for noodles and spiced bean curd, cut into squares and fried, and for dumplings— good northern fare to keep the cold out. There were bathhouses, fortune-tellers, professional letter writers scribbling for the illiterate, pavement barbers who cut hair before an audience. These barbers knew everything, heard every piece of gossip doing the rounds. Impromptu Peking opera singers, child acrobats and bearded magicians performed on the streets and then passed a hat round the crowd. A few cars fought their way between clusters of rickshaws, and when it rained, the rutted roads were ankle-deep in mud. In a sign of modernity, overhead wires were bringing the first electricity to the Tartar City, but the older residents distrusted these snaking, humming cables.

As a scholar, Werner wanted to observe as much of Peking's street life and traditions as possible, and being a skilled linguist, he was keen to engage people in conversation. He was also of the belief that a stiff daily walk kept you young. In winter he would wrap up in a long gabardine coat he had used on research expeditions to Mongolia. He attracted attention—an elderly but straight-backed white man, invariably wearing specially made wraparound dark glasses of his own design to protect his eyes from Peking's dust storms. Werner maintained all his life that these glasses had allowed him to retain his excellent vision.

His usual route took him south from his house, through the teeming collection of *hutong* and across Hatamen and Flower streets, then along Embroidery Street and past the Goldfish Ponds, where scholars came to contemplate amid their tranquility. From there he walked towards the ancient Temple of Heaven, where countless emperors had once come to pray for good harvests.

Occasionally he would wander westwards from his house, along the Tartar Wall to the Hatamen Gate. Here cars and rickshaws had to slow to a crawl to pass through the narrow archway into the Legation

Quarter, whose eastern boundary was formed by the gate. The Quarter's western boundary was marked by another gate—Ch'ienmen, home to Peking's main railway station—and also by Hubu Street, teeming with restaurants specialising in boiled mutton. In Liulichang, just outside Ch'ienmen, Werner might browse among the old bookstores and curio shops. Or he sometimes wandered to the northern border of the Quarter, which was the grand sweep of Chang'an Avenue and the Forbidden City. The southern boundary was the Tartar Wall.

Aside from his scholarly work, Werner's main concern in life was Pamela, and he doted on her. People who knew Pamela always commented on her independence; how she was able to take care of herself when her father left on long research trips, her excellent Chinese language skills, the fact that she seemingly had no really close friends. In a tight-knit, often socially incestuous small foreign community, Pamela's independent, self-contained character marked her as somewhat different from the run-of-the-mill foreign girl in Peking. She had been an orphan, abandoned at birth by an unknown mother and adopted by Werner and his English wife, Gladys Nina, who were childless. Before Pamela could get to know her adoptive mother, Gladys Nina died, and Werner had raised his daughter alone.

While Pamela had grown up outside the Legation Quarter, first in a house on San Tiao Hutong in the Ch'ienmen district and then on Armour Factory Alley, she enjoyed the Quarter's skating rinks and hotel tea dances. She went to see Hollywood movies at the cinemas on Morrison Street and around Dashala Street, an area known as 'Peking's Broadway,' and listened to big-band music broadcast on a Shanghai radio station. But she also spoke fluent Mandarin, and moved more comfortably and more frequently in Chinese society than did most of her white contemporaries. She regularly visited the teeming food market of Soochow Hutong and ate at the cheap Chinese restaurants patronised by Chinese university students near her home.

Pamela had become that rare thing among the city's foreign community—a white girl who enjoyed both the European lifestyle of the Quarter and the life of Chinese Peking. Her ease in conversing and her interest in China's culture, no doubt fuelled by her father's work, meant that she tended to roam widely across Peking on her bicycle, exploring parts of the city other foreign girls never ventured into. When younger she had been known to disappear for hours, arriving home out of breath but just in time for her tea. Like her father, Pamela appeared to be largely content with her own company. When he disappeared into the remote hinterlands on expeditions and research trips, she amused herself. The household servants looked after her, although they couldn't discipline her, and with her mother dead and her father away for long stretches, Pamela was forced to be decidedly more independent of mind and spirit than most of her contemporaries.

Still, hers was a privileged life, of school, of tiffins—light snacks—with other foreigners at one or another of the grand hotels in the Quarter, and long summers picnicking in the Western Hills outside Peking. The worst weeks of the city's heat and dust were spent on the beaches of Peitaiho, a seaside resort where Werner kept a cottage. There the pitch-black nights were lit by fireflies and lanterns on the porches; the days were consumed by languorous swims in the salty Yellow Sea and donkey rides along the beach.

Much as he loved her, Werner had his difficulties with Pamela. She'd been a problem at her first school, the Convent of the White Franciscans, where she was rebellious, answered back and infuriated the teachers. Then she'd gone to the French School, where she was asked to leave, after which she was refused admittance to the American School. Though troubled, Pamela was intelligent. She took exams for a scholarship to the Peking Methodist School and won a place, but there too her behaviour was rebellious, and again her father was asked to remove her.

Finally, in 1934, unable to control his daughter and at his wits' end, Werner sent her off to board at a grammar school in Tientsin. It was run on strict English public school lines and was known for its discipline. Those who knew Pamela gave her some latitude. After all, she was an only child with no mother and an elderly father who left her alone in Peking for long periods while he went off on expeditions, looking for the lost burial tomb of Genghis Khan in Mongolia or pursuing rare artefacts in the wilds of Muslim western China. It was hardly surprising that she was a little wild.

狐 狸 精

Pamela was fifteen when she was sent to Tientsin, a city nothing like Peking. Since the 1870s it had been a treaty port, where foreigners controlled their own concessions and lived outside Chinese law, policing and judging themselves. There were four major concessions, British, French, Italian and Japanese. Without doubt the British dominated, with their trademark Bund along the Hai River and the British Municipal Council, but Japan was taking an increasingly uppity second place in the power rankings.

Nevertheless it no doubt felt a little provincial to Pamela after Peking. The city had its share of history and tradition, but it wasn't imperial Peking. For a long time Tientsin had been compared unfavourably to the other great treaty port of the China coast—Shanghai. However, by the start of the twentieth century Tientsin was growing prosperous, trading everything from coal to camel hair, Mongolian cashmere to Tibetan mohair. Tientsin was now northern China's richest port, with a population of over a million people. Now there were theatres and cinemas, good restaurants, an ice-cream parlour, a German café, and a branch of the Laidlaw & Co. department store on Victoria Road. There were even nightclubs featuring White Russian singers, occasionally patronised by northern warlords come to town for the bright lights. Tientsin also had its share of vice—brothels, bars and opium dens—but it still couldn't quite hold a candle to louche Shanghai.

The students at Tientsin Grammar were British, American, White Russian, stateless Jewish refugees, wealthy Chinese and Indians, and many other nationalities—some twenty-nine in total when Pamela was there. With its stone walls, highly polished floors and

English uniforms with a Union Jack, it was the most traditional of traditional English schools, transplanted to the East. Its students were, by and large, the pampered children of the privileged.

The girls wore the drab 'gymnasium costume' of England, adorned only by their house badges; the boys wore caps, ties and blazers; and they all studied the English curriculum. The entire student body assembled in the wood-panelled auditorium every morning, boys to the left, girls to the right, before the headmaster, who stood on the stage in don's robes over tweeds. A ritual morning greeting was followed by a hymn, perhaps 'There Is a Green Hill Far Away,' and then a rendition of 'God Save the King.'

Classes started at 8:50, broke for lunch at noon, then resumed at 2:00, ending at 4:00. The school fees were eighty silver dollars a month, 50 percent more if the pupil lived outside the British Municipal Area of Tientsin, and an additional eighty-five dollars a month for boarders like Pamela. Tientsin Grammar was a little slice of England in warlord-wracked, Japanese-threatened northern China. Pamela and her classmates studied for the gruelling Cambridge matriculation exams; there was a lot of Latin. There was also a drill instructor and constant sports—hockey and netball for the girls; cricket, football and swimming for the boys.

Most of the students were day pupils from Tientsin; Pamela was one of only a half-dozen or so boarders. She lived at the School House, a sombre Gothic-style building that doubled as the home of the headmaster, who traditionally took in boarders to supplement his income. Students rose at seven, breakfasted at seven forty-five, left for school at eight thirty. After school there was high tea at five, then prep, reading and hobbies at five thirty. Bedtime was between seven and nine, depending on age.

It was a set routine with little to break it. Cocoa and biscuits were served at bedtime; guests could be invited to tea on Wednesdays and also visit on weekends, subject to approval. Pamela's new friends in Tientsin were unaware she had been thrown out of schools in Peking.

They knew her as a plain, quiet girl and a keen sportswoman, and assumed she was boarding because her father, whom everyone had heard of, travelled a lot for his work.

And it was true that Pamela had been turning over a new leaf, trying to behave and stay out of trouble, but her life was not all cocoa at bedtime. There was a boyfriend. Michael 'Mischa' Horjelsky was Polish-Jewish, Tientsin Grammar's star athlete, a good-looking swimmer with a body that would have set the girls of the Upper Sixth on fire. Mischa had thick dark hair and a charming smile. He was cheeky and funny and a good scholar.

For Pamela he was a catch. Line up the boys of her year, and anyone would have tipped Mischa as the matinée idol, the one to have girls swooning in the aisles. And he doted on her—the two were inseparable, said some who knew them, and were rarely seen apart during the school day.

In early 1937, Mischa was planning to visit Peking for a few days. Mischa lived with his family in Tientsin, while Pamela had gone to stay at her father's on Armour Factory Alley when term finished. Mischa's visit to Peking was to be the first time Pamela brought him home to meet her father, but tragedy was to strike before that could happen.

狐 狸 精

'*Pamela!*' At the base of the Fox Tower, Commissioner Thomas moved quickly to where Werner lay on the cold ground.

The two men had known each other for many years, both veterans of Peking. Thomas effectively ran the Legation Quarter on a day-to-day basis, holding down the offices of Commissioner of the Legation Quarter Police and Secretary of the Administrative Commission of the Peking Diplomatic Quarter. He was more or less a mayor, chief of police and administrator, all rolled into one.

Thomas had seen Werner's note only shortly before being called by Han to the Fox Tower. He'd thought nothing more of it, assuming it was a mystery probably already solved even as he read the note. But

now both he and Colonel Han were aware that the horrifically mutilated dead girl lying before them was Pamela Werner.

Crime scenes can quickly become circuses, and this one was no
exception. Colonel Han was swift to bring in extra constables to rope
off the entire area at the base of the Fox Tower and push the onlookers farther out of range. The officers then canvassed the area, and in
the ditch some distance away found an oil lamp, which was entered
into the record as possible evidence. Han had ordered still more straw
matting to be placed over the body to prevent gawking, but he was
not going to remove the corpse until he'd made a thorough examination of the scene.

That was becoming difficult. Word had spread like wildfire that a
dead white girl had been found at the Fox Tower, a place known for its
bad spirits and sorcery. Curious locals continued to arrive, along with
the press, both Chinese and foreign, tipped off perhaps by a constable
looking to supplement his pay packet. The Reuters pressman had a
camera; there was a local stringer for the Shanghai-based *North-China
Daily News*, and also reporters from the *Peking and Tientsin Times*, the
most widely read paper north of Shanghai, and its rival, the *North
China Star*. Han ordered them to stay back from the body while his
own photographer from Morrison Street documented the crime scene.

Two young constables had meanwhile accompanied Werner back
to his house on Armour Factory Alley. Han and Thomas now had to
make sure that the dead girl was indeed his daughter—they needed a
formal identification, and that, ideally, should come from a family
member. Werner had seemed certain, but he was in a state, and many
foreign women had fair hair, not least the legion of Russian women,
the most likely foreigners to be found dead in the city. They needed
confirmation. If the corpse was Pamela, then a British subject had
been murdered on Chinese territory, and the daughter of a former
British consul, no less.

Thomas suggested calling Constable Pearson at the British Legation, who knew Pamela personally. Pearson was sent for, and he got

to the crime scene at 2:15 p.m., but was unable to make a definite identification, such was the degree of facial mutilation.

Then Han had an idea. He sent a constable to Werner's residence to bring back Yen Ping, the gateman. The old man, when he arrived, reported that Pamela had still not returned home. Werner himself hadn't spoken a word since coming back, and he was now resting in a state of shock, with pains in his chest. A doctor had been called to examine his heart.

Han showed the gateman the silk chemise found under the corpse, but Yen Ping was unable to identify it as Pamela's. So Han showed him the body. Like everyone who saw it, he reacted with shock. No, he said, he could not identify the face, but the hair was unmistakable. Moreover one eye was less damaged than the other, and Yen Ping recognized the unusual greyness of the iris.

Constable Pearson, who was still there, confirmed that Pamela indeed had rare grey eyes, and he also recognized the expensive diamond-set watch, as did Yen Ping.

It was enough. The corpse at the Fox Tower was officially recorded as Pamela Werner, British subject, resident of Peking, daughter of E. T. C. Werner, the former British consul at Foochow, now retired.

狐 狸 精

Winter nights in Peking draw in fast and early, and it was already getting dark. Han sent for a coffin and gathered up the evidence: Pamela's loose clothing, including her tartan skirt, which had fallen off as the body was lifted, her belted overcoat, a pair of torn silk stockings, a comb, her shoes, a handkerchief, the bloodied card for the French Club skating rink, and the wristwatch. When the coffin arrived, four constables carefully placed Pamela's body inside. A sheet was found to cover her below the waist.

It had once been Chinese tradition, and the law, that a murdered body should not be moved until the murderer was caught. But the

Peking police force now prided itself on its contemporary practices, taught in the modern police academy. Han placed the recovered items inside the coffin and put the lid on it. The constables then carried it to a small, deserted temple inside the Fox Tower until an ambulance arrived. From there the body was taken to the Peking Union Medical College for the autopsy.

Wild Dogs and Diplomats

$\mathcal{J}$t was Commissioner Thomas who grasped the ramifications of the murder first. Thomas had joined the British diplomatic service in Peking in 1898, aged just nineteen, then resigned due to ill health a few years later. But he'd stayed on in China, finding a job with the administrative commission and building a reputation as an efficient, skilled hard bargainer, a trait perhaps gained from his father, a canny Shrewsbury cattle dealer. Thomas knew well that Werner was seen as a friend of China by the Chinese government, and the pressure would be on the Peking Detective Bureau to solve this murder quickly.

When a foreigner died under suspicious circumstances in Peking, it was standard procedure for the appropriate legation to be invited to nominate an envoy to monitor the investigation. The envoy had no rights as such; he couldn't arrest anyone, nor could he question suspects without permission from the Chinese police. His role was purely that of an observer, a go-between.

Thomas knew that this was an investigation for which the British would want to appoint an envoy, and that it would be someone from the legation staff. As Pamela was the daughter of a high-ranking foreigner, the case would be high profile. Things would be further complicated by the fact that the British consul had a dislike for Werner; the two had fallen out some years ago during the course of their work.

For Han, though, the idea of an envoy from the British Legation was problematic. An envoy would interfere, he protested to Thomas while both men were still at the crime scene. And this was no casual back-alley stabbing, no mugging gone wrong or heart attack in a bar; this was something horrific, unfathomable. Domestic arguments that turned tragically violent, disputes over money or women or both that flared into murderous rages—these were bad enough, but the killing of a young English girl at a time of tension in the city was alarming to the authorities.

Thomas, aware they had to act quickly, suggested a compromise. Han should outflank the British Legation by nominating an envoy himself, someone the British could not object to. The commissioner knew there was no one attached to the legation who was senior enough, or experienced enough, for something like this anyway. Nor, given the magnitude of the crime, could it be anyone from the Legation Quarter police.

Thomas thought the legation might want to bring in someone from Shanghai, where law and order in the British-dominated International Settlement was run by the tough and experienced chief commissioner Major Frederick Gerrard, a Highland Scot who'd served with the Indian army and the British police in India before a stint as deputy commissioner of police in Basrah, Mesopotamia. Thomas knew Gerrard was good, a copper's copper, but thought that in these darkening days he'd have one foot in the police and the other in British Intelligence and Special Branch in Shanghai. He'd also have his hands full battling the city's rival gangs, who were fighting for control of lucrative narcotics and prostitution rackets with Chicago-style shootouts on the streets. Recently there'd been a rash of kidnappings of prominent Shanghai citizens, and more than enough trouble with an increasingly belligerent Japanese community. Gerrard had plenty of murders on his own patch and would be loath to spare any of his men, let alone himself.

Fortunately, Thomas told Han, he knew of a police officer with the perfect background for the investigation—Detective Chief Inspector Richard Dennis, chief of police, British Concession, Tientsin. DCI Dennis was a most capable man, experienced and independently minded. He had trained at Scotland Yard.

The legation couldn't easily argue against the qualifications of a senior ex–Scotland Yard detective. Moreover, since Dennis was with the British Concession authorities in Tientsin, he didn't technically work for the British government. The legation might apply pressure, but Dennis would be able to resist it. He was a seasoned policeman of the old school, the sort who wanted to get at the truth, and he'd been trained by the best.

In other words, Thomas managed to convey to Han, Dennis wasn't a diplomat, he wasn't part of the old boys' network, he wasn't political. He was a copper, pure and simple.

Colonel Han agreed, and left Thomas to call the British consul in Tientsin to formally request that DCI Dennis be temporarily assigned to Peking.

狐 狸 精

Later that evening, Han made his way through the *hutong* behind the Morrison Street station to the Peking Union Medical College, a short distance away. This college was Peking's most advanced centre of medicine. Established with the help of missionaries in 1906 and now funded by the American oil magnate John D. Rockefeller and his foundation, it had always mixed Western doctors with Chinese, sending bright young Chinese to be trained in the United States and recruiting American and European experts to work at the college, going so far as to build a series of Western-style houses for the foreign personnel. By Peking standards the college was modern, clean and efficient. There was no medical facility like it in China, outside of Shanghai.

Han entered the mazelike complex, which was laid out in traditional Peking style but with newer Western buildings on all sides. The place could have been in New York or Boston, four or five floors high and purely functional, until you looked up and saw that the architects had incorporated Chinese flourishes—green saddleback roofs and traditional floating swallowtail eaves. What Han wasn't to know was that these adornments had been added after a suggestion by one of the members of the committee that established the college, a man who was an expert on Chinese architecture and who believed deeply in preserving Peking's traditional skyline—E. T. C. Werner.

The complex was silent at night. The gatemen were warming themselves around a charcoal brazier in a hut at the entrance. Han made his way to the pathology department, where he was met by Dr Wang, the medical superintendent. This was good—Han knew that Wang always worked with Cheng Hsiang-hu, chief professor of pathology and a man Han admired. Cheng was a graduate of Harvard Medical School, and very experienced.

Superintendent Wang escorted Han to the autopsy room, where the contrast with the outside world was stark. There were spotless white tiles, gleaming stainless steel, bottles of chemicals on shelves, a tray of scalpels catching the light, along with other medical instruments Han didn't know the name of.

Professor Cheng nodded acknowledgement to Han as he washed his hands. Wang stood ready with a clipboard and pen to record the details. Attendants wheeled in Pamela's body on a trolley and lifted it onto the autopsy table, which was slightly angled and had gutters to catch any blood. The smell of antiseptic and cleanliness gave way to the smell of the dead and damaged—the familiar metallic tang of dried blood that caught in the back of the throat was mixed with a smell not unlike that of the fried pork in the Soochow Hutong market. Chinese or foreign, the odour of the dead was the same.

Pamela's body had been undressed and washed but was still an unsightly mass of cuts, slashes and bruises. Her sternum was still the same gaping hole Han had seen at the Fox Tower. In fact, with most of the blood and mud cleaned away, he could see just how many stab marks there were—they seemed numerous to him. The naked body was strangely wide where it had been cut open across the chest. Han found it hard to picture Pamela's face—he had yet to see a photograph of her—but under the intensely bright lights, he could now see that she was freckled. He noticed too her small hands, clenched rigidly tight, her thumbs locked inside her fists, trapped there by rigor mortis.

There was a second pathology expert at the autopsy, Dr William Graham Aspland, a senior consultant who had formally ordered the postmortem and appointed Cheng as Pamela's chief pathologist. Both men wore green gowns with Western suits, shirts and ties underneath. Like Han, they thought this was one of the worst cases of mutilation they'd ever seen, and that was saying something. Cheng conducted postmortems almost daily, and Aspland, an English physician who specialized in opium addiction, had cleaned the dead from the battlefields of France and Belgium during World War I.

It was now past ten p.m., but Han had asked for the autopsy to be done this evening so that the investigation could get under way. Tradition decreed that he had twenty days to solve the case—after that it got much, much harder, as detectives got reassigned and the bosses at police headquarters lost interest. Aspland had agreed to the late-night procedure and called in Cheng immediately.

They began. First they weighed the corpse—nine stone, four pounds—and measured her—five foot, five inches. Distinguishing marks? None, though Cheng noted her uncommon grey eyes and long eyelashes. The estimated time of death was somewhere between ten p.m. and two a.m. the previous night, but Cheng could be no more precise than that. The specific cause of death was several blows with a blunt instrument to the area around the right eye, which had split the skull and caused massive haemorrhaging in the brain. Death would have taken perhaps two to three minutes from the first blow. Most of the horrific wounds had been inflicted postmortem.

Superintendent Wang's account for the night showed that Pamela had to have been standing and facing her attacker when she was hit, suggesting that she knew him. The fatal blows were delivered from a short distance away and were extremely powerful; Pamela and her killer had been up close to each other, probably in a confined space. He had most likely been taller than she: the blows had been struck down on her skull, cracking it like an egg. The flow of blood from the wound had no doubt blinded her, causing her to sink to the floor and die where she lay. In all probability, Pamela's killer had looked her in the eye as he'd ended her life.

Cheng catalogued all the injuries for the record. Han confirmed with the doctors that the blood loss caused by them would have been significant, and because there'd been little blood at the Fox Tower, this substantiated his suspicion that Pamela had been killed elsewhere. Somewhere, there had to be a lot more blood.

The knife used to slash the body after death had a blade approximately four inches long, Cheng estimated, possibly with a double edge. The throat had also been cut postmortem; the windpipe was completely severed. The slash and stab marks appeared random and were of different lengths and depths—Cheng described them for the record as 'frenzied.' Han noted that although Pamela's tartan skirt and Aertex blouse had been ripped, there were no slash marks on her clothing: she had been stripped before being repeatedly stabbed.

Pamela's right arm was also nearly severed from her body, the muscles cut clean through. Cheng speculated that two different, very sharp blades had been used for this. The humerus—the long bone running from the shoulder to the elbow—had been fractured in two places by blows from a blunt and heavy instrument that Cheng couldn't identify. The lack of extensive haemorrhaging in the tissue around the wound led him to believe that the attempt to sever the arm was also made postmortem. Aspland concurred.

All four men looked at each other with one thought—the murderer or murderers had tried to dissect the body, to dismember it before disposing of it. The cuts to the shoulder could not have been made with an ordinary knife, by someone hacking at the flesh and muscle; some sort of specialist cutting tool must have been used.

Next Cheng moved to Pamela's chest, which had been opened almost from her throat to her pelvic bone, the entire length sliced and pulled apart. Cheng noted, 'The general nature of the cutting suggested that the flesh had been taken away in a single piece.' A large piece of skin was missing, including part of Pamela's breasts.

Han remembered the woolen cardigan the girl had been wearing at the Fox Tower. It had been bloody, but not that bloody—he thought this meant that the killer had undressed and then partially re-dressed his victim after her massive blood loss, leaving off her undergarments and stockings and loosely pulling back on her torn skirt, blouse and cardigan. He was positive now that the Fox Tower was not where Pamela had been murdered and butchered; the kill site was somewhere else, somewhere they didn't know about yet.

Cheng was finding it hard to record his findings, so bizarre and impossible did they strike him as being. After removing the skin from Pamela's chest and stomach, the killer had carved open her chest to expose her ribs. He had then broken all twelve of her ribs, six on either side. Each had been broken outwards, and then the killer had removed her heart, her bladder, her kidney and her liver.

To break a rib inward was not difficult. A blow to the side of the chest would achieve this, and people broke ribs all the time, falling, fighting or in accidents. But to snap something with the thickness and strength of a rib outwards, against the natural curve, was much more difficult and suggested the use of great force.

The medical men were disbelieving, despite the evidence before them. The motive for such an act was impossible to imagine, and none of them were willing to hazard a guess as to why this had been done. Not content with opening the rib cage, the mutilator had reached in and removed the organs. It seemed that Pamela had been killed by a madman.

The autopsy continued. Cheng noted that two clean incisions had been made through the diaphragm below the lungs and at the abdomen. He believed these had been done with either a surgeon's scalpel or a professional amputation knife. They were not the hack job of an amateur. Pamela's stomach had also been cut away, at the oesophagus and the small intestine—it was inside her body but no longer attached to anything. The medical men now removed it for further examination.

Han had a question. Could dogs or animals have caused this internal damage? He was thinking of the reports of the *huang gou* skulking around the Fox Tower that morning, until chased off.

But Cheng thought not. The cuts in the diaphragm and abdominal cavity were the result of sharp instruments. They were too clean and neat to have been made by animals, and there were no signs of dog bites anywhere on the body. The *huang gou* were innocent.

Han considered the nature of Pamela's injuries. In a sense it was a relief that the majority were postmortem; the idea of such atrocities being committed while the girl was still alive made them unthinkable. There were scratches on her lower arms that were premortem, perhaps signs of a struggle, though it appeared to have been brief. It seemed Pamela had been killed, bled and butchered in that order, but not all in one place.

When Han asked whether Pamela had been raped, Cheng couldn't say, and although it was now past midnight, Aspland called out another colleague, Dr James Maxwell, the medical college's professor of gynaecology and obstetrics. Maxwell had caused a storm several years earlier with a paper he wrote on the use of meat hooks by unqualified midwives in rural China, and the subsequent deaths of both mothers and babies.

Now he examined Pamela for signs of sexual activity or interference, and concluded that she'd had intercourse at some time in the recent past—she was not a virgin. But he was unable to say whether this was consensual or not, or whether it was pre- or postmortem. The science just wasn't advanced enough. Pamela's vagina had also been mutilated, but again Maxwell was unable to determine when this had taken place. Han asked him whether he thought this was the work of a sexual maniac; Maxwell thought it quite possibly was.

The final doctor to examine Pamela that night was Harry Van Dyke, a brilliant physician who'd been hired to establish the college's pharmacology department. Van Dyke swiftly ruled out poisoning and could find no traces of chloroform; Pamela had not been drugged, and while she had been drinking alcohol, the level in her blood wasn't high. Van Dyke also determined that at some point during the previous evening, Pamela had eaten Chinese food.

The autopsy completed, Cheng noted for the record that prior to her murder Pamela Werner had been 'a healthy and normally developed woman of approximately 18–19 years of age.' He noted her teeth as healthy, though two in the back had been removed professionally at some point, and there were recent chips to two of her front teeth, which he assumed had occurred in the struggle.

The men discussed what they knew and what they didn't. Pamela's injuries suggested rage, a frenzied madness, but also someone competent with a surgical knife and who had a basic knowledge of anatomy. Cheng thought that if the murderer was skilled, then the mutilations could have been done within half an hour; if less skilled, then two to three hours.

Han asked whether all this could have been done in the open, or whether the killer had required light and an indoor location. Cheng couldn't be sure but thought some light would have been needed, even if the killer was skilled, although perhaps a butcher or a hunter might be capable in the dark.

As to the process, Cheng believed that following death the chest was the first to be mutilated. This would have caused the loss of a massive amount of blood, and the killer or killers could not have avoided becoming soaked in it themselves. However, the blood had been drained from the abdomen before that was cut, accounting for the lack of blood in the abdominal cavity—Pamela had effectively been bled dry before having her internal organs removed. There was no evidence of clotting in the blood vessels, and this indicated to Cheng that the bloodletting had occurred soon after death rather than later—no more than five or six hours at the most.

Around dawn, the body was taken to the nearby mortuary. When Colonel Han left the medical college the press were waiting for him outside, mostly foreign journalists, stamping their feet in the cold. Han was in no mood to talk, and besides, he knew better than to reveal the details of what he'd just seen on the slab. His only statement was, 'No comment.'

The early editions of Saturday's China-coast papers all led with Pamela Werner's murder. The Shanghai-based *China Press* ran the headline Ex–British Consul's Daughter Discovered Dead, Badly Mangled. The reporters were scrabbling for facts, Han having told them nothing for now, and the story was riddled with inaccuracies. That didn't stop it being repeated across all the newspapers in China and then across the world. Pamela was described as anywhere from fifteen to nineteen years old, and all the papers included the erroneous detail that wild dogs had savaged her body.

Much was made of her father's career, and the fact that her body had been found at the Fox Tower, as close as 250 yards from her home as the crow flies, and right next to the foreign enclave of the Legation Quarter. Much, too, was made of the local superstition that the Fox Tower was haunted; fox spirits had made the front pages. Peking was reportedly mystified—that much, at least, was true. But it was widely presented as fact that Werner himself had discovered his daughter's body—he had stumbled across her corpse while out looking for her and had had to throw stones at the *huang gou* to stop them tearing at her flesh.

Nobody at the medical college had talked to the press, who had not been informed of the details of the mutilation or the missing organs, but dark hints were made that this was an awful slaying in the extreme. The journalists relied on interviews with people at the scene. Colonel Han Shih-ching of the Peking police was listed as the investigating officer in charge; no mention was made of Scotland Yard's involvement, no comment given from His Britannic Majesty's British Consulate.

Across the Pacific, on the American continent, the *New York Times* reported, 'Peking was shocked to learn that the body of a British girl had been found under the Tartar Wall, between Hatamen

Gate and Fox Tower.' That too was correct—Peking *was* shocked. You could feel the fear ripple across the city.

Even though Peking had been living with the threat of invasion for months now, even though everyone knew that when the Japanese arrived, they would be brutal, the city's dread had just been ratcheted up a degree. The murdered body at the Fox Tower seemed to graphically symbolise the spiral into barbarism. This was not an assassination, not part of a political feud; it was the butchering of an innocent. The city's terror was coalescing, and now there was a name to embody the horror that would befall them all—Pamela Werner.

The Investigation

*D*uring that Friday night, two policemen from Tientsin, Inspector Botham and Sergeant Binetsky, had arrived to prepare the ground for their boss, Detective Chief Inspector Dennis, who was due in Peking later on Saturday. Botham set about arranging accommodation for Dennis at the Grand Hôtel des Wagons Lits, and for himself and Sergeant Binetsky at the slightly less expensive Hôtel du Nord.

Meanwhile Sergeant Binetsky went to the Morrison Street police station, which had also had a busy night. The front desk had been dealing with crank callers and those deranged Pekingers who confessed to every murder in the city. One such call ran:

> **Desk sergeant:** 'What did you do?'
> **Caller:** 'I strangled her.'
> **Desk sergeant:** 'Why did you kill her?'
> **Caller:** 'She was a filthy Russian prostitute.'
> **Desk sergeant:** 'What did you do to the body?'
> **Caller:** 'I left it to the dogs.'

Desk sergeant: 'What had she ever done to you?'
Caller: 'She was a fox spirit and she possessed me.'

None of the confessions, even the less outlandish ones, matched the crime, and they kept coming on Saturday morning. Once Han was called from his office to the front desk to confront a wild, ranting White Russian woman who was demanding that her husband be locked up and charged with the murder. The desk sergeant couldn't understand her, and Han too had trouble making out her words through her thick accent. She wore heavy makeup, and spittle flew from her mouth as she shouted. Her good-for-nothing husband was a killer, she insisted; he was infatuated with *batončiks*, young blond prostitutes. He spent all his money on those 'small buns' in the bars and whorehouses of the Badlands. He was at home right now, still covered in blood. The police must do something.

They had raced round to the house and found the man hung over and with his old tsarist medals on display. He was as wild and ranting as his wife, and screamed all the more wildly when he saw her at the heels of the police, but he had no idea what they were talking about. He hadn't seen the newspaper his wife had read that morning. He was bloody, but it was his own blood, he told the police, spilled courtesy of an American soldier's fists and boots in a Russian bar, where the vodka had flowed a little too freely. Tempers had flared. Two other Russian men living in the same *hutong* verified that the man had been drunk and fighting, that this was nothing unusual, that his wife was a crazy harridan he'd have done better to have left in St Petersburg, that they were both a little unhinged after having to flee Russia with nothing and live destitute in a strange country.

A constable dispatched to the marines' quarters at the American Legation returned with an alibi for the Russian. A burly marine admitted hitting the man for insulting his girl and the fighting honour of the Fourth Marines. He didn't regret his actions, but he didn't think the Russian, asshole though he was, deserved to face a murder charge.

Then there was the case of the scared and cowering rickshaw

puller who'd been brought into Morrison Street on Friday, after being caught close to where Pamela's body was found. The rickshaw puller, a country boy called Sun Te-hsing, had been washing out a bloodstained cushion cover from the seat of his rickshaw. When Han had got back to the station that day, he had the boy put in a cell while he examined the cover—it was bloody, but not bloody enough for the dead girl's injuries, Han determined. After questioning the boy, he let him go. The rickshaw puller was sent on his way, back out onto the cold streets, and told to disappear.

Most of the calls coming through to the station, and most of the newspapermen crowding the lobby of Morrison Street, mentioned one man—Pamela's father. And indeed, that was the procedure in a murder investigation—first look close: to the family, the husband, the wife. Murderers invariably knew their victims; randomness was rare. That was a detective's mindset—think the unthinkable, and statistically you were likely to be closer to the truth.

狐 狸 精

After missing lunch, Colonel Han found himself standing on the platform of Peking Central Railway Station in the early afternoon chill, waiting for DCI Dennis. The station was European in style, on the southwestern edge of the Legation Quarter, close to Ch'ienmen Gate. It had a high, arched roof and a distinctive Western clock tower at one end of the platform.

Han had been pleased to find that no journalists were gathered round the ticket gate; it meant the press hadn't got hold of the story that a British policeman was being brought in from Tientsin. The colonel was in two minds about Dennis's involvement in the case. The detective was experienced and British, and both those things were called for in this instance. Better a detective than an embassy spy, or even worse, a dullard who just got in the way. But a part of Han resented the involvement of any foreigner in a Peking murder case—this wasn't Shanghai or one of the other treaty ports, this was sovereign Chinese territory.

But he'd decided to be rational and accept that this was no ordinary Peking murder, if such a thing existed. A foreigner had been killed, and Dennis, or someone like him, was an inevitability.

Han expected the train to be late. The journey from Tientsin to Peking normally took two hours, but it had become dangerous, with bandits and saboteurs and roaming Japanese troops. Han shook himself to get his blood moving against the chill; it wouldn't do to shiver in front of a Scotland Yard man.

To arrive in Peking, Han knew, was to be awed somewhat. The train, known as the International, came into the station under the walls of old Peking, virtually alongside the towering Ch'ienmen Gate. The tallest and most southerly of the city's ancient gateways, it marked the entrance to the inner part of Peking, the old Imperial City. Occasionally camel trains setting out for Mongolia, the old tea-trade routes and the Silk Road still wandered past it.

When Dennis's train, only slightly behind schedule, pulled into the Water Gate platform and disgorged its passengers, Han realised he had no idea what DCI Dennis looked like, apart from foreign. He was one among many—most of the passengers appeared to be foreigners, at least in the first-class carriages at the front of the train.

Then he saw him. He would have known the man was a policeman regardless of race or nationality. It was Dennis's bearing: erect, purposeful, exuding authority even in civilian clothes—a dark, worsted double-breasted suit, starched white collar, black tie and coat, ubiquitous fedora. Shoes so polished you could almost see your face in them. It helped that Dennis was tall, standing a good few inches above anyone around him, Chinese or foreign. At six feet himself, Han nonetheless pushed his shoulders back involuntarily.

The DCI, familiar with the uniform of the Peking police, strode towards Han, and the two men appraised each other. Han was powerfully built, with close-cropped hair, angular cheekbones, and a longer chin and a sharper, more highly bridged nose than many Chinese. Dennis, while taller than Han, was somewhat gangly beneath his winter coat, but he had enough brawn to deal with anyone troublesome. He had slightly outsize features—a thick brow, long nose, large hands, large ears. Everything about him stamped him as a man of authority.

'DCI Dennis?'

'Colonel Han.'

'I have a car. Shall we?'

'Indeed.'

They walked through the ticket barrier, where the railway functionary was smart enough to know when not to demand a man's ticket, and strode out under the archway at the entrance, across to a parking area occupied by a few cars and a host of rickshaws. Dennis had only a small suitcase. Han's driver, a young constable, jumped out of the police Chevrolet and opened the back door for the men.

'To your hotel?' Han asked.

'Straight to work, I think.'

On the way to Morrison Street, Han briefed the British officer on the results of the autopsy, admitting to Dennis what he would later admit to journalists: he had as yet found no important clues. The two men agreed that in the absence of such they should follow procedure and reconstruct the victim's last days: start with the last known sighting of Pamela and work back carefully but swiftly. Murder investigations had to move fast, or they ground to a shuddering halt. Trails ran cold, witnesses disappeared, the killer escaped.

And then of course there was Han's twenty-day limit, not to mention the number of anonymous tip-offs and crank calls already received, which proved that the Peking rumour mill had swung into action. That morning, after a few hours' sleep on the foldout cot he kept in his office, Han had recalled all available constables for duty, cancelled leave across the board and issued instructions for everyone to take to the streets and look. Look for what? Look for blood. Find the blood, and they'd find the killer.

So commenced the formal investigation into the murder of Pamela Werner.

狐 狸 精

Detective Chief Inspector Richard Harry Dennis—Dick to the boys—was just shy of forty, a butcher's son from West Ham on the fringes of London's East End. His mother was reputedly from a well-to-do family, one of the stodgily respectable lower middle class of the Edwardian decade. As a young man, Dick Dennis found the world plunged into World War I. He rushed to join up. He was fit, smart, and somewhere along the way he had picked up good French, so he signed up with the newly formed Royal Flying Corps and flew over the battlefields of France. He was shot down in 1917, invalided out and sent home, his war over.

In 1920, perhaps missing the action, the discipline, the uniform, he joined the Metropolitan Police, where he rose to the rank of detective sergeant, stationed at Paddington on the edge of the West End, and then at Scotland Yard. He married, and a son—Richard junior—soon followed. But the marriage collapsed. Dennis married again in 1930, this time mildly scandalously, to his son's nanny, an East End woman named Virginia whom he always called Violet. Richard junior thought she was his birth mother.

Dennis liked police work, but he didn't much like struggling in London with a wife and child on a copper's lowly wage. With a reference from no less than Lord Trenchard, marshall of the RAF and commissioner of the Metropolitan Police, he took the job of chief inspector of police with the British Municipal Council in Tientsin, arriving to take up his duties in July 1934 with the new rank of DCI. It was a step up in rank and an even bigger step up in pay and conditions, from grimy West London to a sizeable house in Tientsin's British Concession and a force of men working under him.

Life on the north China salt flats suited Dennis just fine. His house was on well-to-do Hong Kong Road, and he also had a beach house in the seaside resort of Peitaiho. His son attended the Ecole Municipale Française and took riding lessons at the Tientsin stables with a

White Russian who'd once taught the children of tsarist nobility. His wife oversaw the servants, and there was enough money left over for a stout Mongolian pony, Heathfield, which he entered at the Tientsin racecourse. The pony was a winner, making the front page of the *Peking and Tientsin Times* when it came in first at the Peking Maidens.

It was a life unimaginable in England on a policeman's wage, and Dennis was a respected man in Tientsin. The police work was routine, but his position required him to attend civic functions and welcome the British ambassador when he came to town. Dennis was granted an automatic place among the worthies of British Tientsin. The city was better connected than it had been too, with tramp-steamer links along the China coast and a branch line of the Peking–Hankow railway.

There was the threat from the north to be monitored, of course, and the population was inevitably nervous. But the foreign concessions protected themselves with regiments of troops, which guaranteed some security from the rapacious warlords, the predatory Japanese, and the elusive and secretive White Lotus Society that terrorised the sorghum fields around the city. In fact Tientsin was a comparatively peaceable place, and it was only sometimes necessary to control the nightlife. It certainly wasn't anything like Paddington on a wet Friday night at chucking-out time.

And then Dennis was called to the old Chinese capital to investigate a crime that had all Peking, and soon Tientsin, talking. It was the most savage murder of a foreigner in China in living memory. But the DCI arrived with his hands tied.

Late on the night before he left, he had been summoned by the British consul in Tientsin, the veteran China hand John Affleck, and told to confine his investigation to the Legation Quarter, by Foreign Office order.

There were to be no searches, no investigations outside the Quarter. Affleck was blunt—Dennis was to liaise with Colonel Han as he must, but he should be in closer contact with Commissioner Thomas and the legation staff. For a copper as independently minded as Dennis, this placed a severe limit on his ability to operate.

Dennis thought Affleck seemed unusually nervous during his visit, although the official line was clear as a bell—don't mess with anything outside the Quarter. Moreover, the girl might have gone to school in Tientsin, but this case was nothing to do with that city. Dennis was on loan to Peking as a favour. He was to do his job and then get back here; this murder was not Tientsin's problem.

Pamela

When Pamela returned to Peking for the 1936 Christmas holidays, the telephone at Armour Factory Alley had rung constantly. Young men called to ask her to tiffins, dances, dinner parties, concerts. Retracing those final days, DCI Dennis and Colonel Han learnt that, in the main, her suitors came to pick her up at the house. They were often friends of the family, and when they weren't, they met her father.

Politically, it had been a fraught Christmas and a tense New Year. All Peking had followed the incredible events surrounding what came to be known as the Sian Incident. On 12 December, Chiang Kai-shek had been kidnapped in Sian, a sprawling, ancient city at the start of the Silk Road. The kidnapper was a warlord and former dope addict called Chang Hsüeh-liang, also known as the Young Marshall, whose father, a former warlord, was the Old Marshall, better known as the infamous Tiger of Mukden, who'd been assassinated by the Japanese in the late 1920s.

The Young Marshall hoped to coerce Chiang into a united front with the Communists against the Japanese. For a fortnight during the standoff and the dead-of-night negotiations, the entire nation held its breath. Chiang was eventually released on Christmas Eve, to fireworks across the country. The action had its desired result—Chiang was forced to accept the formation of a united front—but the kidnapper paid a high price, remaining under house arrest for the next fifty-seven years.

Politically active foreigners like the Snows, Werner's neighbours on Armour Factory Alley, followed every twist and turn of the drama to write about it. But Pamela seemed more interested in boys and dances than in world events. Tense faceoffs, encroaching Japanese, rogue warlords—she was keener to go ice-skating. And this Christmas there was a new skating rink, set up for foreigners by the French Legation. It was near the French Club, closer to home and less crowded than the frozen lakes in the shadows of the Forbidden City, or the Pei-ho Lake, or the YMCA rink on Hatamen Street. Pamela had been introduced to the new rink by family friends, and liked it so much she joined the club.

As well as skating, there'd been a whirl of parties and dances and the Western New Year. And Peking was also getting ready for its own major annual event, the lunar Chinese New Year. Nineteen thirty-seven would see the arrival of the Year of the Ox, the year of the element of fire, and traditional red-paper and fish-skin lanterns were already being hung in preparation for the celebrations. Many people had noted, as 1936 made way for 1937, that the partying was a little more frenzied than in previous years, as if the revelers sensed the end of something, and the coming of a kind of madness.

On the final afternoon of her life, after her father had gone out for his walk and she had finished writing her letters, Pamela donned her heavy overcoat and woolen mittens and pushed her straw-fair hair up into a beret. She took her ice skates and her bicycle and told Ho Ying, the household's cook, who'd known her since she was a baby, that she'd be back by seven thirty. She said she would like meatballs and rice for dinner, and Ho Ying said he'd be sure to go to the nearby Tung Tan Pailou Hutong and see the butcher. Pamela left through the courtyard's moon gate and cycled off along Armour Factory Alley to meet a friend for tea.

Ethel Gurevitch was from a White Russian family who'd been living in Peking for five years. At fifteen, she was younger than Pamela, but the two had gone to the same school, until Werner enrolled his daughter at Tientsin Grammar. The girls had run into each other the day before at the skating rink, where they caught up on news about school, their lives and mutual friends, agreeing to meet again the following afternoon.

They arranged to meet outside the Grand Hôtel des Wagons Lits at five o'clock. Ethel arrived a couple of minutes past the hour, and Pamela turned up a few minutes later. They walked their bicycles round the corner to the Gurevitch family home on Hong Kong Bank Road, where they had tea and gossiped with Ethel's mother, who also knew Pamela. Around six o'clock the girls headed over to the rink.

They skated together for an hour or so, wrapped up warmly under the bright arc lights the club had set up. A mutual friend, Lilian Marinovski, another White Russian girl who'd been at school with Pamela, was there too. At seven o'clock Pamela said she had to go home. She told Ethel and Lilian she'd promised her father she would be back by half past seven, and she knew he would worry if she was late. He was a worrier, a rather traditional father.

It had long been dark by seven, and it was freezing, with a bone-chilling wind through the blacked-out streets at the edge of the Quarter. The girls stood around the coal braziers that had been set up by the rink.

'But aren't you afraid to ride home alone?' Ethel asked Pamela, while Lilian wanted to know if she was scared of the dark. They both lived nearby, within the Quarter, and were staying out later than normal on account of it being Russian Christmas, but Pamela would have to ride a mile or so outside the Quarter to Armour Factory Alley, skirting the notorious Badlands by riding along the Tartar Wall. Then she'd be pedaling through the Tartar City in the dark, down unlit *hutong*, with not even moonlight to help. From the Tartar City, looking back into the Legation Quarter, the only landmarks at night were the spindly spires of St Michael's Church, the lights in the upper windows of the Wagons Lits and the Hôtel du Nord, and the black frame of the radio tower at the American Legation.

Pamela made what would later be considered an odd reply, one that was endlessly reported and mulled over. 'I've been alone all my life,' she told her friends. 'I am afraid of nothing—*nothing!* And besides, Peking is the safest city in the world.'

With that, she left her two friends to retrieve her bicycle. It was the last they saw of her, waving as she disappeared into that bitter January night.

狐 狸 精

Peking was populous, but it was not a nighttime city to rival Shanghai. It was more conservative, reserved. Apart from the Badlands.

Lying in a narrow strip between the Legation Quarter and the Tartar City, the Badlands was a network of twisting *hutong* devoted to sin and vice. This part of Peking was sleepy and calm during daylight hours, but at night it grew raucous with those seeking illicit pleasures. Anything was available in the Badlands, at a price.

It had been known until the fall of the Qing dynasty in 1911 as the Glacis, a military term meaning a piece of land kept open to provide a buffer zone, where attackers would be forced to expose themselves. Back then it was a no-man's-land between Chinese and foreign Peking, a place where European troops were put through their drills and privileged foreigners exercised their horses. Since then the Glacis had become developed, and the polo fields swallowed up. Yet it retained its no-man's-land feel, neither completely Chinese nor completely foreign, although technically it was under the jurisdiction of the Peking police.

Into this vacuum moved the dive bars, brothels and nightclubs, the gambling and drug dens, most of them run by stateless White Russians or, increasingly, Koreans acting as fronts for the Japanese. Effectively beyond the law, it had become the playground of the foreign underworld of Peking. The stiff-backed authorities of the Legation Quarter ignored the sin on their doorstep, and the Peking police turned up only to receive their 'gifts' from the various criminal elements.

By the 1930s part of the old Mongol Market had also been absorbed into the district, which was now commonly known as the Badlands. Along with low-life Chinese and foreigners, it drew curious visitors, and also played host to the U.S. Marines and the British, French and Italian soldiers who guarded the nearby legations. Its rookeries of vice catered for all tastes, no matter how exotic or depraved.

The Badlands felt impermanent, hastily thrown together, with buildings that had been knocked up from rough wood or cheap brick, then slathered inside with plaster to make them appear more robust than they were. Inferior lodging houses clustered on the fringes, with rooms to rent for incognito assignations. There was rotgut and hooch in the flophouses for the destitute, which were home to Peking's foreign driftwood—men and women who'd come about as far as possible to escape something they mostly kept to themselves. On the streets were Chinese beggars with suppurating sores, missing limbs, milky eyes, and goiters protruding from their necks. White Russian down-and-outs with straggly beards and frayed tsarist uniforms wandered aimlessly. The Badlands' flourishing trade in flesh, narcotics, and sleaze, wrapped up in desperate poverty, was the end of the road for many.

The Badlands' northern border was Soochow Hutong. By day this was a busy food market of butchers, sweetmeat vendors and purveyors of fruit and vegetables. At night it became a cluster of street restaurants, whose deliverymen ran meals to nearby bars and brothels. The heart of the Badlands was Chuanpan Hutong, a winding street of jerry-built structures, fetid and dank lodging houses for the transient, and all-night restaurants where pimps met their girls. Those too old, ugly or strung out to work in the brothels walked the street, touting for business. The presence of red lanterns and bouncers outside a joint indicated a late-night bar with a tacky cabaret show, or a protected brothel overseen by a fearsome madam who'd accommodate any request—white girls, Chinese girls, Chinese boys. The Olympia Cabaret was a popular spot, as were the Manhattan nightclub, the Alcazar, the Olympic Theatre and the Roma, White Russian–run Kavkaz and the Korean-run White Palace Dance Hall.

About halfway along its length, Chuanpan Hutong formed a junction with Hougou Hutong, which ran down to the Tartar Wall. The wall formed a natural southern border of the Badlands, extending all the way to the Tartar City and the Fox Tower. On Hougou Hutong, street sellers sold opium, heroin, along with the works to inject it, and cheaply printed pornography of pubescent Chinese and White Russian Carole Lombard lookalikes.

The only piece of goodness in the area was the church of the China Inland Mission. Converts were few and far between, but unwanted babies were daily arrivals. The Protestant missionaries had dubbed their church the Island of Hope.

The 'better' class of foreigners thought the Badlands typified Chinese depravity; the Chinese thought it symbolic of barbarian foreign ways. Both mostly pretended it didn't exist. They were fooling themselves.

狐 狸 精

From the moment Colonel Han and DCI Dennis began talking about Pamela, during that short car ride from the train station to Morrison Street, it was clear they were talking about two different Pamelas. Both men realized that they knew far less about her than they'd thought.

Dennis knew her father by reputation, as a former diplomat and Sinologist. He also knew that Werner had a holiday home at Peitaiho, as did the DCI himself. And while his son attended the rival Ecole Municipale Française, Dennis was aware of the status of Tientsin Grammar, and he assumed that Pamela was a typical student—polite, well mannered, somewhat standoffish, as the school tended to think rather highly of itself. Pamela was probably mostly interested in sports and studying.

Dennis had brought photographs from Tientsin. One showed Pamela in an end-of-term photograph, a relatively plain-looking girl with yellow-blond hair pulled tight to her head, parted from right to left and bunched about her ears in curled plaits. Her shapeless Tientsin Grammar smock and regulation blouse did nothing to enhance her appearance; neither did the thick school stockings and functional black shoes—her legs looked stocky, her ankles fat.

There were other photos of Pamela in the school hockey team, crouching down in the front row, and in the netball team, standing stiff and formal, still with those stocky legs. The photos were between a year and eighteen months old, and in them Pamela was sullen, rigid. She was looking away from the camera, uninterested, unsmiling.

Han, on the other hand, had discovered a very different Pamela. He'd been asking questions, reading accounts of the phone calls that had come into Morrison Street, the anonymous letters, the reports from his detectives. And he had a photograph of his own to show Dennis, one he'd had his detectives secure from the Werner household. Over the coming days, it was to appear on the front pages of Chinese and international newspapers under the simple heading MISS PAMELA WERNER, MURDER VICTIM.

In this photograph, Pamela was less a girl and more a woman. It was a posed studio portrait, taken at Hartung's, the best-known studio in Peking, and showed Pamela standing before an art-deco curtain, alongside a vase of flowers on a shelf draped with patterned Chinese silk. Her hair was fashionably slicked down, parted in the centre and curled under, à la Norma Shearer or Claudette Colbert. She was wearing a modern, stylishly tailored dress, only slightly lowered at the neck and suggesting a flat chest—in vogue in the 1930s Hollywood movies Pamela queued up to see at the cinemas around Dashala. The dress was pulled in tight at the waist to accentuate her gently curved hips. If her legs were still stocky, you couldn't tell; they were hidden under the full-length dress. One small foot clad in a delicately embroidered shoe poked out below.

This time Pamela was looking straight into the lens of the camera, with a confidence the school photographs lacked. Her lips were painted, her eyebrows plucked; there was a little kohl under her eyes. She was emerging as a good-looking woman who commanded attention.

Han had sent his men to Hartung's on Legation Street and learnt that the photo had been taken on Monday 4 January—three days before Pamela was killed. The people who knew Pamela in Tientsin were shocked by her glamorous portrait when they saw it in the papers, and those who knew her in Peking were surprised to see her looking so drab and plain in her Tientsin Grammar uniform. Han reviewed the case so far for Dennis: the horrific preliminary results of the autopsy, and the usual crank calls, false confessions and accusations, including the worthless drunk White Russian who was ratted out by his jealous wife.

Dennis was interested in the story of the rickshaw puller, Sun Te-hsing, who'd been seen washing his bloodstained cushion cover by the Fox Tower. Han told Dennis that the puller had picked up a late-night fare on the evening of Russian Christmas, a foreigner who'd been drinking in the Badlands and had got into a fight. He had bled on Sun's covers, and the puller had to wash them; nobody would hire his rickshaw with a soiled cushion.

The puller had been scared during questioning, Han claimed. He was a nineteen-year-old peasant who'd come to the city with no other options than pulling a rickshaw. He and some sixty thousand other pullers working in the city managed half a million fares among them daily, through cold or heat, for mere pennies.

Han described the business for Dennis. A country bumpkin, unwise to the ways of the big city, was charged high rent for a rickshaw and so had little left over after a day's work. Only the toughest made it through more than a few Peking winters plying the streets and alleyways. It was easy to imagine a puller growing desperate enough to grab a chance at a drunk foreigner's wallet, but that didn't make him a deranged killer who sliced open young white girls' bodies. And anyway, this wasn't a case of robbery. The watch would have been the first thing to go.

Han told Dennis he had sent his detectives to the Legation Quarter address the rickshaw puller had given. There they'd rousted a hungover American from his bed, a member of the Horse Marine Guards that protected the American Legation. He confirmed he'd been drinking and fighting at one of the bars on Chuanpan Hutong, where he got a busted nose for his trouble and a few cuts. He'd bled on the seat of the rickshaw on his way home. Han had seen the stains himself, and they were nothing like what would have come from Pamela's wounds.

The lead had gone nowhere, Han told Dennis. They should forget about it.

狐 狸 精

The two detectives divided up the interviews according to their backgrounds. Han would interview Werner's Chinese servants and also try to trace shopkeepers, rickshaw pullers, taxi drivers, staff at the skating rink, neighbours, and anyone else who could shed light on Pamela's last days. Dennis would talk to Pamela's foreign friends, starting with Ethel Gurevitch, and try to work out her movements. The murder was barely two days ago; memories should still be fresh.

Han went to Werner's house on Sunday morning, where he started with Ho Ying, the cook. On the day Pamela was killed, Ho Ying had prepared a lunch of macaroni for her and Werner. Around three that afternoon he went to the nearby market on Tung Tan Pailou Hutong to buy, among other things, the pork for the meatballs Pamela had requested, as well as some traditional Peking sweetmeats. Pamela loved sugary preserved fruits and the glutinous rice dumplings known as *hsiao chih*, and regularly asked him to buy them for her.

Everything was in accordance with what the cook had told one of Han's constables on Friday. Pamela had said she'd be going out around four and would be back at seven thirty. Ho Ying had prepared the meatballs and rice, which she never ate, and the master had grown increasingly anxious when Pamela failed to return. Ho Ying, who went home at the end of the workday to his family a few *hutong* away, had stayed later than usual at the house that night. Eventually Werner asked him to enquire after Pamela at the skating rink, but it was closed. The Chinese workers who were sweeping the ice told him that two hundred skaters had used the rink that night, but they didn't know Pamela. Ho Ying dashed back to Armour Factory Alley to give Werner the bad news, and then went home.

Next Han talked to the sixty-four-year-old gatekeeper, Yen Ping, who confirmed that Werner and Pamela had had lunch together at one o'clock that day, and at two o'clock Werner left for his regular afternoon walk. Pamela went out shortly after three, by which time Ho Ying had left for the market. Werner returned at five, later coming and going several times to look for his daughter. Yen Ping remained at the gate throughout that night; he was there from noon on Thursday until Friday morning, keeping watch for her. He saw her leave just after three o'clock, and then he never saw her again.

There was little more Han could do at the courtyard residence until he returned with Dennis to interview Werner, a prospect neither of them relished. The old man was still recovering from shock. His doctor had told Han that Werner's heart had suffered a severe strain.

That morning it was Dennis who was hearing new information—at the Gurevitches' house on Hong Kong Bank Road. Ethel had already given a statement to police, claiming she'd reached the Wagons Lits a little late, just after five, and Pamela had turned up a couple of minutes after that. Pamela had told Ethel she'd been there earlier, but as Ethel hadn't arrived yet, she'd gone for a walk. The two girls then had tea with Ethel's mother and father, after which they went skating. Pamela had ridden off on her bicycle; Ethel had stayed at the rink with Lilian Marinovski until it closed at eight.

What had they talked about over tea? Dennis learned for the first time about Pamela's boyfriend in Tientsin. According to Ethel, Pamela was excited that he was coming to Peking for a few days, although she didn't say what his name was. Ethel assumed he'd be staying at Armour Factory Alley. Next Dennis asked what Pamela had eaten while she was with Ethel—had she eaten any Chinese food? No, said Ethel, just a little bread and butter and a slice of cake with tea. Her mother confirmed this. Pamela had eaten and drunk very little, claiming she wasn't hungry, but she didn't say when she'd last eaten. Nor did Pamela have any Chinese food at the skating rink.

What about Pamela's clothing? Dennis asked. What had she been wearing that afternoon? Ethel recounted the tartan skirt, the fashionable Aertex blouse, the woolen cardigan, along with a belted blue overcoat, mittens, beret and stockings. No, Ethel didn't know the names of any of Pamela's friends in Peking, except Lilian Marinovski, whom they'd met at the rink that night. Ethel told Dennis she thought Pamela had seemed different—more outgoing, grown-up. She had new friends and new pastimes. She was invited to parties and dances. She was interested in boys; she hadn't been when Ethel had known her in Peking. At school she'd been quiet but occasionally rebellious; she'd got into trouble and been sent to Tientsin.

From the Gurevitches' house, Dennis went across the Quarter to visit Lilian Marinovski, but this time learned nothing new. At eighteen, Lilian was closer to Pamela's age and still a student in Peking. She had done most of the talking at the skating rink, and hadn't asked Pamela many questions. Pamela hadn't mentioned any boyfriends, but Lilian too thought she seemed more confident, more grown-up. It had been a chance encounter with a girl she vaguely knew, nothing more.

Han and Dennis met back at Morrison Street at lunchtime, where there was nothing to be had but bitter police-station tea and a tin of Hatamen cigarettes. Apart from the boyfriend, there was precious little new information—everyone questioned had confirmed the times and details they'd given the previous day. Dennis made a note to ask Werner when they interviewed him if he'd been expecting Pamela to bring anyone home in the next day or two. Then he telephoned the station in Tientsin and asked one of his detectives to find out who Pamela's boyfriend was, and where he'd been between seven in the evening on 7 January and early the following morning.

'Dig around a bit,' he told the detective on the phone. 'Find out who her friends were, what her teachers thought of her, what her behaviour was like.' The boyfriend was the closest thing they had to a suspect, though there was no apparent motive, and they had no idea if he'd been in Peking at the time. Or even if he existed, and wasn't just a youthful girl's fantasy to impress her friends.

There was one hole in the story. Pamela had left Armour Factory Alley just after three and had met Ethel Gurevitch shortly after five. The Wagons Lits was little more than a twenty-minute ride from Pamela's house, or half an hour maximum along the Tartar Wall, her preferred route to avoid the Badlands. That left an hour and a half unaccounted for that afternoon.

Han gave his men pictures of Pamela and sent them to fan out between the house in Armour Factory Alley and the Wagons Lits. Show the picture to everyone, he told them, every shopkeeper, café owner, market-stall trader; every hawker, hotel receptionist, gatekeeper. Someone must have seen her. And sure enough, someone had.

The break came quickly—Sunday evening. A concierge at the Wagons Lits had seen Pamela between three and four on the Thursday afternoon. One of Han's uniformed constables phoned to say he'd found the man.

The detectives drove across the Legation Quarter to the hotel, where the constable was waiting in the lobby with the concierge. Han showed him the photograph of Pamela again, and he identified her as having come into the Wagons Lits on 7 January to enquire about taking a room there—he remembered that it was some time between three and four o'clock.

The concierge's desk was about twenty feet from the main reception, and the girl had entered the lobby, gone to the reception desk and taken a leaflet on the rates. She had been alone. The concierge couldn't remember exactly whom she'd spoken to on the desk, but he was sure it was Pamela—the blond hair, the grey eyes.

But why was she interested in a room at the Wagons Lits when she lived just a mile or so away? Was she planning a rendezvous with her boyfriend from Tientsin? Or had she argued with her father, and wanted to leave the house on Armour Factory Alley?

The detectives needed to talk to Werner in depth. That could wait until tomorrow, Monday, not just the start of a new week but also the day of the official inquest at the British Legation into the death of Pamela.

That night Colonel Han went home to sleep after nearly three days of nonstop work. Dennis returned to the Wagons Lits, where he spent a few hours in the hotel bar tapping into the old China hands' rumour mill, and the nightly session of gossip and tip swapping among Peking's foreign bright young things. He told Inspector Botham to do the same at the bar in the Hôtel du Nord. Dennis knew that the only subject on anyone's lips would be Pamela Werner.

If there was anything useful to be learned about her or her father, the hotel bars were where tongues would loosen.

An Old China Hand

*T*he inquest into the death of Pamela Werner began Monday morning at the British Legation, standard procedure in the questionable death of a British national.

The British had the largest of all the foreign legations, a spacious compound of twenty-two buildings, guarded by soldiers of the King's Royal Surrey Regiment and by two oversize stone lions at the gates. Britain's imperial power and prestige radiated not just over Chinese Peking but over the other legations in the Quarter too. The British Legation was the place where besieged foreigners had huddled for their last stand against the Boxers in 1900. The vengeful slaughter and looting of Peking by the foreign troops had begun later that year on the same site.

A cold, functional, unadorned room inside the main building had been set aside for the inquest, which was presided over by His Britannic Majesty's consul, Nicholas Fitzmaurice, this morning acting as HBM's coroner in Peking. Fitzmaurice, the man with whom Werner had clashed in the past, was a career diplomat, formerly the consul in Kashgar, in China's restive far west region of Turkestan, before coming to Peking in 1933. He was the archetype of the humourless, formal British envoy, although his aides said he was shaken at what he had been told of Pamela's injuries. Still, his British stiff upper lip was on display now.

The consul had the only comfortable chair in the room; everyone else was relegated to hard-backed wooden seats behind a row of black-suited legation flunkies. Han, dog-tired, attended as the investigating officer, Dennis as official British liaison to the Peking police, and Commissioner Thomas represented the Legation Quarter police. The public gallery was crowded with the gentlemen of the press—the English-language papers of the China coast, stringers for the *Times* of London, the *New York Times* and a host of other international papers looking for a story. Pamela's death had run on front pages syndicated from Adelaide to Winnipeg—pretty European girls being murdered in the Orient was big news in the wider white world.

The proceedings that morning were perfunctory. Just a single witness was called—Pamela's father, E. T. C. Werner, described by the press as 'bent and white-haired,' a man broken in his grief. Fitzmaurice saw Werner as a cantankerous irritant; the two had fallen out in Kashgar, when disputes had arisen over the expeditions of the archaeologist Sir Aurel Stein across Central Asia, and specifically his acquisition of many ancient scripts from the Caves of the Thousand Buddhas near Dunhuang. These had been taken to the British Museum, and the Chinese were not happy about it. Werner, who'd become involved in the matter as a noted scholar, thought Stein's removal of the ancient documents was tantamount to looting, and he argued about it with Fitzmaurice, who backed Stein and the museum. Now the old man sat before him as the bereaved father of a murdered daughter. It was awkward.

Dr Cheng and the other doctors at the Peking Union Medical College had held back their findings while they continued to examine Pamela's body for clues, the new scientific term being *forensics*. Han had encouraged them to keep the medical details out of the inquest, and therefore out of the newspapers. Right now, making the details public would only up the number of crank calls and do nothing to assist the investigation. Han already had a steady stream of lunatics claiming to have murdered Pamela; he didn't need a line of heart thieves outside the door too.

And there was public security to think about. Organ theft was a delicate subject in China—rumours ran riot of unnatural medicines, strange rituals, triad ceremonies. All the more so when it was a young foreign girl. Peking was ever closer to tipping over into blind panic and chaos; Han didn't want to give it a further push.

Formalities. All Fitzmaurice had to do was convene the inquest and call on Werner to positively identify his daughter. Because of her disfigured state, Werner did this through her clothing and her watch.

Pamela's name was then entered into the record by Fitzmaurice's clerk. When asked his daughter's age, Werner gave it as nineteen years and eleven months. The press scribbled away—every newspaper thus far had got her age wrong.

With that, Werner sat down. Fitzmaurice declared the body to be that of Pamela Werner, British subject. He noted that Colonel Han of the Peking police was the investigating officer and adjourned the inquest, pending further medical testimony. Dennis's presence was not formally noted. Fitzmaurice then asked Han when Pamela's body might be released to her family for burial.

Han, standing before the bench with his hat in his hands, wearing his black dress uniform and leather boots for the occasion, said he would ensure the body was released the moment the doctors at the medical college had completed their work. Fitzmaurice nodded and banged his gavel.

The procedure had lasted barely twenty minutes. The crowd filed out of the cold room. More press were massed outside the front gate, milling between the acacia trees that lined British Road. Flashbulbs popped and Han repeated his customary 'No comment.' Werner slipped out a side door to avoid the scrum, a small courtesy arranged by Fitzmaurice. The press was left with no headline but WERNER INQUEST IS HELD.

Han and Dennis headed back to Morrison Street. Dennis had

arranged to meet Werner at Armour Factory Alley that afternoon, having decided against bringing him in to Morrison Street for questioning. It wouldn't look good, and besides, Dennis wanted to see the house, Pamela's room, get a feel for her and her father in their own environment. Both detectives had the sense that the Werner household had been far from normal.

Now they sat smoking in the incident room. Han's officers had cleared some space, pushed back the regulation blackwood furniture, and pinned up the photographs taken at the crime scene. Black-and-white photographs with thick black arrows pointing to where the body had been found; close-up shots of Pamela's wristwatch, her silk chemise, the bloodied skating-rink card, her shoes, the oil lantern that had been recovered nearby. Han kept the photos taken at the medical college in a bland manila envelope locked in his desk drawer. He had shown them to Dennis, of course, but they were too gruesome to be put on display, and the risk was too great that some constable looking for extra money at New Year would sell them to the press.

狐 狸 精

Han had been hearing gossip about Werner, and what he'd learnt he now told Dennis.

The servants' talk was that Pamela's father was a strange man, though a respected one. He paid fair; he didn't mistreat his staff. He could speak more Chinese dialects than they could; he knew their culture, was a scholar. But with no mother's influence, the daughter had been wild, and there was trouble at school. The old man couldn't control her; he went off on long expeditions and left her alone with the servants. It wasn't a harmonious household.

Her return home for the Christmas holidays had been a fraught time, according to the local gossip—the servants reported arguments, shouting, even a fight between Werner and one of Pamela's suitors, on the street outside the courtyard. She'd been dating men, going out for tiffins, dinner, dancing, late nights. Werner had not been happy about her newly independent social life; he was old-school, saw it all as too modern. He'd been particularly concerned about one suitor, a half-Chinese, half-Portuguese man called, oddly, John O'Brian, who had become obsessed with Pamela in Tientsin and apparently proposed to her. This man was now living in Peking.

Pamela had rejected him, but the whole affair worried her father. Then he'd taken against a Chinese student who'd called for her several times. The gossip was that Werner told him to go away and stop bothering Pamela, and it had escalated into a fight out on Armour Factory Alley, a spectacle witnessed by the neighbours. Werner, in his seventies, had rapped the boy across the face with his cane, breaking his nose.

It seemed that Pamela's father had a temper.

狐狸精

Edward Theodore Chalmers Werner was born in 1864 aboard the passenger liner *Black Swan* when it was anchored at Port Chalmers, New Zealand. His Prussian father and English mother had added the name Chalmers to his birth certificate as a joke.

Joseph and Harriet Werner were comfortably off, thanks to his father's family trust fund, and Joseph had a wanderlust. He took his own family travelling far and wide, across South America, the United States and continental Europe. For a decade they were a well-heeled gypsy band, until Werner, his three older sisters and one older brother all came of school age. Eventually they settled in England, where Werner attended a respectable public school, Tonbridge. But the scholarly young Werner didn't much care for this school, which put the physical before the intellectual and was Spartan rather than scholarly—a factory for the production of empire builders.

Joseph's early death in 1878, at the age of sixty-four, meant that when Werner finished his schooling he had to find a career. He passed the entrance exams for a Far Eastern cadetship with the Foreign Office and was sent to Peking as a student interpreter for two years, to get his Chinese up to scratch.

Peking in the late 1880s was a very different place from the Peking of 1937. It was a city slowly recovering from multiple devastations, one of which was the Taiping Rebellion. The Taiping rebels had been intent on overthrowing the Qing dynasty and establishing a theocracy in China. Their charismatic leader, Hung Hsiu-chüan, declared himself to be the half brother of Jesus Christ, and anointed himself the Heavenly King of the Taiping, ruler of the Heavenly Kingdom of Great Peace. Rarely was a kingdom less aptly named—Hung's rebellion lasted fifteen years, from 1850 to 1864, and left as many as fifteen million Chinese dead. There'd also been the Opium Wars, which ended in 1860 with the sacking and looting of Peking; and in the late 1870s, northern China was stricken by a great drought and famine.

The foreign community of Peking at the time Werner first went there was small and tight-knit, with far fewer Europeans than in Shanghai or Tientsin—really only diplomats, the men of the foreign-run Chinese Customs Service and missionaries. In the late 1880s a trip outside the Legation Quarter by a foreigner would cause crowds to assemble, and cries of 'Yang guizi' ('Foreign devil'). The Legation Quarter was also significantly smaller in area; not until after the Boxer Rebellion was it enlarged. There was Kierulff's general store and the Swiss-run Chamot's Hotel, and that was just about it. Peking was a remote, strange city, a hardship posting, but Werner knew immediately that he had arrived in the country he would devote his life to.

He sucked up the sights and smells of Peking, the carts jostling around the crowded gates, the imperial inner city and the sprawling, teeming outer city that lay beyond the mighty walls. He loved the street hawkers, the stalls selling everything from dried fruits and iced sweets to baked yams and rice-stuffed lotus roots. He suffered the periodic blinding dust storms and the flooding when the rains came, the infernal summer heat and the bone-chilling winter cold.

Once his two years as a student interpreter were up, Werner moved from posting to posting, steadily climbing the diplomatic ladder. He did a spell in the chancery at the Peking Legation, then a year in Canton, two in Tientsin, and another couple in Macao, before a furlough home to attend law school at London's Middle Temple, where he qualified as a barrister. Back in China he was promoted through the minor treaty ports—Hangchow, Pagoda Anchorage, the steamy tropical island of Hainan, then a couple of years on the Gulf of Tonkin, in the remote Pakhoi. He was pushed up the ladder to officially open the new treaty port of Kongmoon—not much of a place—and this was followed by another year's furlough in England. He was rewarded with an appointment as consul at the busy tea port of Kiukiang, where he served four years.

During all this time Werner remained single. Then, at the age of forty-five, he met his future wife.

Gladys Nina Ravenshaw was the twenty-three-year-old daughter of an old and wealthy English family. Born in Brighton in 1886, she was the second oldest of four girls. Her father, the blue-blooded Lieutenant Colonel Charles Withers Ravenshaw, was an old-school British Empire hero. He had been a member of the famed Indian Political Department, was in the British Army in India, and was a veteran of the Second Anglo-Afghan War, part of the forces that fought at Kandahar and occupied Kabul. He was also a former British ambassador to Nepal, a good sportsman and a crack shot. Werner admired him greatly, describing him as 'the best sort of Englishman.'

Gladys Nina's childhood had been lived mostly outdoors, either in the picturesque Sussex village of Turners Hill or at one or another hill station in the Raj. She and her family followed her father through his various posts, in Rajputana, Secunderabad, Mewar on the Persian Gulf, Mysore, the hill district of Coorg, until he became the British Resident in Gwalior and then in Nepal. In 1906 he retired, and the family returned to Sussex.

Gladys Nina was a girl of the British Empire. She was sporty; she loved tennis, ice-skating, golf and particularly horses—anything equestrian. She had raced across the South Downs of Sussex and played polo with the young blades of the British Army in India. She also played violin and piano, recited poetry and was good at languages. And while she had never been more than a perfunctory churchgoer, she developed a strong interest in Theosophy, the movement of Madame Blavatsky, which was something of a fashion at the time among upper-class English girls. Theosophy held that all religions contained a portion of the truth, quite a radical idea back then, and the Ravenshaw girls certainly knew it annoyed the old lieutenant colonel.

Accomplished and attractive, Gladys Nina was known in the society columns as the last of the unmarried 'pristine Ravenshaws.' She had a well-proportioned face, lustrous hair, dark brown eyes, good skin and an elegant neck, and it's hard to believe that she didn't have other suitors chasing after her, young men her own age. Nevertheless she fell for Werner, who, though older, was deemed suitable marriage material by the Ravenshaws.

The two had met at a Theosophy lecture in Aldeburgh; Werner had been in the genteel Suffolk seaside town to visit his now elderly mother. As he had to return to China to take up a posting as consul in the important treaty port of Foochow, he was forced to court Gladys Nina by mail. Eventually he proposed. She travelled to China, and the couple were married in Hong Kong's cross-shaped St John's Cathedral in December 1911. The newlyweds honeymooned in Macao before returning to Foochow, where Werner remained as consul until he retired in 1914.

That they chose to stay on in China afterwards raised a few eyebrows. Retirement to a cosy fireplace on the English south coast was the usual route. Werner, his pension rendering him relatively wealthy in China at the time, rented a large four-storey house on Peking's San Tiao Hutong, an ancient street of jade and antiques vendors near the Ch'ienmen Gate. Being central, it allowed Gladys Nina to easily explore the streets and familiarise herself with her new town.

Childless, in 1919 Werner and Gladys Nina adopted Pamela from the Catholic-run orphanage at the Cathedral of the Immaculate Conception of the Blessed Virgin, known also as the Portuguese Church or the South Church. Here the nuns took in the unwanted babies of Peking's indigent foreigners, mostly White Russians. In those years of turmoil, as the White Russians fled the Bolshevik revolution, travelling across the steppes of Siberia and down into Harbin, Tientsin, Peking and Shanghai, the orphanages became crowded with discarded white babies. For the mothers, their money gone, their husbands and brothers still in Russia fighting in the White Army, babies were an encumbrance or a mortifying embarrassment.

狐 狸 精

What was it about that one baby girl, among so many, that led the Werners to choose her?

Perhaps Gladys Nina stared into her grey eyes and the decision was instant. Grey eyes, more so than other colours perhaps, seem somehow to look deep into you. Whatever the reason, the Werners took her home to San Tiao Hutong and named her Pamela—Greek for honey and all things sweet. They did not know her birth mother, her birthday or her exact age, since the nuns had not known either. The date of birth listed on the passport issued to her by the British Legation was 7 February 1917.

As she grew up, Pamela never kept her adoption a secret. When people commented on her distinctive grey eyes or questioned her about her heritage, she would say that she supposed her birth mother had been Russian, as grey eyes were most commonly found in Russians.

In 1922 tragedy struck. Gladys Nina passed away at the age of just thirty-five, leaving five-year-old Pamela motherless and Werner a grieving widower.

He began to dedicate all his books to his dead wife, and mostly avoided the social life of the Legation Quarter in favour of scholarly work. If he was considered reclusive, it was because he preferred his study and library, considered one of the best in Peking. He built a name for himself as a China hand and writer, and was a gifted linguist. On top of the several Chinese dialects he spoke, he was fluent in French, German, Spanish and Portuguese. He was given a position with the Chinese Historiographical Bureau and was considered a Friend of China by the academic establishment at Peking University.

As for Pamela, Gladys Nina had left her $20,000 in silver dollars, which she had been able to access on her eighteenth birthday. That made her a rich young woman.

It accounted for the platinum and diamond watch—a treat to herself from the exclusive Sennet Frères jewelers on Legation Street. Platinum was then *the* choice of society ladies. Wallis Simpson, making headlines as the Duchess of Windsor, declared, 'After seven p.m. all you can wear is platinum,' and prices soared as the metal became fashionable.

The watch had cost $450 in silver dollars, and Ethel Gurevitch told DCI Dennis she didn't know anyone else with one like it, not even close.

Pamela's inheritance was no secret.

狐 狸 精

When a police officer from Tientsin's Victoria Road station visited the house of Pamela's boyfriend and informed him of her death, the boy was at first disbelieving and then distraught.

Superintendent Bill Greenslade, Dennis's deputy, had later gone to fully interview the good-looking Mischa Horjelsky—sports star and head prefect of the Upper Sixth—and thought the boy was genuine. He had an alibi, one that was backed by his family—a good family—and their servants. He'd been at home in Tientsin all the time Pamela was in Peking.

Mischa had no idea who could be responsible for Pamela's murder. He had been planning to travel to Peking that week, he said, to spend a few days with her and meet her father.

Tientsin was in shock at the news. Werner was well known to many people in the city, and Pamela was known as a quiet student in her mid-teens.

狐 狸 精

Now Dennis and Han had two questions that needed answering.

First: Where was the murder scene?

The autopsy had confirmed beyond a shadow of a doubt that this wasn't the Fox Tower. Han detailed all available men to search out hotels and lodging houses in the Tartar City and the Badlands, anywhere people rented rooms, and collate the names of all guests for the evening of 7 January and the following morning. They were to ask about any rooms found with blood in them, or whose sheets had disappeared, or where two people had checked in and only one checked out.

Pamela's photograph was to be shown to all doormen, night watchmen, gatekeepers, concierges, receptionists and porters who'd been on duty that Thursday night and Friday morning—and if they were currently off duty, the officer was to have them come in or go to see them. Don't miss anyone, Han told his men, Chinese or foreign, from the Grand Hôtel de Pékin to the worst flea-bitten flophouse in the Badlands. The Grand Hôtel de Pékin, although it was patronized exclusively by foreigners, was situated just outside the Legation Quarter, and so technically Han's territory.

The policemen were ordered to check every bar, nightclub, restaurant—somewhere that evening, Pamela had eaten Chinese food. The men started in the eastern district and then fanned out.

More constables were sent to check anywhere that was secluded and quiet at night—temples, parks, warehouses, right along the desolate Tartar Wall. Every place within the radius of each police box, starting from the Fox Tower and moving out, was to be searched.

As Han's authority didn't extend to the protected island of the Legation Quarter, Dennis requested the right to conduct house-to-house searches there, but the Administrative Commission of the Diplomatic Quarter, backed by the British Legation and Consul Fitzmaurice, refused. What was DCI Dennis insinuating? A search of Chinese Peking would be sufficient.

The second question concerned transportation.

Dennis and Han were assuming the killer had used a car. He could have pulled up on City Road, which passed by the Fox Tower, dragged the body down to the ditch and then driven off. There were over two thousand private cars registered in Peking in 1937, and they all needed to be checked, along with the city's fleet of taxis. Han was aware that the registration of cars was haphazard at best, but still, the checks had to be done. Traffic police were told to stop all cars with non-Peking licence plates and check them as well.

Han also sent men to scour the city's flea markets, junk shops and any other places the killer might have disposed of those items of Pamela's still unaccounted for—her ice skates and bicycle, her mittens and coat and beret.

It was not possible to search every room in every house in Peking, and a search of the Legation Quarter had been officially ruled out. But somewhere in the city was a room with a lot of blood, and Han and Dennis were betting that the killers would not have transported the body far—they felt sure that the murder had happened in the Tartar City.

They were working on a number of assumptions:

The killer or killers lived alone, or had access to a private place where they wouldn't be disturbed by other residents or servants.

They had access to a car to move the body and someone to drive it. In order to avoid discovery, they would not have driven the dead body farther than was necessary.

They'd had a lot of cleaning up to do, and it was unlikely they'd have been able to remove all traces of blood from the room and their clothing.

Meanwhile, somewhere out there were Pamela's internal organs.

Armour Factory Alley

*D*CI Dennis went to Armour Factory Alley to interview Werner, accompanied by Inspector Botham and Sergeant Binetsky. It was a tricky situation.

Werner was a grieving father, and it seemed that foreign Peking felt his loss. It had certainly been stunned to read in the newspapers that wild dogs had mauled the body, statements which, while false, were taken as true. Had people known the full extent of Pamela's mutilations, they would perhaps have been beyond shock and in sheer panic. But Dennis had only been in Peking for a matter of days, and already he was exceeding his strictly imposed Foreign Office limits by taking the investigation outside the confines of the Legation Quarter. His copper's instincts left him no choice.

With no firm leads or suspects as yet, and with robbery ruled out, experience told Dennis that Werner was the prime suspect. London, Peking, it made little difference—few people were killed by someone they had no acquaintance with. Murder was personal. Nine times out of ten, people were killed by people they thought loved them—wives by husbands, children by parents, lovers by lovers. For now, Werner, whatever his former high office, whatever his age, was their prime suspect.

Dennis knew he had to be careful. Werner might be retired, but he remained well connected, right to the top of the British establishment in China. And that establishment was watching this case like a hawk; it still saw Britain as chief among the foreign powers in China, and it prized British prestige above all else. It would not want to see a former British consul put on trial for killing and butchering his daughter. The legation had begrudgingly accepted Dennis's involvement in the case—they had little choice, given his qualifications—but it didn't mean they liked it, and it didn't mean they wouldn't pull the old-pals act and try to influence him. He'd been waiting for their call since he'd arrived.

So a light touch was needed, at least initially. Dennis walked along Armour Factory Alley, getting a feel for the street. The older, less modernised houses had windows of thick translucent paper rather than glass. One or two new concrete buildings had appeared in recent years, with more solid masonry. Both ends of the alley led on to more alleys, forming a network that ran from the Peking Academy back to the fetid canal and the Fox Tower. Armour Factory Alley ran west into Soochow Hutong, which then continued to the Badlands, and through to the edge of the Legation Quarter.

Dennis hadn't realized how close to Pamela's home her body had been dumped, and how close that was to the Quarter, with the Badlands forming a no-man's-land between the two areas.

He did know that Werner had been one of the first foreigners to move into Armour Factory Alley. The scholar had rented the whole courtyard house for himself, a space that perhaps four or five Chinese families might have occupied in these cramped times, as people flooded into the city from the surrounding countryside.

The three police officers were admitted by Yen Ping, the gatekeeper, and shown through the courtyard and into the house. That first look at a suspect's home was important. Dennis saw traditional dark Chinese furniture, red-lacquered pillars, features of latticework and bamboo. It was gloomy inside, with few lights to illuminate the decor. There were objets d'art Werner had collected from his expeditions around China and Mongolia, but they were placed like exhibits in a museum, which only made the place seem even more austere. It felt like an old man's house, not something a nineteen-year-old girl would enjoy. Or maybe home was home, and Pamela hadn't noticed the atmosphere.

Dennis was shown through to Werner's study, leaving Botham and Binetsky to wait outside. The room faced south for maximum sunlight and was lined with floor-to-ceiling bookshelves thick with Chinese and English titles. Off to one side was Werner's private library, where Dennis could see more shelves, more books.

The old man was slumped in a chair at his desk, which was made of heavy mahogany and teakwood. Its drawers must have been lined to preserve their contents: Dennis could smell camphorwood or sandalwood. He'd seen Werner's photo in newspapers, and had once attended a lecture he'd given in Tientsin on Chinese myths. He'd also seen him on the beach at Peitaiho, sitting under a sunshade, reading a book. Perhaps he'd even seen Pamela there too—playing in the sand, riding the donkeys, swimming—without knowing who she was.

Dennis was aware that many people found Werner difficult to like, though they respected his learning and his years in China. He knew too that the old man was a committed atheist, which annoyed both the missionaries and the Sunday pious who saw church as duty. Werner certainly had his peculiarities—he was a virtual teetotaler in a community that drank regularly and in large quantities, and he was known for having eschewed company in all his postings, however remote, as well as in Peking and Tientsin. 'The socially popular man is intellectually poor!' Werner had once written.

So he wasn't one of the clubbable, social Brits. Dennis was—he had to be, his job demanded it—but he drew no immediate conclusions about a man who wasn't. In Tientsin he moved in higher social circles than he had in London. A Scotland Yard detective wasn't everyone's ideal Pall Mall club member, but out of the straitjacket of English class conventions, and with a higher rank, he'd found himself in the surroundings of the Tientsin Club. He'd had to visit a tailor to have a dinner jacket made. Fortunately his job gave him an excuse to skip church and the more boring committee meetings. But if Werner preferred not to retire to the club for rounds of whisky sodas, reheated gossip and a fortnight-old copy of the *Times*, well, that was hardly the hallmark of a murderer.

Dennis expressed his condolences to Werner. He intended a conversation rather than an interview. He was on Chinese soil, and without Han present he could not formally question, caution or charge anyone. But the old man was uncommunicative and, the DCI felt, somewhat dismissive. Why was Dennis in Peking? Surely the case was under the Chinese police and Colonel Han?

Dennis explained his involvement, saying that he and Han were working together. He didn't mention that the British Legation did not trust the Chinese, or that they were pressing for a result. He didn't mention the limits that had been placed on his involvement, or that he was stretching them already.

Werner seemed to accept it all. He said little and hardly looked at Dennis, his eyes ranging instead along his bookshelves. What Dennis didn't know was that Werner rarely looked directly at anyone he addressed, and when he did make eye contact with Dennis, the DCI couldn't help feeling that instinctive tug that told him someone was looking down their nose at him. He shrugged it off. Werner had spent the best part of his life in the diplomatic service, where snobbery was an occupational hazard.

Werner laid out his movements on Pamela's final day with the dispassionate precision of the barrister he'd trained as. He had last seen his daughter in the afternoon, and when she did not return home he had gone to the Gurevitches' house, then to Commissioner Thomas's office to report her missing. He'd sent his cook to the skating rink, then he'd wandered the city looking for her.

Dennis knew that Han had already pinned down the exact time Werner was at the Gurevitches' and the time the note to Thomas had been recorded at the Legation Quarter police station, but that left a lot of time unaccounted for, the alleged searching time. Time enough for Werner to find Pamela, lose his temper, commit a murder and return home.

Dennis asked Werner to list the route he'd taken once more, and noted it down:

South to the Temple of Heaven and its adjacent park
Through the Legation Quarter
To the northern end of the city and the Lama Temple
The Confucian Hall of Examinations
The Mohammedan Mosque
The Portuguese Church

And then home. When Pamela still wasn't back next morning and no word had come, he'd gone out looking again. This time:

To the Hatamen Gate
Back along the Tartar Wall
Through the German Cemetery
Then to the Fox Tower . . . and Pamela

At this point Werner broke down.

Dennis sat back. He reminded himself that Han had told him Yen Ping was adamant Werner could not have left the house in between these two searches without the gateman knowing.

Now it was Werner who wanted details. He'd learnt nothing at the inquest. In terms as gentle as possible, Dennis described what had happened to Pamela, but it was impossible to spare the old man certain facts—the missing organs, the cutting and slashing. Werner broke down again, and looked all his seventy-two years and more. His reaction seemed real to Dennis, his grief genuine.

When could he have her body for burial? Werner wanted to know.

Soon, when the doctors had finished—it wouldn't be long now. Dennis tried to comfort the old man.

Then the DCI asked to see Pamela's room. Werner instructed the amah to show him while he remained at his desk. Dennis was taken to a small bedroom adjacent to Werner's own. After opening the door, the amah burst out crying and rushed off.

Standing in Pamela's room, Dennis could only think of the studio portrait she'd had taken just days earlier: the glamourous dress, the knowing look. Her bedroom struck him as a nunlike cubicle; there was a bed, a simple bureau, a desk and a chair. No frills of any kind. It was cold, bare, unlived in, not a young woman's room.

In her wardrobe he found the black evening dress she'd worn for the photo, and a couple of the Japanese-style silk kimonos that most foreign women kept to wear in Peking's stiflingly humid summers, but the rest of her clothing was simple—skirts, blouses, cardigans.

At that point, Werner entered the room. He looked around, seemed to sense the emptiness.

'We were to return to England soon,' he told Dennis. 'Her furniture has gone ahead, along with some books, personal items and summer clothes.'

Dennis nodded; an imminent move would explain the asceticism. But why go to England? he asked. Surely Pamela had the rest of the academic year to go, exams to take?

'I would have thought you would have known?' said Werner.

Dennis looked at him questioningly.

'She was unhappy at school in Tientsin,' the old man explained; 'she didn't want to return. There'd been trouble at schools here before. Tientsin should have been better. England was the only place for her. Perhaps with her family she would have ... settled. They were looking forward to meeting her.'

Dennis took the opportunity to ask about the suitors, the men who'd been calling for Pamela over the holidays, taking her out. Werner, not bothered by the question, gave the names and addresses for most of them, who were old family friends by and large.

Dennis mentioned the Chinese student and the incident that had ended in a broken nose. Werner admitted not liking the boy, who had briefly been one of his pupils, and moreover had a wife back in his hometown of Mukden in the northeast. Werner conceded that he might have overreacted, saying that the student and Pamela were just friends.

Then he broke down again. Dennis had wanted to ask about the half-Chinese, half-Portuguese suitor called John O'Brian, who'd reportedly become infatuated with Pamela in Tientsin and followed her to Peking. But the old man was too distraught.

Dennis called Botham and Binetsky into the room and told them to collect evidence. Werner was unable to watch as the two men started picking up his daughter's scant belongings and putting them in their overcoat pockets—a jade comb, a hair clasp and her diary. Distraught, he left the room.

Nobody had told Dennis that Pamela was leaving school and returning to England. He needed to know more, but now was not the time to ask. The more he heard about Pamela, the less he knew, it seemed. A plain schoolgirl who nevertheless had the power to infatuate boys; a troublesome daughter who was seemingly popular socially— Pamela was more of a contradiction than ever. Dennis needed to bring her into clearer focus before he could ask the right questions.

He headed back to the Wagons Lits, after telling Botham to get out that night and listen to what foreign Peking was saying about the Werners. Then he phoned Bill Greenslade and asked him to go over to Consul Affleck's office, to find out why Pamela had been going to leave school, whether there'd been trouble at Tientsin Grammar too. Dennis wanted to find out what Werner had assumed he already knew.

Cocktail Hour at the Wagons Lits

*D*ennis had arranged to meet Commissioner Thomas after dark at the Grand Hôtel des Wagons Lits, for a quiet chat before the place got busy. The bar of the Wagons Lits was still a centre of foreign gossip and intrigue, despite being increasingly taken over by the Japanese. The newcomers swaggered about, got belligerent, threw their weight around—it would all be theirs soon enough.

Elsewhere in Peking, Japanese soldiers were strutting around and treating the city as their own; their armoured cars were already on the streets. Tokyo claimed it was simply regular troop rotations, but nobody believed that. Stay long enough at the bar, and you'd hear the more drunken, but perhaps honest, opinion: the Japs would clean house in China; they were the only Orientals who understood discipline and efficiency. They'd given the Ruskies a bloody nose in 1905 and checked the tsar's expansion. It might be brutal, but in the long run the Japanese would be the best thing that could happen to China, and they'd clear out the Communists too. Or rather, they were the best thing that could happen from the point of view of London or Paris and their trading interests.

Commissioner Thomas had already given Dennis the official biography of E. T. C. Werner, the one the British Legation would stick
to come hell or high water. Whatever the internal feuds, the grudges,
the hidden skeletons, Pamela's murder had brought the diplomatic
shutters down.

Thomas warned Dennis that the legation would not be helpful;
indeed, they would be quite the opposite. National prestige came
first. Dennis knew the mind-set—the Duke of Wellington's 'That
which we require now is not to lose the enjoyment of what we have
got.' Meaning, What we have, we hold on to, and don't think a dead
girl or two is going to change that. Reputation and face had to be
upheld, come what may, even the slashing and dumping of an English
subject barely a mile from the British Legation.

And indeed the legation had not been helpful. Dennis had asked
them for any information they had on Werner and got in return a
one-sheet résumé stating his date of birth, the bare bones of his career
in China, a retirement date, and little else—a bland *Who's Who* entry,
and a scant one at that. At least Dennis received something—Han
had been getting the runaround from the legation, with nobody bothering to return his calls.

But Thomas, it seemed, was willing to talk—off the record. The
commissioner had probably known Werner longer than anyone else
in Peking. Thomas was a Peking veteran, but Werner had arrived
some fifteen years before him and was now just about the oldest of the
old China hands.

Dennis and Thomas found a table out of sight to all but the
white-suited, silent-slippered Chinese waiters who brought whisky
sodas and replaced the big brass ashtrays on stands next to each man.
The spittoons on the floor, though unused by foreigners, were standard Peking fixtures. The ladies and bright young things among the
palm fronds were drinking the Wagons Lits' signature champagne
cocktails, or gin rickeys and sherry flips; there was a background noise
of ice on metal from the cocktail shakers behind the bar. A string
quartet played light, faintly recognizable mood music—the greatest

hits of 1935 had eventually made it to Peking. The city tried, but it couldn't help being behind London, Paris and New York.

Dennis and Thomas stuck to whisky. Thomas wasn't usually a prodigious imbiber, but tonight he was knocking them back. He was still shocked by what he'd seen at the Fox Tower; Pamela's corpse was seared in his memory. Dennis too was having a few, although he was more used to corpses and had developed a stronger stomach. When he showed Thomas the autopsy report, the commissioner skimmed it, threw back his whisky and ordered two more—large ones.

Now Dennis casually asked Thomas if he knew anything about Pamela being unhappy at Tientsin Grammar. The commissioner had no idea. That was more Dennis's bailiwick than his, Thomas said; if anyone should know, he should.

That was the second time today Dennis had been told he should know something he didn't. It made him a little uneasy. He had learned nothing new from reading Pamela's diary. There were tales of summer picnics, gossip about tiffins and dances—the usual frivolities of a young woman, it seemed to him. The entries were lighthearted rather than deeply confessional, and there were gaps between them. The diary hadn't yielded any suspects.

He moved on to the gossip that was circulating about Werner, and here Thomas was much more forthcoming. Not surprisingly, the old scholar's unofficial biography—the one based partly on fact, partly on interpretation, and sprinkled liberally with innuendo and a little backstabbing—was very different from that supplied by the legation. Stories of his past were resurfacing and doing the rounds once more, by way of anonymous calls to Morrison Street, notes left with the desk sergeant and talk in the hotels and bars. It seemed Peking had something to get off its chest regarding E. T. C. Werner. He was a man everyone had a story about.

Not everyone saw him as a harmless elderly former diplomat, a scholar or a grieving father. To some he was a man of violent mood swings, an odd character who alienated people, and who'd given them cause to gossip for decades. A highly intelligent man, to be sure, but one considered by some, at the highest levels of the British government in China, to be seriously unstable and unfit for duty. A vain man of strange and radical ideas, a man they officially wanted to be rid of but who had fought back and made enemies. A man who was possibly capable of murder and who may just have committed murder before.

狐 狸 精

The social set of foreign Peking had a mantra they repeated to visitors over cocktails at the Wagons Lits, in the members' enclosure at the Peking Race Club, on long weekends in the temperate Western Hills: 'We don't worry much about pasts in Peking.' But in reality pasts were everything. The city's gossip rested fundamentally on people's histories—why they were in Peking, where they'd come from, what they were hiding from. For nobody's closet was skeleton-free, and digging out those skeletons was the social sport of foreign Peking.

Werner's diplomatic career in China had seen him rise quickly, only to fall dramatically. He had been dogged from early on by an unpopularity he could not shake, and did not try to. A few old China hands still recalled him famously taking his riding crop to a group of monks in Peking's Lama Temple, after an argument over his camera. That had been back in 1888, when Werner was just twenty-four and working in the British Legation.

The story was written up by Werner's companion that day, a sensationalist London hack called Henry Normann who worked on the *Pall Mall Gazette*. Normann had made Werner appear to be a furious brawler, and the British public got a good read over their kippers.

Had Werner acted violently? Perhaps, but the Lama Temple was still considered a dangerous place for foreigners fifty years later, in the 1930s, and the monks regularly extorted money from visitors.

More than any burst of anger nearly half a century before, it was Werner's inability to coexist with the small foreign communities of his postings that had condemned him in the eyes of the gossips and the old China hands. In Macao he'd been reprimanded by no less a personage than Sir Claude MacDonald—the uptight British ambassador to Peking during the time of the Boxers—for his failure to 'mix,' and for apparently insulting the Portuguese chief justice in Macao in some way, one that was never quite stated. Werner had been forced to apologise but had reputedly not done so with grace. He gained a reputation for being 'abrupt'—a damning indictment in expat English society.

Some said it was his posting to remote Pagoda Anchorage, upstream from Foochow, that seriously unhinged Werner. Here he was virtually alone, with no foreign community to speak of. The consul's office and residence were nothing more than a cramped houseboat, and the nearest town of any size was miles away. It was a tense place. Chinese merchants, angered by what they saw as unfair treatment, had boycotted British goods, and there was little to see beyond the dubious sights of the Plum Garden Prison and the Mercy Hospital.

Sequestered on a houseboat no bigger than a canal barge, Werner spent his time learning obscure Chinese dialects and poring over ancient texts, while the few other foreigners living in the area went hunting, danced and got royally drunk. The place had a reputation for undoing men: Werner's predecessor had succumbed to his loneliness and begun imagining diabolical plots against him by his Chinese servants. He had to be sent back home to England, to a padded cell in an asylum. The rumour mill said Werner had lost his mind in Pagoda Anchorage too, had got into fights with the handful of other foreigners there. Once again Sir Claude MacDonald had to step in and sort out the mess. Within the Foreign Office, the word was that Werner was trouble.

As punishment, even more obscure postings followed—Kiungchow on Hainan Island, where only an irregular steamer from Hong Kong visited; Pakhoi, from where not much apart from sugar, aniseed and dried fish was shipped to Macao; and Kongmoon, which was as lonely as Pagoda Anchorage. Werner suffered them all, keeping himself to himself, studying his little-known dialects and the local superstitions and traditions.

And then came Kiukiang, a posting that led to a national scandal. When a Chinese man was killed on the Kiukiang Bund in 1909, the Chinese accused an Englishman called Mears, who just happened to be the head of the British police in the treaty port. Werner, as consul and judge, held a hearing in camera, calling only one witness, a British doctor, and declared Mears innocent.

The Chinese protested. Was this British justice? It smacked of a cover-up. There was a boycott of British goods. The other foreigners in Kiukiang, mostly merchants who needed to remain on good terms with the Chinese, thought Werner was arrogant to have provoked local anger in this way, and the vocal business community demanded his sacking. Not that Werner could have won, whatever he'd chosen to do. Had he offered up Mears for jail, British face would have been lost.

George Morrison, otherwise known as 'Morrison of Peking'— who was also a vicious little gossip—wrote to his *Times* of London editor in 1910:

Unfortunately we have a very inferior Consul at Kiukiang, an eccentric named E.T.C. Werner, a man not on speaking terms with the majority of the community. When I was last in Kiukiang the British Commissioner of Customs feelingly complained to me that though stationed in the same port with this poisonous Consul he received no extra pay for so being. Werner has largely contributed to the trouble and will have to go home.

The case went higher, to Sir John Jordan, His Majesty's ambassador envoy extraordinary and plenipotentiary to China, a tough and proud Ulsterman who wanted no troublesome consuls on his watch. And from there it went to the British Parliament in London. It became a national embarrassment. The maintenance of British prestige meant that Werner was given a pass in public, but behind the scenes it was asked whether he was fit for duty.

His final posting was Foochow, where in a defiant and typically British stand he was simultaneously promoted and given a warning: Here you are, but now hear this—no more trouble.

These were chaotic times across China. The last of the imperial dynasties, the Qing, had been tossed out and a presidential republic ushered in. The ailing and impotent Qing government had become too corrupt and too weak to resist the increasingly rapacious territorial and preferential-trading demands of the European great powers. By 1911 the Chinese army had had enough, and in October that year it revolted. Chaos ensued until Dr Sun Yat-sen returned to China from exile in the United States. He pulled together the fractious opposition, and in February 1912 proclaimed the formation of the Republic of China, becoming its first president.

The Forbidden City was thrown open as the imperial family and their eunuchs were sent packing. Chinese men cut off their pigtails, which had for so long symbolised Manchu dominance over the Han Chinese. But through all this turmoil, Foochow remained relatively quiet, becoming a backwater as the tea trade slowly died.

Despite Werner's recent marriage to Gladys Nina, he was not happy in the port town, describing the posting as 'earthly purgatory.' He spent his time collating statistics on Foochow's falling tea exports, and the minutiae of the port's major trade in bamboo shoots and lacquered furniture. He was reputedly not on speaking terms with half his staff. He refused to fit in, pointedly avoiding the Foochow Club, the centre of English expat life, and making it known that he didn't drink and thought little of people who did. It was all bound to come to a head.

And it did—spectacularly so. Werner was reputedly in open argument with eight of the thirty-five male members of the Foochow Club and had strained relations with the rest of them. In 1913 he became convinced that one, a man called Blackburn, a popular type, highly regarded and married with a family, had been spying on Gladys Nina as she undressed in her bedroom at the consulate. Werner accused the man of being a Peeping Tom.

Then he got into a fight with a British official at the Customs Service over some trifling matter. It escalated, and eventually Werner and Gladys Nina stormed the Foochow Club together one night with riding crops in their hands, upsetting tables, startling the regulars, disrupting the bridge games. They then proceeded to beat and whip the Customs Service officer as he scrambled around the bar-room floor on his knees, trying to escape their blows.

It was too much. The pair were undignified, they appeared deranged; the British community in Foochow complained loudly to Ambassador Jordan in Peking. This was the second time he'd had trouble from Werner, and Jordan decided he was too unstable and had to go.

Werner had risen higher than any of his contemporaries among the 1884 intake of Foreign Service cadets. He'd been the youngest of them all and had become the most successful. And he had married extremely well. But he also fell the furthest. Actually getting fired from the British diplomatic service in China was a difficult thing to achieve, and in fact only one official had previously ever been ousted—a man called Higgs, who was sacked by John Jordan in 1913 for marrying a widow. The staunchly Presbyterian Jordan thought that was unbecoming of a man in the service. To hush it up, a job was found for Higgs and his new wife with the British Military Mission in Siberia, and the disgraced Higgs wrapped himself up and headed north to the frozen wastes of the Russian Empire, there to contemplate the sin of loving a widow.

Shortly after the Foochow incident, Werner was recalled to London and virtually accused of being insane. He fought his detractors, but Jordan was determined not to have Werner back on his watch—the man was a confirmed atheist, for goodness' sake. He'd dabbled in Theosophy, attended lectures by Indian mystics.

The government declared Werner sick; he found doctors who pronounced him fit as a fiddle. The government looked for excuses; Werner believed he was the wronged party and protested loudly. But nobody listened. Werner was friendless, the government resolute.

Whitehall forced the issue, but made sure Werner was decently pensioned.

Werner saw conspiracies in all this—his German heritage was being used against him as the war clouds gathered over Europe. He offered himself for service at the front but was turned down by the War Office, who claimed he was too old. He saw prejudice; he grabbed at the role of outsider, assuming his usual belligerent damn-the-consequences attitude. He was the product of a wealthy family, an English public school and the diplomatic service, but somehow—smart, dedicated and determined as he was—he'd never quite been part of the Empire clan, was never really a fully paid-up member of the Establishment, never invited into the old boys' club. He had placed himself in juxtaposition to them, and now he was being left outside and the doors were closed. It was members only.

Werner was retired just as World War I commenced. He was forty-nine. He received a full and generous pension, but with his reputation for being unsociable, unstable, stubborn and dour, there was no way back in to service with the British government for him. Frustrated, angry and bitter, Werner and Gladys Nina booked a passage back to Peking and a new life.

狐 狸 精

Bar-room gossip. Foreigners drinking too much in their closeted and tight-knit clubs. Dennis knew the signs, and took every tale about Werner with a grain of salt. Wherever there was too much booze and too few people, petty jealousies and rivalries intensified. Small places, especially the goldfish bowls of foreign Peking and Tientsin, were highly combustible. And how much more explosive were the tiny, claustrophobic postings like Pagoda Anchorage, Kiukiang and Foochow of twenty and thirty years ago; these were smouldering pits where bored expats had nothing to do but twist the knife.

A resistance to fitting in with the foreign community in those places was definitely odd, rare for sure, but it wasn't a crime. And striking a monk or horsewhipping a Peeping Tom was hardly a precursor to grotesque murder. But the rumours around the death of Gladys Nina were harder to shrug off as the result of petty rivalries and jealousies. These rumours had surfaced immediately at the time of her death, and now, following the murder of Pamela, they were swirling again.

It wasn't just Gladys Nina's death that had been hotly debated for years in Peking, but her life with Werner. None of the gossips agreed on much, but they did agree that she was a beauty, a catch for Werner. The snobbishly inclined, of which Peking had more than its fair share, noted that he had punched well above his weight and she had married beneath her station. The Ravenshaws were one of England's oldest families, and plenty of foreigners in Peking believed that marrying Werner had been the undoing of Gladys Nina.

Just as there seemed to be two Pamelas, split between her seemingly mundane existence in Tientsin and her fast-paced life in Peking, so there appeared to be two Gladys Nina Ravenshaws—one an attractive woman who lived life to the full, the other a bedridden invalid. Those who'd known Gladys Nina since her girlhood reflected on her once vibrant personality and her sudden deterioration. Werner, when he wrote or spoke about his wife, always referred to her long years of suffering, her weak constitution, her incapacitating illnesses. The two Gladys Ninas, just like the two Pamelas, were hard to reconcile.

Commissioner Thomas had given Dennis a copy of a book Werner published in 1922 called *Autumn Leaves*, a strange miscellany ranging from essays on the social Darwinist Herbert Spencer to Theosophy and spiritualism, the nature of the universe, and symbolic disfigurement among certain tribes in China. The book's frontispiece consisted of a full-page portrait of Gladys Nina Chalmers Werner. An earlier photograph, taken on their wedding day on the steps of St John's in Hong Kong, showed Werner looking a full twenty years older than his bride. She was taller than he, and neither was smiling; they seemed more resigned than anything. Perhaps it was just the times, the stiff formality of the British upper classes in 1911, combined with Hong Kong's humidity, even in December. If there were any guests at the cathedral that day, they were not recorded.

When the couple returned to Peking in 1915, following Werner's forced retirement, things seemed to go well at first. Werner filled his days working on his books and papers, and lecturing at Peking University. Gladys Nina was thought to be happy—she was considered one of the best dancers in Peking, and on the few occasions when the former consul and his wife had to move in society for appearances' sake, she showed she was still lively and active. The couple seemed to have put the horsewhipping and Peeping Tom episodes behind them.

But then Gladys Nina changed. People said it was as if the life was seeping out of her. She was 'like a frightened sparrow in a painted cage,' recalled one person who knew her well. She grew pale, became listless, found herself confined to bed. She consulted the best foreign doctors in Peking and for a while was under the care of a French practitioner named Dr Bussière, who had been personal physician to the Chinese republic's second president and successor to Dr Sun, Yuan Shih-kai. But just as he'd ultimately done nothing for the president—China's so-called Strong Man died in his bed—so he could do little for Gladys Nina, and her health continued to slide.

Nobody could say what was wrong with her. Gladys Nina had a brother-in-law, John McCreery, who was regarded as one of the leading physicians in the United States. He too was consulted, but could give no answers. Werner claimed that his wife had had a cardiac condition since she was a child, but people who'd known her dismissed this as nonsense. Werner was insistent, and claimed she also had neurasthenia, an illness which, in the early part of the twentieth century, was thought to be psychopathological, affecting mostly women and causing bouts of fatigue and depression.

Exactly why Gladys Nina and Werner chose to adopt a child was unclear. Some rumours had it that she became too sickly to conceive, others that the marriage was never consummated. Whatever the reason, if Gladys Nina had hoped that bringing a new bundle of energy into her life in the form of Pamela would prove a tonic, she was wrong.

As her health continued to spiral downwards, she could not find the energy to care for her daughter, a task that was relegated to amahs. The supposedly eminent Dr Bussière prescribed solutions of salt and gold, which were injected straight into Gladys Nina's veins. The needles were thick, the veins hard to find, and the puncture wounds left large yellow bruises on her arms, but the treatment actually seemed to work.

Werner then sent her to the United States for several months' rest with her sister Eileen and brother-in-law Dr McCreery. They lived on an estate called Quiet Water in Greenwich, Connecticut, and there Gladys Nina seemed to rally. But when she returned to Peking, she suffered an attack of influenza, and then was hit by meningitis. This was too much for her frail body, and she died, aged just thirty-five.

Her mother in England died shortly afterwards, some said of a broken heart at losing her. In the space of a couple of months, eight-year-old Pamela had lost both her mother and grandmother.

While Werner mourned, Peking gossiped. Tragedy and disaster followed him, people said. He had nearly drowned as a boy in Mexico, in the shark-infested harbour at Vera Cruz during a storm. Later he had survived a railway crash in London, and after that a collision of ships during fog in the English Channel. Visiting Naples, he had fallen through a skylight onto the roof of an office building, but miraculously got up and walked away. In Hankow in 1898 he escaped a terrible fire that engulfed the city, destroying a square mile of housing and killing over a thousand people.

He led a charmed life, it was said, while those around him died. In Tientsin in the 1890s he'd been caught in the British Concession as a mob retaliated after a Chinese was killed in a fracas. Ten French nuns were slaughtered, and half a dozen other Europeans killed. In the turmoil of 1911, as the Qing dynasty collapsed, Werner escaped the massacring rebels while others around him were beheaded and disembowelled.

He had faced down bandits while on a solitary horseback tour of Mongolia and returned to tell the tale of his search for the tomb of

Genghis Khan. He'd encountered more bandits while attempting to travel the length of the Great Wall. On the island of Taiwan he had fallen ill in the jungles of the hinterland but managed to walk to civilisation unaided.

Werner seemed to attract death and destruction, yet was always able to escape. Whenever he was asked about this, he would mockingly recite from *The Rubaiyat of Omar Khayyam*: 'When you and I beyond the veil are past / Oh, but the long, long while the world shall last.'

And it seemed he could kill, too. In remote Kiukiang Werner had been caught up in a violent anti-British insurrection: a mob of angry Chinese surrounded the small and poorly defended British Consulate compound. Werner found an insurrectionist pouring petrol on the roof, intending to burn it down with all the staff and their families inside. Werner did not hesitate: he shot the arsonist dead at point-blank range.

The fact that Werner, following Gladys Nina's death, continued to claim that she'd been sickly since childhood only fuelled the gossip. Her friends continued to vehemently deny it, but Werner remained insistent, calling her death an 'inexplicable act of God' and a 'blessed relief,' and declaring himself 'desolate' without her.

The truth was that Gladys Nina had died from an overdose of Veronal, confirmed at her inquest and recorded as such by the British Legation's assiduous record keepers.

狐 狸 精

In 1922, death by an overdose of Veronal set alarm bells ringing. A barbiturate, Veronal was an upper-class drug of choice and had been since it hit the market in 1903. It was medically prescribed for everything from toothache to insomnia, influenza to depression, but anyone who read the newspapers knew it was also a way for the better-off to end it all.

There had been a lot of precedents. In 1912, in a seedy room above Jimmy the Priest's saloon in New York, playwright Eugene O'Neill, his marriage on the rocks, attempted suicide with cheap whisky and Veronal. A year later, a depressed Virginia Woolf also tried to kill herself with the drug, having been given it in a nursing home to help her sleep. In 1917 Stephanie 'Baby' Primrose and Catharine 'Topsy' Compton-Burnett, sisters of the popular novelist Ivy, died in a suicide pact after taking Veronal in their locked bedroom on Christmas Day. It was the celebrity drug for the new century.

But while Veronal was a popular choice, it could take more than twenty-four hours to die from an overdose. The Compton-Burnett sisters died because they locked themselves away; Virginia Woolf and Eugene O'Neill survived because people found them. Would not Werner, who claimed to be forever at his wife's side in her last days, have noticed an overdose in the space of twenty-four hours?

People wondered. And they drew their own conclusions. For every suicide attempt with Veronal, there was another story of murder. DCI Dennis had known sensational cases of murder by Veronal while at Scotland Yard.

Werner had appeared to be the grieving husband as he stood by the graveside at Peking's British Cemetery, where she was to be buried, so Werner said, 'beneath the trees and flowers she loved so well.' On that cold February day in 1922, the child Pamela stood beside her father, doubtless not quite understanding what was happening. Werner recited 'To the Mothers,' a poem by Marion Couthoy Smith, Gladys Nina's favourite poet, who'd been popular during World War I:

> *Mothers of men, have you not known*
> *That the soul of the child is not your own?*
> *If God has sealed him for palm and cross,*
> *To hold him close were your bitter loss.*

And now, in yet another tragedy, Werner was preparing to bury Pamela, in the same cemetery, in the same grave. Dennis knew there could be no reinvestigation of Gladys Nina's death, but the story gave him pause for thought.

Dennis couldn't help thinking too of Pamela's own tragic life—being given up for adoption and then so quickly losing her adoptive mother, followed soon after by her maternal grandmother. Her maternal grandfather, Charles Withers Ravenshaw, died at the family estate in Essex two years before Pamela was murdered, never having met his adopted granddaughter or seen his daughter's faraway grave.

Among the photographs of Pamela that Dennis brought with him from Tientsin was one he'd found in the Tientsin Grammar School publication the *Grammarian*. A humorous piece had students submit pictures of themselves as young children, and there was Pamela, 'P.W.,' around the time of Gladys Nina's death, looking happy enough outside the Werners' home on San Tiao Hutong. It was the house where her adoptive mother had decided to end her life with an overdose, or so the official record read. Was it suicide or assisted suicide? So-called mercy killings were not unknown in the 1920s, but there was little public sympathy for them, whatever people might have thought in private. They were considered murder by the courts, and there was definitely no dispensation from the church.

One thing DCI Dennis did note was the $20,000 in silver dollars that Gladys Nina had left to Pamela, with Werner as guardian. On Pamela's death, the money reverted to her father. It was a significant sum, one that went an especially long way in Peking. Dennis's Scotland Yard training had been based on the theories of the legendary Sir Basil Thomson, a criminologist who for many years was head of the Criminal Investigation Department at the Yard. Thomson's words were mantras for his men: 'The search for the motive should be kept up incessantly, for no murder was ever committed without a motive, except one done by a maniac. There is always an underlying motive.'

Pamela's father had motive. But the frenzied stabbing that had been inflicted on her body after death, the carving, the missing organs—that was the work of a maniac, surely. Was Werner a maniac? Dennis considered him odd—more than odd, he was so distant. But that didn't make him a killer.

It was a lot to think about as the men retired for the evening, leaving the Wagons Lits to the younger set of foreign Peking, who seemingly had fewer concerns and perhaps less to do the following day.

The music was starting to pick up the pace as cocktail hour moved into party time. There was a postdinner crowd that came here, and to the other hotels and bars in the Quarter, who enjoyed the edginess of life in a city on the brink. They were living like kings on their trust funds, way above anything they could afford back home. There were Germans who didn't have to worry about Herr Hitler and his SS, Americans rich as Croesus thanks to the silver-backed dollar, all and sundry glad to be away from the Great Depression. This corner of the Far East was still a playground for a select few, for a little while longer anyway.

Into the Badlands

Colonel Han was sticking with his trademark 'No comment,' but the journalists were fishing. The inquest had given them nothing either, and Han was forced to admit that the police had no clues. He did manage to keep Dennis, Botham and Binetsky out of the papers, evading questions about who was helping him with the investigation. The press declared him 'reluctant to talk,' and insinuated that the Peking police weren't up to the job.

Han appealed for anyone with any knowledge to come forward, citing the reward being offered by the Legation Quarter police for information that led to the capture and conviction of the murderer or murderers. Notices in English to this effect were handed out to the press. The amount, $1,000 in Chinese dollars, was the equivalent of about $330 in American dollars, and to the vast majority of Chinese Peking it was a fortune. A typical family survived on less than $100 a year in American dollars.

But Werner attacked the handling of the reward. He argued that the leaflets should also be printed in Chinese, and that it should be possible to claim the money through a bank, under promise of protection and anonymity, so that local Chinese would not suspect a trap. The Chinese public had a general distrust of authority. Consul Fitzmau-rice refused point-blank, insisting that anyone, Chinese or foreign, must claim the reward from him personally.

Han had tracked down most of the men who had been reported as having known Pamela in Peking, and all of them had alibis—they had been out of town and had the hotel reservations and train tickets to prove it, or at home with parents and colleagues. Inspector Botham, on Dennis's orders and with Han's agreement, had questioned each of them and taken their statements. Han had then dispatched his men to double-check their stories. All of them checked out. All the men were horrified by Pamela's murder.

Still, the picture of Pamela became clearer as a result. The men reported her as gay, fun. A girl who enjoyed going out for tiffins, to cafés, skating. A girl who liked dancing and laughing. She had been dating freely, and many of her dates found it hard to believe she was still at school. Pamela hadn't mentioned it, and they had considered her a woman, not a schoolgirl.

The officers had ticked off the boyfriends from Werner's list one by one, with two exceptions. They were unable to find the Chinese student who'd called for Pamela only to have his nose broken by her father for his pains. Werner had told the police that the student was from Muk-den in the northeast, that his name was Han Shou-ching, and that he'd attended the Kao Tang Shih Fan College in Peking's southern suburbs.

The police visited the college, but Han Shou-ching was no longer enrolled there—he had gone back to his father's home in Muk-den. They also looked for John O'Brian, the young man who'd become obsessed with Pamela in Tientsin and who was now thought to be in Peking, but with no luck. Another dead end.

Tuesday morning saw the revelation in the press of the involvement of DCI Dennis of Tientsin in Colonel Han's murder investigation. The foreigners were happy. 'Optimism prevails,' wrote the Shanghai-based *North-China Daily News*, greeting the wires' report that a British policeman—a 'Scotland Yard man,' no less—was on the case.

The journalists besieged Morrison Street but were forced to wait around on the steps to the station entrance. The pack of foreign newsmen attracted curious locals, and a large crowd soon swelled. Morrison Street was always crowded at the best of times. A broad, acacia-lined thoroughfare just to the north of the Legation Quarter, it was one of the few streets where foreigners and Chinese mingled. Fashionable Europeans and wealthy Chinese ladies browsed at the department stores and curio shops, bought sweet buns or cream cakes at the Russian bakery, went to the dry cleaners and the drugstores, while the less well-off local Chinese ambled along to the food stalls and hawkers in the nearby Dongan Market, or headed to the Lung-Fu Temple with its hundreds of stalls selling porcelain, jade, lacquerware and silks alongside toys, food, dogs and cats.

Cars and trolleybuses competed with rickshaws, pedestrians and bicycles on Morrison Street. Traditionally dressed blue-gowned men wearing felt trilby hats squatted on the corners or stood around smoking in deep discussion. White-gowned amahs with foreign babies in their charge strolled for fresh air. East met West on this street, which was also home to the headquarters of the Salvation Army, whose uniformed members marched from one end to the other with drums and trombones, playing 'Onward Christian Soldiers'; bemused Chinese refused to be converted to anything.

When Han finally appeared, he stood at the top of the station steps in full police uniform, cap on, pistol holstered. Dennis stood slightly behind him, with no need to hide now, in his civilian suit. Protocol dictated that Han address the press—it was his case, his station. But he still had no details to give, no motive to suggest, no suspects to name, only a message he wished to convey to the victim's grieving father.

'I will do my best to bring Pamela's murderers to justice,' he told the assembled crowd.

That was all the papers got. Colonel Han was a man who never gave the press more than was necessary. He was not a glory hunter. And he did not want to set himself up for a fall. Dennis tended to agree; the less said, the better.

But it was almost a week since Pamela's body had been found at the Fox Tower, and the journalists were starting to bay for blood. Flash-bulbs popped as they threw questions. Han simply smiled, opened his arms to them, palms outward, showing that he had nothing to give but his humble apologies, and then the detectives disappeared back inside the station.

That evening, Dennis was at the Wagons Lits having a hot stew dinner after a day of getting nowhere. Werner's movements on the night of the killing had all been verified. His servants, the Gure-vitches, the desk sergeant at the legation police station, and the vari-ous gatemen at the locations he'd visited across the city all confirmed seeing him. Dennis didn't buy Werner as the killer anyway—the at-tack was just too vicious, too manic. He knew in his guts that the old man wasn't the murderer.

As Dennis was eating, the restaurant manager came to tell him he had a telephone call from an Inspector Botham. Dennis took it on the heavy Bakelite phone in the manager's office.

Botham was excited. 'They've got a foreigner with blood on his clothes,' he told Dennis. 'More blood in his lodgings. We've sealed the room, and he's now at Morrison Street. He won't talk.'

'Do we know his name?'

'He's saying nothing, but Han says he knows him—name of Pinfold.'

'I'm coming straight there.' Dennis said, an emptiness in the pit of his stomach. They'd found blood.

Han's rousting of every lodging house and boarding room in the Badlands had paid off. The man had been found in a dingy flophouse infested with rats, cockroaches and typhus, where rooms were rented by the hour, the day or the week—cash in advance, no questions asked. This was where poor white Peking lived alongside those Chinese who wanted to be anonymous, and it was as low as it got for a foreigner. The man lived in one small room with no toilet and one paper-covered window looking out onto a back courtyard strewn with rubbish.

Han had recovered items from the room. A pair of shoes with bloodstains on them, and—what had alarmed the White Russian landlady enough to call the police when she went in to check that her lodger hadn't skipped on the rent—a dagger with bloodstains on the sheath and a torn handkerchief with yet more bloodstains. Han had taken them all, along with the man's clothing, put them in brown paper bags, and sent them over to the Peking Union Medical College, where the pathologists were called out for another long night's work. There was no doubt it was blood—but whose?

When the occupant of the room, Pinfold, was brought into Morrison Street, a young Chinese constable pulled Colonel Han aside. He recognised the foreigner. The constable had been on duty a couple of days after Pamela's murder, protecting the crime scene at the foot of the Fox Tower as instructed. Among the curious locals who passed by was this man. The constable remembered him as one of only a few foreigners to linger. He had seemed agitated, scraping his feet on the ground as he stared at the spot where the body had lain, and was notably more down-at-heel than the average white man in Peking.

The interview room at Morrison Street where Pinfold was questioned had a hard brick floor and a marble-topped table with the ubiquitous stained white-enamel spittoon underneath. Han and Dennis sat on one side of the table, Pinfold on the other, both policemen and suspect alike on stiff-backed chairs that weren't meant to be comfortable. Botham stood by the door.

A single lightbulb hung from the ceiling on an electric cord, and the temperature in the room was kept low to ensure that the suspect stayed awake. The window was set high so that nobody could see outside, and from the courtyard only the shouts and jeers of the constables changing shifts could be heard. The whitewashed walls were bare but for a large portrait of Dr Sun Yat-sen above Han's head.

This was Han's station, Han's suspect and Han's interview. Strictly speaking, Dennis was not supposed to be involved—he was supposed to confine himself to the Legation Quarter—but Han let him take the lead. There were no lawyers, no reading of rights, no recording equipment. The interview was not conducted under oath.

Dennis sat surreptitiously casting glances at the man, noting that he looked unfazed, used to the environment. You didn't spend fifteen years in Scotland Yard without knowing whether or not a man had seen the inside of a police station before, and this man clearly had.

Before they'd entered the interview room, Han had given Dennis the background—the lodging house, the destitute state of the man's room, the landlady's suspicions. He said he believed the man was called Pinfold, but he'd never spoken to him before. He thought he was Canadian, maybe British, possibly American.

Dennis learnt that the man had arrived in Peking in the late 1920s, in better shape back then and with a job. He'd worked as a bodyguard for one of the many warlords who'd based themselves in Peking during that time of chaos, when allegiances and territory changed hands between men with private armies, before Chiang Kai-shek pacified the northern warlords and before the Japanese arrived to finish off the last few stubborn holdouts in Manchuria.

The warlord Pinfold worked for had a large courtyard residence on the edge of what was then the open ground of the Glacis, before it was built over as the Badlands. His property extended almost to the Tartar Wall, and he came under Han's jurisdiction. A lot of the northern warlords liked to hire foreign bodyguards because they didn't have ties to any clan, and so tended to stay loyal as long as they were paid. They usually had soldiering experience, and they added a little glamour and status to a warlord's retinue. These mercenaries were mostly White Russians, ex-tsarist cavalry officers with nowhere else to go, and no skills to sell except their ability to fight. But there were a few other rogue foreigners mixed in, and this Pinfold was one of them. Han had seen him many times, up on the Tartar Wall guarding the warlord's property.

Then that warlord had gone. Han didn't remember how—whether he'd been assassinated, or there'd been a coup, or whether he'd given up the renegade life and taken his troops and his allegiance to Chiang and the Kuomintang. Maybe he'd just retired, and was now safely in Shanghai with his mistresses and his opium pipe and a large bank account. Since then Pinfold had hung around the Badlands, but what exactly he did wasn't clear. What did any of the foreign driftwood in the Badlands do? Work as muscle for the dive bars or brothels, manage the casinos or cabarets, a little pimping, gun running? Sell a little dope to the marines and other foreigners?

Han had put in requests for any details on Pinfold to the Canadian, American and British legations, but he wasn't hopeful. Men like Pinfold didn't leave trails or register their presence.

Pinfold's lodgings had yielded nothing to identify him, no passport, no bankbook, no papers. The officers had turned the room over, but the man had few possessions beyond the suit he was wearing. There were a couple of soiled shirts, some underwear, a heavy winter overcoat, and a battered old suitcase, which was empty. The only shoes he owned were the blood-spattered pair Han had confiscated, which had been replaced by some Chinese straw and cloth slippers a couple of sizes too small.

Apart from clothing, his sole belongings were a cheap, cracked wristwatch and a paltry amount in Chinese dollars—no wallet. The furniture and objects in the room—a bed, a small table and chair, a wardrobe, a chamber pot and a scorch-marked copper ashtray—were the property of the White Russian landlord. There were no photographs of loved ones, no letters from family, no mementos or knick-knacks, none of the ordinary acquisitions of life.

The landlady had confirmed that the dagger recovered was the man's—she'd seen it in his room before. Han had him empty his pockets, which revealed a few Chinese coins, amounting to little more than next week's rent, a pack of cheap cigarettes, and a matchbook from the Olympia Cabaret, a new joint in the Badlands owned by an overseas Chinese—Han would check it out later. Pinfold also had a second set of keys, which didn't fit the lodging-house doors. He refused to say what lock those keys fitted.

Dennis wondered whether he had belongings somewhere else, away from the Badlands, stashed with a friend until he got back on his feet. The marginal and the transient sometimes did that.

Now the man looked calm, accepting cigarettes, smoking them down to the butt. Dennis guessed his age as about forty, the same as his own, and could tell that he'd once been strong, had probably served some time in someone's army. He was now skinny, underfed; his dry, pallid skin was loose and pockmarked and he was out of shape, wheezing sometimes like an asthmatic. Maybe he was a doper or maybe he was just broke. His hair was short but cut badly—he'd probably done it himself to save the money—and it was greasy and in need of a wash. His teeth were in a bad way, tobacco-stained and rotten; his fingernails were chewed to the quick, his knuckles covered over with hard skin.

Whoever he was, he was down on his uppers, coughing up an unhealthy amount of brown phlegm into the spittoon.

So far, the man had refused to say his name, declined even to confirm with a nod that he was Pinfold. Dennis introduced himself and tried again, asking the man for his name, nationality, age and address, each time getting no response.

'Can you tell us where you were on the night of 7 January?' And when he still got no response, 'The Russian Christmas? Why were you at the Fox Tower on 9 January?'

The man said nothing.

He didn't ask why he was in an interview room at Morrison Street, he didn't ask what this was all about. He didn't demand to know why his shoes, knife and handkerchief had been confiscated, or whether he was being formally charged. He didn't mention Pamela's name, despite his being seen at the crime scene, despite her being front-page news. He refused to account for the bloodstains on his shoes, or why he had a bloodstained dagger in his room. He did not ask for any consular official, lawyer or anyone else to be contacted.

He did not squirm, he did not complain. He simply did not speak at all. Stalemate.

At length, Colonel Han had the man put in one of the ice-cold cells at Morrison Street. Let him spend the night with the dope dealers, addicts and petty thieves; see if that loosened his tongue.

狐 狸 精

The China coast newspapers reported an arrest, confirming that it was a European and not a Chinese but giving no name. It was Inspector Botham, the journalists claimed, who had made the arrest, but he was refusing to talk to them. Reuters reported the bloody shoes, the handkerchief, the dagger and sheath. Clearly they'd been given inside information.

Nothing had come through from the pathologists at the medical college yet, but back in the whitewashed interview room with Sun Yat-sen staring down, Dennis, Han and Botham resumed their former positions. Pinfold was looking older after a night in the cells. Grey stubble peeked through on his chin; there were dark sacks under his eyes. He might have been tired, but he still wasn't talking; it would take more than one night to change his mind. Still, they ran through the questions again, patiently repeating the ones they'd asked the day before.

Nothing. The man barely acknowledged that the detectives were in the room with him. Dennis tried another tack. He showed Pinfold the day's newspapers, with Pamela on the front page under the headline HUMAN MUTILATOR OF BRITISH GIRL—EVIDENCE INDICATES FIENDISH INDOOR CRIME.

Dennis thought he detected a flicker, a second glance before the man's head sunk back down. The DCI laid out the details—the Fox Tower, the cuts, the mutilation, the missing organs, the sexual interference. Still nothing. They broke for lunch. Let him sweat.

That afternoon they received corroboration of his identity. The Canadians said they thought he was indeed named Pinfold, one of their nationals and a man of interest to them. According to the grapevine, he was a deserter from the Canadian Army; the consul was contacting the Royal Canadian Mounted Police Security Service in Ottawa for more details. Rumour had it that Pinfold had skipped his barracks in Canada for the United States, got himself a criminal record, maybe in Chicago, and then crossed the country to San Francisco and got a boat to China via Manila. A note in the Canadians' file stated that he regularly attended public executions at Tien Chiao, something few foreigners did, considering it ghoulish.

The Canadians were liaising with the Americans to see if anything came up there or in American-run Manila, which had its own white criminal underworld with casinos, girls and dope. But it would take time.

One thing the Canadians threw in about Pinfold struck the detectives. He was usually seen down around Chuanpan Hutong, and particularly at a White Russian dive bar along that street. It was a place with no name, at number 27, run by a couple called Oparina. There was a brothel next door at number 28.

Chuanpan Hutong—the main drag of the Badlands, east of the Legation Quarter, west of Armour Factory Alley—was right between where Pamela was last seen alive and her stated destination of home. Everyone said she always avoided the Badlands by using the Wall Road, a path that ran sometimes along the bottom of the Tartar Wall and sometimes along the top of it, and which was inaccessible to motor vehicles, available only to pedestrians, bicycles and rickshaws. Her father, too, had insisted that Pamela didn't know the many twisting *hutong* in the Badlands and she feared getting lost in them, but no witnesses had come forward to confirm that was her route on the night she was murdered. The police had assumed she'd taken the Wall Road, as was her habit.

But what if she hadn't taken her usual route after all? What if she had cut straight across the Badlands to get home, along Chuanpan Hutong, busy with the wild Russian Christmas? If she had, then she would have passed right by number 27, right by the Oparinas' joint.

They needed to recanvass—place Pinfold on Chuanpan Hutong, place Pamela passing by, see whether it was possible for the two to have crossed paths—and then get the pathology results on the shoes, handkerchief and knife.

That was what Dennis called a case, if he could find a motive.

狐 狸 精

That Thursday night, the police of Morrison Street rousted 27 Chuan-pan Hutong. Colonel Han led the charge, with twenty constables alongside him. Dennis kept out of it, retreating to the Wagons Lits. A Badlands bar was a little too public, and any involvement by him was bound to get back to the legation in Peking and to his bosses in Tien-tsin. That would be followed by a reprimand, or even a recall, for taking the investigation outside the Quarter.

But no one had mentioned anything about Inspector Botham's remit, so Dennis told him to go along for the ride and observe what he could. If there was any flak later, Dennis would take it as his superior officer.

On the west side of Chuanpan Hutong were the bars and broth-els, and on the east side cheap Chinese eateries and late-night cafés. You could buy chunks of mutton on wooden skewers, called *chuanr*, as well as *bing*—wheat cakes fried in oil seasoned with spring onions— and *jian bing*, rolled pancakes with an egg cracked onto the batter. The indigenous street food of Peking was cheap, filling and popular with both the Chinese and the foreigners.

The eateries catered to the working girls on breaks, giving them a place to rendezvous with their pimps or meet up with clients outside the brothels for off-the-books negotiations. The Badlands had no streetlights, but major haunts like the White Palace Dance Hall had lightbulbs strung up outside, while red lanterns advertising bars and restaurants glowed right along the *hutong*. Rickshaw pullers walked up and down in the cold, looking for fares.

While this was technically Chinese Peking, foreigners were in the majority: a mix of criminal elements, dopers, drinkers and whoremongers, along with a few groups of curious, better-heeled foreigners slumming it. The area was the domain of White Russian and Korean prostitutes, with just a few Chinese among them. The main Chinese action went on elsewhere, mainly on the western side of the Legation Quarter.

Most of the brothels sat behind courtyard walls, hastily plastered, and impossible to see past. The entry gates were manned by a mixture of White Russian heavies and tough-looking Chinese men. The latter were usually from Shantung, in the northeast, and were the biggest and toughest China had to offer. Neither group was to be messed with. The dive bars were open to anyone who fancied their chances. Here peroxide-blond White Russians past their prime raised their sketched-on eyebrows and offered 'business' to the semicomatose, the paralytic, the close to broke.

Twenty-seven Chuanpan Hutong was nothing out of the ordinary. It consisted of one big room with a chest-high bar, wooden chairs and rickety tables. It was thick with cigarette smoke; the drinking was serious but not top quality—cheap Crimean wine and Georgian brandy. The bar was manned by the Oparinas and took cash only, no chits, no credit: don't insult by asking. There were a few smaller side rooms for card games, where there was more smoke, more drink. Some prostitutes on the wrong side of desperate hung around looking for business, but not on the premises. The brothel next door was closed and in darkness when the police arrived, but there were plenty of other places for girls to take clients.

It was no secret that the Oparinas' joint was also a front for prostitution, opium and heroin, and probably other shady deals, including arms for the warlords and gangsters. But as it was frequented exclusively by white foreigners who weren't being targeted by General Sung's political council in its anti-dope campaign, it hadn't been raided before.

Still, the Shantung bouncers on the door of number 27 knew better than to get in Han's way; this was his patch. Han ran a classic roust—gramophone off, lights on, everyone told to stay in their seats, several larger constables on the door to prevent anyone leaving. There was no back exit, just a high wall topped with broken glass that separated the lowlife of the Badlands from the high life of the Legation Quarter.

The policemen checked everyone in the bar, questioned them, showed them a photo of Pamela. Those out on the town for an experience were quickly let go, and a group of off-duty Italian Marine

Guards were sent on their inebriated way to their legation. The hard-core drinkers were kept back, along with the Oparinas.

Nobody had seen Pamela, but plenty of regulars knew Pinfold. It seemed he wasn't a man people felt honour-bound to keep quiet about. The Oparinas admitted he was a regular patron. Others said he was a tout, pimping girls to off-duty soldiers along Chuanpan Hutong. But no one could remember whether he was in the joint on Russian Christmas, Thursday 7 January. It had been a busy night, a drunken night.

As for Pamela, there was no shortage of blondes, bottle and natural, in the Badlands, but none of them were English and none of them respectable. The Badlands was White Russian territory, not a place where prim and proper girls ventured unaccompanied.

The constables pulled in some of the girls, brought up a wagon and had them taken to Morrison Street for questioning. Botham wanted to check out the brothel next door, but the Oparinas told him the place had closed down, the owners gone.

After leaving number 27, Han and Botham headed across the Badlands to the Olympia Cabaret, the source of the matchbook found in Pinfold's pocket. Han knew the place, and the Chinese owner, a Pekinger who had gone to Paris and made a lot of money. He'd run various joints around the edge of the Legation Quarter and throughout the Badlands, but now stayed mostly in France, looking after his business interests there. In his absence, the cabaret was run by an American.

The building was new, another hastily thrown-together Badlands specialty, but a lick of paint, some table linen, dim lights and a permanent layer of cigarette smoke hid the jerry-built nature of the place. It was pretty small but typical of its type, with a dozen tables, a discreet entrance, waiter service, a small stage with a Russian two-man band and singer who kept it low-key, and a half-dozen Russian dance hostesses. The latter spoke broken French to appear classy, and claimed to be former Russian nobility.

The Olympia was an after-hours joint, even for the Badlands, with nothing doing until midnight or later. It was a place for prostitutes to unwind, cozy up with their pimps; a place for men to bring women they shouldn't be seen with. They huddled at the back tables, ruby-red table lamps obscuring their infidelities.

Han and Botham were seated at the bar by the Russian doorman while he went to find the manager, a short, stocky man in his mid-forties called Joe Knauf. Han nodded to him in acknowledgement and introduced Botham. The American ordered a round of whiskies, which the detectives accepted—it had been a long night. They chinked glasses and downed them in one. Another round, uncalled-for, appeared in front of the policemen.

Knauf already knew about the roust at number 27—news travelled fast in the Badlands. He said the place was a dive, and Madam Oparina a White Russian bitch he wouldn't trust farther than he could throw her. The whorehouse at number 28 had been a poxed dump.

He also knew Pinfold, who had come into the Olympia a few times. The two had been out hunting together in the Western Hills. There was a bunch of them, Knauf said, who did that now and then, to get a break from the city. It wasn't so easy now, though, with the Japs nosing around.

Knauf was a solid-looking tough guy, but he was all helpful big smiles and back-slapping bonhomie with the coppers. But when it came to the Russian Christmas, he couldn't remember whether he'd seen Pinfold. He gave the same story—that had been a crazy night, with a lot of drinking. Those Russians really knew how to celebrate—it was very good for profits. Anyone could have come into the place and picked up a book of matches from the bar, Knauf wouldn't know. He shrugged. Then he asked if this was about Pamela Werner, and when Han confirmed it was, the American said it was a terrible crime, and according to the papers she'd been a pretty girl. He'd read about it in the Tientsin papers too, when he'd gone there a few days before on some business.

There wasn't much more to be learnt. Knauf ordered another round of drinks for the detectives, and they stayed to take in the show, a White Russian jazz quartet that persuaded a few punters to get up for a smooch. Han and Botham kept drinking.

The Fox Tower looms over eastern Peking: only the narrow ditch separated the tower from Pamela's home on Armour Factory Alley

Pekingers walk their songbirds by the city's ancient walls

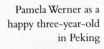

Pamela Werner as a
happy three-year-old
in Peking

E. T. C. Werner at thirty-five
in 1900 (above) and at sixty in
1924 (right)

Exerzierplatz Gesandschaftsviertel Peking.
Drill Place. Legation quarter

The Legation Quarter as rebuilt after the Boxer Rebellion of 1900: the exercise
grounds were soon to be covered over and become the Badlands

Legation Street, the premier thoroughfare of the quarter

Peking Central Railway Station: to arrive was to be awed by the imperial city

The Grand Hôtel des Wagons Lits

Above: Inside the compound of the British Legation

Right: The gates of the French Legation; the ice-skating rink was adjacent

Below: Peking Union Medical College

The Hatamen Gate, the main gateway to the Tartar City

Street vendors in the Tartar City

STREET VENDORS, PEKIN.

16. PÉKIN — Rue Han-Chsé, cité Tartare

The Tartar City, a mere stone's throw from the Legation Quarter yet startlingly different

Ch'ienmen Street, home to Peking's police headquarters

Gladys Nina
Ravenshaw

Gladys Nina and Werner on the steps of St John's Cathedral, Hong Kong,
after their wedding, 1911

DCI Dennis with his wife and son at home in Tientsin, 1935

DCI Dennis (on the right) with the British Ambassador to China,
inspecting Tientsin's British Municipal Police

Pamela in 1936:

Left: In uniform at Tientsin Grammar School

Below: With the school netball team (second from left)

Opposite: The much discussed studio portrait

Tientsin Grammar School, the 'best school east of Suez'

The School House, Pamela's home in Tientsin

Mischa Horjelsky
(back row, right)
and the TGS
swimming team

Sydney Yeates,
headmaster of TGS

Helen Foster Snow and Edgar Snow

Japanese troops in Peking, September 1937

Werner at the time of
his daughter's death

Wentworth Prentice

The apartments at 3 Legation Street, which remain little changed today

The present-day entrance to the Werners' former home at 1 Armour Factory Alley; the old courtyards have long been divided up

The Badlands' Chuanpan Hutong (above) and the Fox Tower (left), as they are today

Of Rats and Men

*F*riday, 15 January: one week in from Pamela's murder, with the forty-eight-hour rule well out the window, and the twenty-day barrier getting ever closer. A suspect was in custody, but no forensics had been confirmed, and there were still no witnesses. Werner had been pushing for the release of his daughter's body, and the British Legation had requested it too. Now release was granted, and the burial would take place the next day.

The prostitutes, pimps and drunks rousted from number 27 had been questioned that morning, after cooling their heels in the Morrison Street cells for the night. Then they'd been let go—the station had addresses for all of them, though these would no doubt be useless by noon.

Botham, with a sore head from the night before, gave Dennis a report of the raid, which had uncovered pretty much nothing. Plenty of people knew Pinfold by sight, Botham told the DCI, but there hadn't been a single sighting of Pamela. It looked as though the day would yield little more than the previous week had.

Then Dennis got a call from Commissioner Thomas. The Legation Quarter police had picked up Pinfold several times, on charges of loitering, suspicion of selling stolen goods, living on immoral earnings. None of the charges had stuck, but Thomas expressed his surprise that the British Legation hadn't already been in touch with Dennis—he happened to know that Pinfold was on their Suspicious Persons list.

Thomas had other fascinating details. He suggested Dennis ask the British Legation about a nudist colony that operated in the Western Hills, and specifically an American called Wentworth Prentice and an Irishman called George Gorman. Along with Pinfold, they were thought to be members of the colony, as well as fellow hunters, part of a small group who went after snipe and duck in the paddy fields and hills around Peking.

At first Dennis thought Thomas was joking. A nudist colony in Peking? But one did in fact exist, and had done for a couple of summers, apparently.

Wentworth Prentice had started it. He was a dentist who worked out of the Legation Quarter, a seemingly respectable professional who was involved in some questionable activities with some questionable people. The group rented an old temple in the Western Hills, as did many foreigners on summer weekends, to retreat from the dust and humidity. But this was different, not a base for picnics and rest but a nudist colony. The local Chinese police had let it operate, had probably been paid to do so, and anyway, it was just crazy foreigners being crazy foreigners. Who knew what they got up to?

According to Thomas, Prentice was also rumoured to hold nude dances in his Legation Quarter apartment, where girls were hired to dance naked for a bunch of men. Apparently the British Legation knew about those too. It was all a little bohemian, a little strange, but was it criminal?

As for the Irishman, George Gorman, he travelled on a British passport and had drifted through various Chinese cities before arriving in Peking, where he passed himself off as the local correspondent for the London *Daily Telegraph*, a paper he occasionally freelanced for. He also freelanced for Japanese publications and sometimes wrote for the *Peking Chronicle*. Most people saw him as an apologist for the Japanese military, and many remembered that when Japan occupied Manchuria in 1931 Gorman had been working for the Japs directly, disputing stories by foreign correspondents that Tokyo disapproved of, sowing seeds of doubt and obfuscation.

Hearing all this, Dennis couldn't keep from wondering himself why the legation hadn't mentioned any of it when Pinfold's name became public. He said as much to Thomas, who surmised that since the nudist colony had a few dozen members, it no doubt included some otherwise respectable foreign residents of Peking, and probably a senior-ranking Englishman or three, who wouldn't like the idea of being quizzed by the police about their summer weekend activities. Neither would they appreciate being asked about their patronage of nude dances. It wouldn't do to have it revealed that your erstwhile straitlaced doctor, bank manager or customs official spent his Saturdays running round the Western Hills stark naked.

Dr Wentworth Prentice represented the point at which the two sides of foreign Peking crossed. At his Western Hills colony and his nude dances, the respectable people of the city met the sinful.

狐 狸 精

Dennis had Pinfold brought back up from the cells to the interview room. Han joined him, and Dennis confronted Pinfold with what he'd heard. It was time to go in heavy, provoke a response.

'Let's talk about the Western Hills nudist colony,' Dennis said, and Pinfold blanched. But now that he knew he'd been positively IDed, he finally started talking.

He had been there, he admitted, during the past two summers, up at an old temple Prentice had rented. It was the dentist who ran the place, and he didn't want any Peeping Toms or voyeurs coming over for a look-see, so he'd hired Pinfold to provide security. The local police hadn't been too bothered—the place was for foreigners only, and an envelope with a little cash for their boss ensured they didn't cause any trouble. A bunch of people came out on the weekends and sat around naked, picnicking, playing tennis, swimming—all the usual activities of foreigners in the Western Hills, just with no clothes on. At night they had parties. It was all pretty harmless, and Pinfold had an easy job. The temple was quite remote, with nothing overlooking it.

Who else was involved? Dennis wanted to know. Apart from Prentice, there was the Irishman called Gorman, but Pinfold didn't know the names of any other members. Some were big shots, Legation Quarter types. Others were a little further down the foreign totem pole, and some were women of a 'dubious background.'

How did he get the job in the Western Hills? Dennis asked, and heard that Pinfold had gone hunting with Prentice and Joe Knauf, the manager of the Olympia Cabaret, and a few of their friends a couple of times. The dentist had asked if he wanted to make a little extra money on the weekends. Pinfold was easy with the whole nudist thing, and how hard was it to score some wages while eyeing up naked women? He ran security for the place with Knauf, who, being an ex–U.S. Marine, hired himself out for that kind of work, but Knauf didn't show up every weekend.

As for the nude dances, they were no big thing either. Pinfold would find a girl down on Chuanpan Hutong who wanted to make a little extra cash—maybe a dancer from the Olympia or the White Palace. It was 'gentlemen's entertainment' for a select group of friends at Prentice's apartment on Legation Street, nothing more. It gave a Russian girl or two their dinner money. Where was the crime in that?

What about the blood on his shoes and knife? Dennis asked. Was that from the hunting? And what about his clothing—where were the rest of his clothes? At these questions, Pinfold clammed up.

Dennis broke off the interview for lunch, feeling that something had been achieved. He had names—Prentice, Gorman, Knauf—and details of nudist colonies and nude dances, weekend antics. Maybe it would prove to be nothing, but it was definitely strange. Perhaps Pinfold was right to ask where the crime was. And where was the connection to Pamela? Dennis himself wondered. But there were crossovers, links. He needed to probe deeper, build up a picture of these men and how they interacted.

He headed back to the Wagons Lits for some Western food and a change of shirt. When he got there, the receptionist passed him a note from his secretary, Mary McIntyre, asking him to phone her as soon as possible. Dennis made the call and was told he was being re-called to Tientsin, by no less a personage than Consul Affleck.

狐狸精

Mary McIntyre told him that Affleck, as senior as senior got in the Tientsin British Concession, was raising a storm. He wanted Dennis in Tientsin immediately. There was to be a meeting first thing in the morning, at which the DCI's presence was required. He'd need to get the next train. There were no further details.

Dennis caught the International from Peking, steaming through the monotonous sorghum fields outside the city to Tientsin's East Station, where a crowd of porters, rickshaw pullers and taxis jostled for fares. His driver was waiting for him and drove straight to the British Concession and Dennis's home on Hong Kong Road. He kissed his sleeping son on the head, ate a hastily prepared cold supper, then headed to his office and a pile of paperwork.

There his deputies filled him in on the events in Tientsin since he'd been away. Several cases had gone to court in the past week, and there'd been some fallout from fistfights with troops on leave down on the strip of dive bars and brothels on Dublin and Bruce roads, at the seedier end of the concession. There was some paperwork that needed his signature. Then the Pamela Werner investigation.

On the face of it, there was little to tell. Bill Greenslade had per-sonally checked out the boyfriend, Mischa Horjelsky, and he was off the list of suspects. Greenslade had also paid a visit to Tientsin Gram-mar. It was still school holidays, and the students weren't due back for the new term until the following Monday, but it was the teachers who'd interested Greenslade most—they seemed nervous at the mention of Pamela. It was understandable that they'd be upset, and unsure how their charges were going to handle the situation, but they were downright jittery, referring Greenslade's enquiries to the headmaster, Sydney Yeates.

Since Yeates wasn't at the school, Greenslade went to his home, the School House on Race Course Road, where Pamela had been a boarder. But the servants told him Yeates wasn't there either. Greenslade suspected they were covering for their master. His copper's intuition told him that the man was at home but didn't want to talk to a policeman.

Then Consul Affleck and some of Tientsin Grammar's board members, mostly local bigwigs, had got in touch with Greenslade and in no uncertain terms told him to stop questioning the teachers and pupils, and to stay away from Race Course Road. They also told him that DCI Dennis would be coming back to town. It was all very queer, Greenslade thought. Dennis had no idea what to think.

狐 狸 精

The meeting Dennis had been ordered to attend was scheduled for the following morning at eight o'clock, in his office in Gordon Hall on Victoria Road. The very symbol of British power in Tientsin, the hall was built out of the dark grey stone of the former ancient city wall, which had been pulled down by British troops. It was named after Charles 'Chinese' Gordon, who'd set out from Tientsin to march on Peking with Lord Elgin in 1860. The march had ended in the burning of the emperor's Summer Palace and the looting of Peking by the foreign soldiers.

Gordon then led the defeat of the Taiping rebels outside Shanghai, heading up a ragtag band of volunteers and mercenaries who called themselves the Ever Victorious Army. Lavished with rewards by the grateful Qing rulers, he became 'Chinese' Gordon. Eventually he was immortalised as a hero of the British Empire when he fell under the swords of the Mahdi in the Sudan. 'Chinese' Gordon became even better known as 'Gordon of Khartoum.'

Gordon Hall was the focal point of the British Concession's

authority. It held the offices of the British Municipal Council, the law courts, and the British Concession police headquarters, Dennis's citadel. The building itself was half Gothic castle, half bastion of imperial power, with churchlike arches over every doorway, and a massive front door heavily fortified in case of attack. This door was never used, as everyone entered by the side entrances. If things went bad in Tientsin, Gordon Hall would be where the besieged Brits would make a final stand.

The hall was in a position of prominence on the British Bund, close to the Tientsin Club and the Astor House Hotel, and directly across from the perfectly laid out Victoria Park, which could have been the municipal gardens of any English town. Facing the hall from the opposite bank of the Hai River was the old Russian Concession.

Present in Dennis's office that morning, along with Consul Affleck and Bill Greenslade, were E. C. Peters, chairman of the Committee of Management at Tientsin Grammar, Arthur Tipper, chairman of the Tientsin British Municipal Council, and P. H. B. Kent, legal adviser to the same council. These men were among the most powerful in Tientsin, and ultimately ran the British Concession.

Mary McIntyre brought in tea for them all, and a folder of documents that she handed to Consul Affleck. No one said anything until she had retreated and closed the door, and the tapping of her typewriter keys could be heard. Dennis made to start, wanting to inform the meeting that the investigation had finally got moving in Peking, but Affleck abruptly cut him off. When the consul was riled, traces of his Liverpool accent showed through. His had been a slow rise through the China Service; he'd only recently been elevated to a consulship, at the relatively advanced age of fifty-six.

DCI Dennis exchanged glances with Bill Greenslade, who shrugged to indicate he too had no idea what this was about.

Affleck got straight to the point. He was a blunt talker, despite his rank, and a professed atheist who had controversially married the widow of a British accountant in Tientsin, something that hadn't made him popular with the more traditional and pious elements in the Foreign Office. Times might have changed since 1913, when Ambassador Jordan had ostracised a man for marrying a widow, but prejudices died hard in Whitehall. This morning's meeting was about the headmaster of Tientsin Grammar School, Sydney Yeates. What was about to be discussed must never leave this office—on that, all the men around the table were to be clear. The very reputation of Tientsin Grammar was at stake, as was that of the British Concession in the city, and indeed British face in China.

The consul handed round sheets of foolscap from the manila folder Mary McIntyre had given him. Dennis noted there were none of the usual rubber stampings on the folder to indicate what was inside. The sheets were the formal police registration for Sydney Yeates. It listed his personal details—occupation, address, date and place of birth (1893, Oxford)—and included details of his family. Wife: Louise Ivy, née Barnes, born 1895, Headington, Oxford; children: Barbara, born 1924, Oxford.

Sydney Yeates was a solid fixture of Tientsin's British community. He had studied at Pembroke College, Oxford, then spent time as a teacher in England before moving to Africa to teach. He subsequently became inspector of schools in Nigeria. A stint teaching in Rangoon followed, and he arrived in China in 1923 as assistant headmaster at Tientsin Grammar. He was promoted to headmaster in 1927.

Dennis knew Yeates only vaguely. He'd seen him on the sidelines during the parents-versus-school cricket matches the DCI played in occasionally to make up the numbers, and at municipal council meetings, or on St George's Day, Empire Day and the King's Birthday. Dennis thought the man looked like a headmaster, with his slicked-down hair, dimpled chin, deep-set eyes that accentuated his seriousness, and thin top lip that his pupils said quivered when he was angry. He appeared older than his forty-three years, his thick black spectacles aging him even further. He was tall and strong-looking, and he had an equally strong reputation for being stern.

Not being known as a particularly kind man was one thing, but

Dennis had also heard rumours about Sydney Yeates's excessive discipline. Parents had mumbled, and a few complained openly. The headmaster was fond of doling out corporal punishment on pupils' backsides with a Rangoon cane, sending them home with blue-black welts that blistered and pustulated if they weren't treated. It was said he'd been asked to leave his school in Rangoon for being a little too severe with the cane.

Tientsin Grammar under Sydney Yeates *was* a strict school. If a student was given detention twice in one week, that meant an automatic appointment with the headmaster's cane, but that strictness was part of the reason some parents sent their children there in the first place, and Yeates was hardly the only headmaster in the empire who meted out discipline with a stick.

The pupils themselves had differing views of Yeates. Many liked and respected him; they thought him 'dapper.' Others considered him lazy—he didn't actually teach that regularly anymore—or said he drank, beat them, could be brutal, liked to embarrass and humiliate them, make spectacles of them. Dennis had seen Yeates drinking in the posh Tientsin Club, but couldn't say he drank more than anyone else. Yeates was, to Dennis's mind, a little superior: a little too quick to remind people of his Oxford background, to put on his robes and mortarboard in public.

Affleck now asked Dennis outright if he was sure that the murdered girl in Peking was Pamela Werner, and Dennis said he was. No, he told the consul, they hadn't charged anyone with the crime, but the investigation was ongoing. Why had he been brought back to answer these questions?

Peters, the chairman of the school's Committee of Management, then took over. Certain allegations had been made, he said, the previous year, the previous term. It was impossible to get to the bottom of them, but they were worrying nonetheless. An investigation had been conducted within the school, discreetly of course, and a resolution had been found. However, recent events raised the issue of the press becoming involved, and there were certain facts that, were they to see the light of day, might not be in the school's best interest. And they most surely had nothing to do with the unfortunate and tragic case in Peking.

Dennis was at a loss. He felt that his position had been undermined. What allegations? he wanted to know. What investigation?

Peters looked to Affleck. Affleck looked to the legal adviser Kent, who gave the nod. In his characteristically blunt manner, the consul laid out the events.

The previous term, Pamela Werner's father had approached the school board and claimed that his daughter had been subjected to unwarranted attentions while boarding at the School House—unwarranted attentions from headmaster Sydney Yeates.

She was distressed, upset, and Werner threatened to expose Yeates unless something was done. He used his influence to involve Affleck too, and an investigation was conducted. It appeared that, while perhaps drunk, Yeates had approached Pamela in a manner unbecoming of a headmaster with a pupil. His manner was even more improper given that she was under his care as a boarder.

There had been allegations by others before, but they'd always been withdrawn. Werner, though, was more adamant than most. Yeates had partially admitted that his conduct was improper, and he offered to resign at the end of the school year, in the summer, to avoid a disgrace that would end his career. Werner had pulled Pamela out of school and was planning to send her to England to complete her education. To preserve her reputation, he agreed to Yeates's leaving on the grounds of ill health once the long summer break started. A public scandal was in no one's interest—not Yeates's, nor the school's, nor Pamela's.

Dennis was stunned. He too was a father, and he had a parent's reaction to the news, a horrified dismay that the headmaster had been acting this way towards a student. He made to speak, but again Affleck cut him off.

Pamela's unfortunate death allowed for no choice but to bring forward Yeates's departure, the consul declared. The headmaster had been in Tientsin at the time of the murder, so there was no question of his being a suspect.

If need be, Superintendent Greenslade could make discreet enquiries to validate Yeates's alibi—he'd been at home with his wife and daughter. Yeates had tried his best to avoid Greenslade, but had eventually had to provide an alibi. However, Bill Greenslade would not have described Sydney Yeates as cooperative. For the leaders of British Tientsin, it seemed that the most important thing was for this incident not to become public knowledge; it most certainly was *not* to get into any newspapers.

A decision had been made, Affleck went on, and Yeates would not be returning to school on Monday. Instead he and his family were to leave for England as soon as possible. Peters was to arrange it all, and he would explain to the school that the headmaster was retiring due to poor health. The deputy, John Woodall, would be promoted to acting head. Woodall would have to be told the truth, but apart from him and Werner and those in the room, nobody else would know. Affleck would ensure that the local newspapermen were told to ignore any gossip. The reputation of Tientsin Grammar School . . .

The meeting was adjourned after Affleck had gained an assurance from everyone present that the matter would go no further. Dennis was told he could return to Peking to continue his investigations. As they all got up to leave, none of the men, not even Affleck, blunt as he was, could look Dennis in the eye. There was no other phrase for it— a cover-up had just taken place in the office of the head of the British Municipal Police, Tientsin.

Dennis fumed. He had been rendered impotent to preserve British face. He realized now what Werner had meant by his response to Dennis's question about why Pamela was leaving Tientsin and returning to England. *I would have thought you would have known?*

He *should* have known. And not knowing had not only made him look incompetent, it had taken him away from Peking at a critical moment in the investigation.

The following week, Sydney Yeates left Tientsin with his wife and daughter, boarding the first available ship out of the city. He never returned.

狐 狸 精

Closet investigations, secret meetings, people being bundled out of the city—it all seemed outlandish to Dennis. And despite the pact of silence in his office, the rumours and gossip inevitably increased. There was talk of widespread sexual activity among the older pupils at Tientsin Grammar, and indeed it did seem that there was a fast set at the school, and that Pamela was part of it. Yeates was declared to be a drunk as well as a bully; he'd had an affair with Pamela, had forced her to do things.

The rumour mill went even further: the autopsy had found that Pamela was pregnant, and the baby was Yeates's; he had been seen in Peking on the night she was murdered. In fact he regularly slipped away from Tientsin to cavort in the Badlands. The studio portrait of Pamela appeared in the Tientsin newspapers and was passed from hand to hand for comment. Most were sympathetic to her—she was the innocent victim of a horrific crime that could have been perpetrated on any of them. Others were less so. They read the reports that Pamela was 'not of a placid nature,' that she'd been in trouble at other schools before Tientsin. They discovered she was older than she appeared, and was seeing a number of boys in Peking. They believed she had strung along the popular Mischa Horjelsky in Tientsin and had probably been living an immoral life.

The two schools of thought divided along the lines of the two Pamelas: Pamela as a good girl, a schoolgirl, a plain girl, and Pamela as a woman, too independent, out of control. In numerous comfortable sitting rooms across Tientsin's British Concession, and in the soft leather chairs of the Tientsin Club at Gordon Hall, the question of the two Pamelas was a popular topic of conversation.

The rumours buzzed all the more after Yeates disappeared, along with his wife and daughter Barbara, herself a prizewinning pupil at the school. People wondered why they had left so suddenly. John

Woodall's promotion to acting head and his subsequent move into the School House on Race Course Road had all happened so abruptly, and even though the newspapers fell into line and reported the official reason of Yeates's ill health, the unseemly haste of events was suspicious to many. Tongues wagged, the speculation intensified. Some believed Yeates was guilty of Pamela's murder, and that it was being covered up to save face.

At the end of March, Tientsin Grammar held its annual Speech Day and prize giving, a major event in the school calendar and one that was reported in the *Peking and Tientsin Times*:

> Mr EC Peters—Chairman of the Committee of Management of Tientsin Grammar School—proposed three cheers for the recently departed Mr Yeates. . . . The response to Mr Peters's call was vociferous and unanimous, attesting to the high esteem in which the pupils hold their past headmaster.

Perhaps this was the case, perhaps it wasn't—the paper was still toeing the line. Pamela's absence from the event wasn't mentioned, nor was her murder. There were no condolences for her, no minute's silence.

And in an issue of the school paper, the *Grammarian*, that was published shortly after Speech Day, the new headmaster, John Woodall, wrote an article called 'Mr. Yeates—An Appreciation.' Amidst the praise for his departed colleague was a sentence that was pointed out again and again in the drawing rooms and clubrooms of Tientsin:

> In 1927 he became Headmaster, and for ten years he has held a position which, without exaggeration, must be one of the most difficult and trying ones in the educational world East of Suez, a world where truth is so easily twisted into scandal, where the interests of parents, boards of governors, staff and pupils so often seem to conflict, and where their divergences seem to be emphasized.

Where truth is so easily twisted into scandal. John Woodall was well aware of the gossip about his predecessor, and Tientsin Grammar remained a school with secrets. It was gossip that never went away.

Meanwhile Dennis *had* been away, away from Peking for two crucial days, on a false scent.

Under Peking Earth

While DCI Dennis was taking the train to Tientsin, Pamela's body was being laid to rest in Peking. Some fifty people gathered at the open graveside in the British Cemetery, where the gravediggers had had to work hard to break the frozen ground. It was late afternoon, and the weak sun was already going down, accentuating the unremitting January cold that chilled the lungs of the mourners. Grey clouds swept across the sky; sunset would come before five o'clock, followed rapidly by the gloaming and then night.

Man, that is born of a woman, hath but a short time to live, and is full of misery. He cometh up, and is cut down, like a flower; he fleeth as it were a shadow, and never continueth in one stay.

The British chaplain, the Reverend Griffiths, was presiding at the graveside but Werner wasn't listening, although he remained with his head bowed during the proceedings. He'd rejected organized religion intellectually many decades before, but its formalities were ingrained. Griffiths was there so that form could be maintained. Pamela, too, had been without religion, despite the Franciscan sisters, the school assemblies with the Lord's Prayer.

Thou knowest, Lord, the secrets of our hearts; shut not thy merciful ears to our prayer; but spare us . . .

If Werner had raised his head and looked to the west, he would have seen the Fox Tower looming not a quarter of a mile away. He had stood in this same spot in 1922 and watched as his beloved Gladys Nina's coffin was lowered into the grave next to Pamela's. His daughter had been barely five years old at that time, her blond hair in a pudding-bowl cut, a few of her milk teeth missing. She'd worn a new black overcoat with black woolen stockings as the mother she'd hardly known was buried. Now mother and daughter lay alongside each other.

Forasmuch as it hath pleased Almighty God in his great mercy to take unto himself the soul of our dear sister here departed, we therefore commit her body to the ground; earth to earth, ashes to ashes, dust to dust . . .

Among the mourners at the cemetery were Ethel Gurevitch and her mother, and Lilian Marinovksi and a few other friends from Pamela's Peking school days. The household servants from Armour Factory Alley were gathered to one side, where Pamela's amah was sobbing. Commissioner Thomas was there to represent the Legation Quarter police, but it seemed nobody had made the journey from Tientsin.

There was a small delegation from the British Legation, but nobody senior, just enough for basic duty to be seen to be done. Botham and Binetsky had stayed away to continue with the investigation and the questioning, but Colonel Han was there. He hung back from the group clustered around the graveside, the remainder of which consisted mostly of friends and colleagues of Werner's, come to lend support.

Why the senior staff at the legation had stayed away wasn't clear: Was it because of the lingering problems of Werner's long-ago-terminated diplomatic career, or because of the gossip that plagued the city? Werner had certainly heard the rumours:

The old man did it.

It's his wife all over again.

Death hovers around him.

She was a strange one.

Who's the man they're holding?

Pamela always had a wild streak.

The Chinese say she was a fox spirit.

The cemeteries of Peking, both Chinese and foreign, were all outside the city walls, established there by official order and following rules laid down in imperial times, which prevented burials within central Peking. They were places that superstitious Pekingers avoided; they were the habitats of fox spirits. During the height of the Boxer Rebellion, as the foreign population of the city cowered in the British Legation, fully expecting to be overrun and slaughtered, the Boxers had dug up the graves of the foreign dead, some of whom had lain there since the British Cemetery opened in 1861. They scattered the bones of the corpses around in full view, the desecration yet another horror to the besieged.

The Lord be with you. And with thy spirit.

Reverend Griffiths finished up, and the mourners moved hesitantly away, lingering only as long as seemed fitting. They went back to their waiting cars, then back to the city.

Werner was the last to leave, taking one final look at the grave of his wife and daughter. It had a simple headstone:

GLADYS NINA (RAVENSHAW) WERNER
1886–1922

PAMELA GLADYS CHALMERS WERNER
1917–1937

As he turned and walked away, men with spades began to fill in the grave with the hard and frozen Peking earth.

A Respectable Man of Influence

*T*he pathology lab at the Peking Union Medical College came back with an inconclusive report. The bloodstains on Pinfold's shoes, handkerchief and dagger sheath were most probably from an animal. They couldn't match them to Pamela's blood. The dagger itself was clean, and Pinfold's room had yielded no more traces of blood. They'd tried everything they could, but the science was lacking.

Pinfold had finally admitted to having a second address, one whose locks matched the set of keys found in his possession. It was another lodging house, technically within the boundaries of the Legation Quarter. That put him under the protection of the Quarter, and meant that permission to search the premises had to be granted by authorities there, a procedure that delayed the police. Botham and Binetsky had finally gone to the lodging house, but found little in the room beyond a few clothes.

Han requested that the British Legation allow him to formally arrest Pinfold. Because of the confused and overlapping jurisdictions and agreements between the Chinese and the foreign powers, the colonel needed authorization before he could arrest a foreign resident.

As Pinfold was suspected of being involved in the murder of a British subject, the correct procedure was to apply for permission from the British Legation, even though Pinfold was thought to be Canadian. But Consul Fitzmaurice refused, saying he didn't think there was sufficient evidence to sustain a conviction. Han asked that he be allowed to arrest Pinfold in order to hold him while they gathered that evidence, but Fitzmaurice was adamant; it was a point of protocol. And so Pinfold walked.

He left Morrison Street police station in the early hours of Saturday 16 January. Nobody saw him leave. It was too early for the press, but he walked out the back door just in case anyone was out the front with a camera. His shoes, handkerchief and knife had been returned to him, and he disappeared into the morning rush of Morrison Street. The press never did manage to get a photo of him.

Han issued a press release saying that the suspect had been released due to lack of evidence, and made no further comment.

Half-truths, lies—Dennis knew they hadn't got to the bottom of Pinfold and his secrets, but they had links. He was relieved when Han put out the order for Wentworth Prentice to be brought in for questioning.

狐狸精

Inevitably someone had talked. Someone at the medical college, or a constable privy to the enquiry, perhaps a British official who'd seen the details of the autopsy. Whatever the source, the Sunday newspapers had got hold of the fact that Pamela's heart and organs had been removed.

The news of the stolen heart sent further waves of panic through Peking's foreign community, which was still stunned by the murder. In a world where such a violent killing of an innocent girl was possible, where her body had been eviscerated, carved up and left for the *huang gou,* clearly nobody was safe and nothing sacred.

The superstitious took up the locals' explanation of fox spirits, claiming that their heightened activity was a sign the world was out of kilter. Other sensationalist rumours had it that barbarous Chinese were cutting out foreign hearts for illicit medicinal purposes, or perhaps for use in obscure religious rites. Some residents of the Legation Quarter had no doubt read a few too many Fu Manchu novels late at night, or taken as fact ungrounded tabloid news reports of the return of the Boxers, but still, it made everyone shudder to think about what had happened to Pamela's body.

Colonel Han tore strips off his men, lining them up in the yard behind the Morrison Street station, letting them freeze and shouting himself hoarse. But he knew that if the leak had come from one of his constables, the man would never come forward.

Werner called a press conference on Sunday afternoon outside the British Legation, annoying Fitzmaurice, who was left seething inside. The gentlemen, and a few ladies, of the press gathered obediently, notebooks at the ready, portraits of the grieving but stoic father already half written. Han, hearing of the conference, tapped one of his informants, a Chinese newspaperman on an English-language paper, and told him he wanted to know what Werner had to say, verbatim.

Werner knew how to give a speech. He stood erect and sombre in front of the journalists, who were shaking their hands to keep the blood circulating. Camera bulbs popped and sizzled. With his commanding eyes and a formal dark suit a few decades out of fashion, worn with a crisp white shirt and a black tie, Werner was every inch the former diplomat, the public orator. He was also the grieving father and the wronged man.

He told them that, as far as he knew, the police had made no progress. Suspects had been questioned, but all had been released. Why was this? Were the police incompetent? He hinted that permission to make a formal arrest of a suspect was being refused by the British Legation, and that he, Werner, was being frozen out of the investigation, even suspected himself. Pamela was now buried, but still the full report of her autopsy remained secret, and the inquest had yet to be reconvened to hear the medical evidence.

Werner told the press that he had heard the armchair gossip; he knew the finger of guilt had been pointed at him. He knew too that the hurtful accusations about the death of his poor wife were abroad once more, and that journalists had been looking into his past. He got worked up, he got angry. He was indignant.

And now, he said, unhelpful rumours about Pamela's missing organs and the mutilation of her body were rife. He breathed deeply before continuing. He did not believe the killer of his daughter was Chinese. He'd heard the talk of triads, shamans, thieves seeking human organs for medicine, ritual killings, but it was all nonsense. And the idea that fox spirits had killed Pamela was beneath contempt. Werner, the author of the highly regarded *Dictionary of Chinese Mythology* and the frequently reprinted *Myths and Legends of China*, stated forthrightly, 'Not in sociology, myths and legends nor in art, science or philosophy, has a kinship with the appropriation of human hearts been apparent in this country.'

All this gossip, Werner now told the crowd, was just a distraction. The killer was among Peking's foreign community, and someone knew him; they knew what he'd done but were shielding him, for what purpose Werner could not imagine. He told the gathering that he believed the police were close, that there were men within the foreign community who knew more than they'd come forward to tell.

Then Werner really rattled the cage. Since the offer of a reward from the Legation Police had not worked, he was upping the amount with his own money. The reward would now be worth $5,000 in gold dollars—a currency not commonly used but often held as savings. This was in fact Werner's life savings, and was more than what 99 percent of Peking would make in three lifetimes of toil. The press lapped it up.

狐狸精

DCI Dennis returned to Peking on Sunday evening, and on Monday morning found himself summoned to the British Legation first thing. They didn't issue an order as such, more a polite request: 'In view of circumstances and information reaching the public we . . .' He decided to see what they had to say—the call had been long expected anyway.

The British Legation was technically a consulate now, rather than an embassy, and had been ever since His Majesty's Ambassador Extraordinary and Plenipotentiary Hughe Knatchbull-Hugessen had followed Chiang Kai-shek's government to Nanking. Peking had been reduced to a diplomatic backwater, but Dennis knew the diplomatic corps, and he knew that the staff here, for all their diminished status, would be no less pompous, self-righteous and generally full of themselves. Above all, they were clannish.

The entrance to the legation, where Werner had addressed the press the previous day, was fronted with two stone lions. Once past the guards, Dennis was shown inside to a small library with deep chairs, a bit like a London gentlemen's club but with a pathetic fire in the grate offering little in the way of warmth. Bookshelves lined the walls, except for above the fireplace. Here there was a patch of slightly discoloured wallpaper where the portrait of Edward VIII had hung. It seemed that a portrait of the new king, George VI, who'd held the throne since the abdication of his brother in December, had yet to make it to Peking.

Two functionaries were sent in to greet Dennis. They were effusive with thanks for his coming, but he felt their inevitable condescension just below the surface. Consul Fitzmaurice followed them in, surrounded by his advisers, and bluntly laid out his orders. Dennis was to cease all contact with Werner, since the old man had suffered enough. The legation had already requested that the Chinese police do likewise, and at Ch'ienmen headquarters Chief Chen, chief of the Peking police and Han's superior officer, was cooperating.

The Chuanpan Hutong raid had been a mistake, Dennis was told. One of his officers had been in attendance, and that went specifically against the instructions given to the DCI. Dennis had exceeded his remit.

'Remember,' Fitzmaurice said, 'you have no powers of arrest

here—liaise with Commissioner Thomas before taking any actions in conjunction with Han.'

The British Legation, Dennis was made aware, had theories of its own about the case, and the DCI was overlooking the obvious—the Chinese. The city was full to bursting with immigrants—country boys with no money and little hope, propelled by the regular torments of flood, drought, crop failure and the cancer of poverty, as well as the marauding Japanese. Dennis needed to realise that Peking was a sexual as a well as a political powder keg. Sixty-four percent of the population was male, most of them young, many of them refugees from the countryside. They were probably sexually frustrated, unable to secure wives or afford prostitutes. They were uneducated, uncontrollable, un-Christian, not always capable of self-restraint. Outbursts of maniacal sexual assaults were to be expected in this atmosphere, from such people. Dennis should push Han to look at these men, not go down cul-de-sacs, pursue dead ends.

End of lecture. The DCI was summarily dismissed.

狐 狸 精

Dennis didn't take the advice of the British Legation to heart. Instead, after an update from Han, he went looking for Wentworth Prentice. He didn't have to look very hard—the dentist was in his flat at 3 Legation Street, close to the border of the Badlands.

Dennis and Commissioner Thomas walked the short distance from Thomas's office to Prentice's flat, which was in one of the more modern and upscale apartment blocks, next to the old German barracks. The flats were popular with Americans; they had all the mod cons for high monthly rents, and balconies that looked out towards the Deutsch-Asiatische Bank and the large French Legation. Next to the apartment block was the French Club skating rink.

The dentist's flat was smart and clean, and, surprisingly, the windows were wide open. Prentice explained to Dennis that his landlord had just had the apartment repainted, a rather stupid thing to do in the middle of a Peking winter, but that was Chinese landlords for you. He seemed relaxed and agreed to accompany the two men for questioning. Since the legation police station was tiny, they used Morrison Street, a practice Thomas had agreed upon with Han.

Dennis could see that Prentice was prosperous. Well, everyone knew there was money in dentistry. His hair was neat, cut short at the back. The man's teeth were good—who, Dennis wondered, did a dentist's dental work? He wore a much better suit than his hunting pal Pinfold, a much better suit than Dennis's, truth be told. He appeared to be a fastidious dresser: he had a handkerchief in his top pocket, polished shoes, a perfectly knotted tie.

The American Legation had been a damn sight more helpful than the British when it came to providing information. Wentworth Baldwin Prentice had been born on 6 June 1894 in Norwich, Connecticut, the son of Myron Baldwin Prentice, a grocery shop owner. Prentice had attended Harvard Dental School during World War I, and after graduating had married and moved to Peking, setting up practice in the Legation Quarter in 1918. With almost twenty years' residence in the city, he was perhaps its best-known foreign dentist. W. B. Prentice took care of the teeth of the elite.

It was all pretty standard, but there was a jarring note. Prentice's wife, Doris Edna, and their three children, Doris, Wentworth and Constance, had gone back to America in 1932, settling in Los Angeles. They had not returned to Peking since. The American Legation had no formal record of a divorce, but it seemed that Prentice had been living without his family for some years now.

There was another thing. The Americans had been concerned for the welfare of Prentice's youngest child, his daughter Constance. A file on her had been opened at the legation in 1931, but there was just one line in it: 'Prentice, Miss—Nov. 28, 1931—393.1115/14—Welfare of American in China, Safety of.' There were no details in the file. Nor did the legation have anything more concrete to offer. Dennis didn't know if Doris had left Peking voluntarily, or if Prentice had sent her away, or if she'd fled in order to protect her children from something. Or someone.

While Prentice came willingly to Morrison Street, he was tight-lipped when he got there. No, he said, he was not Pamela's dentist. He was dentist to some of the best and most influential people in Peking, but he had never even heard of Pamela before her murder.

'I have never seen the girl in my life,' he told the police outright.

When asked where he was on the night of 7 January, he said he had finished work and then gone to see a film at a cinema on Morrison Street. No, he didn't have the ticket stub, and yes, he'd gone alone. It was a perfectly natural thing to do, he claimed—he used to go regularly with his wife when she was in Peking, but now had no choice but to go by himself. He missed his family.

Dennis pressed him. 'Weren't you her dentist?' he insisted.

'I was not. I have never seen the girl in my life.'

Dennis terminated the interview, and afterwards looked for confirmation that Pamela had been a patient of Prentice's. It would have been simplest to ask Werner, but Dennis was under strict instructions to make no more contact with the old man. He searched the dentist's records—there was no listing for anyone called Pamela, or Werner. But there was a Gurevitch, Ethel, so Dennis went round to the Gurevitch residence again on Hong Kong Bank Road. Ethel didn't know whether her dentist was also Pamela's or not; she was unable to say whether Pamela even had a dentist in Peking.

Dennis went back to the autopsy notes:

. . . teeth—healthy—26 present, the usual number for a person of her age being 28–32 teeth—two back teeth missing—removed professionally at some earlier time—recent chips to two of front teeth—assumed to have occurred during struggle . . .

Dr Cheng at the Peking Union Medical College confirmed that the removal of Pamela's back teeth had been undertaken some time before her death: the gums had healed, which meant that the extractions weren't recent. Her teeth showed no signs of recent dental work.

Dennis and Han asked Prentice back for a second interview at Morrison Street. The dentist stuck to his story. 'I was not her dentist. I have never seen the girl in my life. Why are you asking me about her?'

Dennis then asked him about his association with Pinfold, explaining that he too had been questioned. Prentice admitted to hunting occasionally with Pinfold, with Joe Knauf too, and a few other men, mostly Americans. And why shouldn't he? He was after all a well-known man about town, a member of several clubs, a Harvard Dental School graduate, a long-standing member of Peking's foreign community. He pointed out, once again, that he looked after the teeth of some of the city's best-known people. Dennis noted the veiled threat in the comment—the connection to influential people.

What about the nudist colony? Dennis insisted. What about the nude dances?

But Prentice didn't even flicker. The nudist colony was respectable; naturism was well established in Europe and America. The detective chief inspector shouldn't be such a prude; some of Peking's most solid and reliable citizens were members. If anything inappropriate was occurring, surely the Chinese police would have objected by now, after several summers? As to nude dances, that was mere gossip. The gatherings in Prentice's flat were simply like-minded men enjoying cultural activities in a private setting.

狐 狸 精

The news that Prentice had been questioned was leaked. The Western Hills nudist colony made the papers, although the nude dance parties on Legation Street stayed secret, or perhaps they were a touch of voyeurism too far for the press. Many in foreign Peking were once again shocked. Prentice was to them a respectable figure in society.

The day after the leak, a long editorial on Pamela's murder appeared in the *Peking Chronicle*, a paper that most of foreign Peking still read, even though it had come under Japanese control. The article was written by George Gorman, fellow member of Prentice's nudist colony. Gorman attacked the police and DCI Dennis for interrogating Prentice, claiming that he knew for a fact Prentice had been at the cinema on the night in question and that he was innocent. He was a man of good character, the Legation Quarter's leading dentist. The police, both Chinese and British, were floundering, with no ideas, and they were therefore pulling in innocent foreigners when they should be looking among the Chinese for the killer.

Dennis felt that Gorman protested too much about the direction of the investigation. He thought it worthwhile confronting the man about his criticisms, so he sought Gorman out. The Irishman lived with his wife and two adolescent children in cramped conditions in the Legation Quarter, something Dennis thought unusual for a regular at the Peking Club bar. Gorman was not at home, but Gorman's wife told Dennis they were all distraught, that Pamela had spent the evening before her murder at their house, taking tea and then going ice-skating with the family. Pamela had left her bicycle at the Gormans' house and collected it after skating. It was the Gormans who had introduced her to the French Club rink near their house. When Mrs Gorman had read that Pamela was last seen a day later leaving the rink, she was shocked.

Dennis left the Gorman home with nothing new, other than now knowing Pamela's movements of 6 January in more detail.

He wanted to question Prentice further, find out more about the hunting in the hills, search the man's flat, which Dennis had noted contained hunting equipment. The sudden departure of the dentist's family didn't sit right with the detective, although it wasn't evidence of anything illegal. Han agreed with Dennis that the nudist colony, too, was strange, but that wasn't illegal either, and there'd been no complaints about it. The nude dancing, if it had occurred, had been in the Legation Quarter and was therefore not Han's territory.

Dennis appealed to Consul Fitzmaurice to let him arrest Prentice for further questioning, but once again the consul refused, citing insufficient evidence. Many men went hunting, and Dennis had no proof that Prentice had known Pamela, or ever treated her. Naturism, nude dances, were all very odd, but they didn't link the dentist to the dead girl as far as Fitzmaurice could see. He was not about to start a tradition of Legation Quarter residents being arrested and taken to Chinese police stations.

Dennis had to concede that Fitzmaurice was right. He didn't have any evidence; he was just going by his copper's guts. There was something about Prentice's manner that was hard to define. Perhaps it was his smile, the way he seemed to mock Dennis with his eyes. It was nothing tangible, more an attitude, an arrogance. And it was far, far from enough.

Dennis was back to square one.

Radical Chic

The investigation had stalled, the days dripped away with no new evidence, no more witnesses, no sign of the blood. Colonel Han's twenty days since the murder had now elapsed, and DCI Dennis was on the verge of collapse. The long hard winter and the bitter cold of Peking were taking their toll. He hadn't had a peaceful night's sleep since the eighth of January. He'd had too many cigarettes, too many whisky sodas, and he'd acquired a nagging cough he couldn't shake. His limbs were frozen from walking the winter streets, and the foul-tasting green medication from the Wagons Lits' in-house doctor was doing no good. Dennis was exhausted but unable to sleep. And he had a detective's inevitable doubt that he was missing something obvious in the case.

Colonel Han was now saying he believed the case would never be solved. As the Japanese moved ever closer, the killer became more distant. Peking was obsessed with its own survival. Assassination had become a daily event; a guerrilla war was being fought on the streets of the city, and the Japanese army was now dug in at the Marco Polo Bridge, a mere nine miles from the Forbidden City and the Legation

Quarter, where it was waiting for orders to advance. In Nanking, Chiang Kai-shek remained ominously silent on Peking's fate.

Dennis's resources were dwindling. Sergeant Binetsky had been recalled to Tientsin—the situation was escalating there also. Dennis too was wanted back, but he'd requested a few more days, pleading to be permitted to stay and see the investigation through. In his sleepless nights and dog-tired days, Pamela was constantly in his mind's eye—schoolgirl, glamour girl. He was almost coming to believe in fox spirits himself, imagining he saw them dancing along the top of the Tartar Wall, loitering in the eaves of the Fox Tower, wandering the endless *hutong* at night. They were laughing at him as they sought their victims, or balanced skulls on their heads. They were as intangible and unreachable as the killer he sought, disappearing into the Peking darkness without even shadows to trail them by. They faded into the air of the Tartar City beyond his gaze, just as the murderer had dissolved into the city.

He put the hallucinations down to the green medicine.

In public, Dennis sought to kill the rumours about fox spirits and organ thieves. He laughed at the talk and attacked the Chinese newspapers who made comparisons with the heart eaters in Boccaccio's erotic and bawdy *Decameron*, a book that was read widely in China in translation at the time. The press were fixated on the stolen-heart angle, egged on by sources unnamed.

But Commissioner Thomas had given Dennis a tip-off on that score. Inspector Botham had been heard holding court in the back bar of the Hôtel du Nord, drinking too much, bragging, enjoying being the centre of attention. Thomas's contacts had also reported the loose-tongued inspector spending too much time in the Badlands, not on official business. Dennis dispatched him back to Tientsin to plug the leak.

The DCI also scotched talk of psychopathological sadists, and declared the gossip around Werner to be 'irresponsible nonsense.' But he kept quiet about Sydney Yeates and his behaviour at Tientsin Grammar School.

Meanwhile he had nothing to link Pinfold to Pamela, or Prentice to Pamela, or Pamela to the Badlands. He had links between Pinfold, Prentice and Joe Knauf, who all hunted together, were all part of the Western Hills nudist colony, and attended Prentice's dances. They were all linked to the Badlands, to foreign Peking's sinful side, just not to Pamela.

Even the dime-droppers were drying up now, or changing tack. There'd been no more cranks confessing to the murder—now they called to say they'd seen Japanese agents poisoning the wells, or Emperor Hirohito walking in the Western Hills with Chiang Kai-shek.

It was time to finish, time to go home. Pamela's murderer was beyond reach now. There remained just the formalities to complete.

狐狸精

The inquest into the death of Pamela did not resume until 29 January. At eleven o'clock on that Friday morning, Consul Fitzmaurice once more took the chair in the British Legation, which had again become an official coroner's court. This time the inquest would hear the testimony and evidence of witnesses and the police, and the full report of the autopsy on the corpse.

Snow had arrived overnight in Peking, and the city was blanketed in a white that was turning rapidly to grey-black sludge. It was if anything even colder in the room than the first time the inquest was convened. Back then it had still seemed that a quick arrest might be possible. Back then the more gruesome details of the killing had not been widely known.

The public gallery had been specially enlarged for the resumption and was overflowing. The benches were packed with witnesses—the Gurevitch family, Lilian Marinovski, Werner's household staff and others who could help with details about Pamela's final days: Chang Pao-chen the old bird fancier, Corporal Kao and Constable Hsu of Police Post 19. Commissioner Thomas and Constable Pearson from the Legation Police were there, and of course Colonel Han and DCI Dennis.

Sitting alone and talking to no one, stiff-backed as a statue, was E. T. C. Werner. He was silently fuming at having been frozen out of the investigation by Consul Fitzmaurice, at being ignored by Dennis.

The inquest into the death of Pamela Werner proved to be the longest in Peking in living memory, its second sitting lasting three days. Snow was still falling outside when the first witness, Chang Pao-chen, stood to retell through a legation interpreter his story of finding Pamela's body. He was followed by the Chinese policemen Kao and Hsu, reading from their notebooks.

Colonel Han told how he had handled the scene at the Fox Tower, leaving out the most gruesome details but trying to finally quash the *huang gou* rumour once and for all. Thomas and Pearson backed up Han's account of the crime scene.

Han then reconstructed Pamela's last day as he knew it, and the gateman and cook at Armour Factory Alley repeated their testimonies. Pamela's amah broke down in tears when she took the stand. The court was adjourned for the day.

The second day, a Saturday, began with Ethel Gurevitch struggling through her story. Her mother and father confirmed Pamela's visit to their house that Thursday. When Lilian Marinovski gave evidence, she distanced herself from Pamela, saying the two of them had been only casual acquaintances. Chao Hsi-men, the receptionist at the Wagons Lits, repeated his story about Pamela's mystery visit to the hotel that afternoon.

It being the weekend, Fitzmaurice broke at lunchtime, announcing that he would hear the last witnesses, the doctors from the Peking Union Medical College, on Monday morning, in camera. The journalists objected; Fitzmaurice ignored them.

On Monday, snow flurries were still whipping Peking, and the streets were icy. Legation guards manned the door to the courtroom, where Dr Cheng was the first to take the stand. He ran through the findings of the autopsy and the cause of death—a fractured skull followed by a brain haemorrhage. He detailed the apparent struggle beforehand, the postmortem mutilation, the almost surgical cuts, the broken ribs, the missing organs, the detached stomach. He tried to remain professional and exact while describing what had been done to Pamela, but he kept pausing, shocked anew at the immensity and horror of what he was saying.

The fatal blow to Pamela's head would have caused death within a few minutes, Dr Cheng told the court, and the butchery of her body had occurred no more than five to six hours after death. If this had taken place out of doors in the dark, it must have been done by someone who knew what they were doing, such as a butcher or a hunter. It was Dr Cheng's opinion that the person or persons responsible had had the intention of dismembering the entire body, but had abandoned their task.

Dr Cheng was followed by James Maxwell, professor of gynaecology and obstetrics at the medical college. Maxwell testified that Pamela's death was 'not the work of an ordinary sexual sadist.' Rather, he said, it 'displayed signs of being the work of a maniac.' Maxwell also said that Pamela 'had been sexually interfered with,' discreetly referring to the mutilation of her genitals, adding that it was 'not possible to state definitively whether this occurred pre- or post-mortem.'

The pharmacologist Harry Van Dyke then testified that no poisons had been involved, and Pamela had not been given chloroform. The last meal she had eaten was Chinese food.

Finally Han retook the stand and told Fitzmaurice that the police had no suspects and had made no arrests. Dennis corroborated Han's statement and then promptly sat down. He chose not to mention that Fitzmaurice had personally refused Han permission to arrest either Pinfold or Prentice, nor that Werner had been made persona non grata to the police by official order. He chose not to mention that he, Dennis, was being pressured to return to Tientsin and his normal police work.

Werner, for his part, had remained quiet throughout. He was not called to give evidence again. He assumed that Fitzmaurice had taken his impromptu press conference on the steps of the legation as a personal slight—as indeed it had been, just as Werner intended. The old man sat through most of day three with his head in his hands.

Having heard all the available evidence, Fitzmaurice declared Pamela's death to be an unlawful killing. His decision meant that the case remained open, an unsolved murder; it was subject to ongoing investigation.

狐 狸 精

The next day, all the most gruesome aspects of Pamela's murder, the very details Fitzmaurice had hoped to suppress by having the evidence heard in camera, became public. The press had managed to get hold of the testimony of the Peking Union Medical College autopsy team.

Peking was horrified to read about the extent of the mutilation to Pamela's body, and about the sexual interference, but interest in the case was beginning to slip. The front pages were dominated by other fears now, and Pamela was relegated to the inside pages, after the bad news from Europe. Franco-German relations were at an all-time low; Göring had been welcomed in Rome by Mussolini; German troops had landed in Spanish Morocco.

Meanwhile, the situation in China as a whole was deteriorating. The Japanese were angry at decisions taken by General Sung's political council, and a Japanese plot to stir up anarchy in rural areas had been uncovered. Agents were everywhere, and people worried that their neighbours were spies. Anyone could be a collaborator in the pay of Tokyo.

One veteran Western journalist in Shanghai described the times as like 'living on the rim of a volcano.' Chiang Kai-shek, who was supposedly in a united front with the Communists, had suppressed a Red revolt in Kiangse Province. And in Peking itself, Japanese tanks had appeared on the streets.

They rumbled through the business districts, down Morrison Street, past the detective bureau. Japanese Zero planes buzzed the skies like mosquitoes, taunting the populace. The Japanese Legation strenuously denied that these were anything other than military exercises, goodwill parades. It didn't feel that way to the residents of the city, where there wasn't much goodwill going round.

Japanese garrisons to the north of Peking were being strength-ened. Mere miles from Peking's outer limits, there were more men and machinery than could be justified for simple replacements. Japanese-smuggled dope continued to pour into the city and be sold off cheaply. The Peking police were busting dens and dealers, but when they caught one, another three took their place, financed by Japanese yen.

Cocktail hour at the Wagons Lits, tea dances at the Grand Hôtel de Pékin, tiffins at the Peking Club, steins at the Hôtel du Nord, were all depleted as people slipped out of the city, getting away while the going was good. Foreign Peking was starting to shrink fast.

DCI Dennis, though, was determined to remain. He argued hard with his bosses on the British Municipal Council in Tientsin, who agreed to give him more time, but he could not remain in Peking indefinitely. He had until the Chinese New Year, and then he had to return to his normal duties.

狐 狸 精

It was all too much for one woman, whose mind had been in turmoil for nearly a month. Eventually, two days after the inquest had ad-journed, she called on the Morrison Street station. She was in a shaken state, asking for the detective in charge of the Pamela Werner investi-gation. Han directed her to DCI Dennis, since she was a foreigner—another rattled white woman.

But this was one white woman who didn't rattle easily—Helen Foster Snow, alias Nym Wales to her readers, aka Peg to her friends, of whom she had many. A vibrant, slim, attractive woman, Helen had a charm many found hard to resist, and she was very popular, a genu-ine beauty who could have been a model in another life. In fact she did occasionally make money modeling for the Camel's Bell, an ex-clusive store in the lobby of the Grand Hôtel de Pékin whose furs, silks and cheongsams made it a favourite stop for rich tourists. Helen was less of a polarizing force than her outspoken husband. Where

Edgar Snow could sometimes be abrasive, it was difficult not to like Helen.

When Colonel Han saw her in the Morrison Street station lobby, he thought she was what Pamela would have come to look like if she'd lived. Dennis agreed; the resemblance was definitely there, though Helen was a decade or so older than Pamela. Neither Han nor Dennis had talked to the Snows about the murder. For Han, the pair would have spelt trouble, and in this case there were no suspicions attached to them anyway. And since they lived outside the Legation Quarter, they were also officially out of bounds for DCI Dennis.

But now he arranged to call on Helen that evening and hear her out. How could he not? Her address, 13 Armour Factory Alley, was just two courtyards down from Werner's, on the same side of the street. As she wrote the address down for him, she said, 'It was me they were after, not Pamela; it was a warning.'

Helen and her husband had been in Peking since 1935, after a few years in Shanghai, where Edgar had rather outstayed his welcome parodying and insulting the American community. Like Werner's, their house was traditional, but unlike his it had plenty of modern conveniences. It was also bigger, covering about an acre, with a conservatory running along the front two wings. There were stables, a tennis court, and a glassed-in pavilion for garden parties. A garden shed had been fixed up as Edgar's writing room, and a towering gingko tree in the courtyard provided shade in the scorching summer months.

Helen Foster Snow referred to her home as 'our haunted house near the Fox Tower.' When Dennis arrived at the appointed time, dusk was settling in. Outside the Legation Quarter, Peking was all grey walls and no street lighting. The Werner house was in total darkness. Armour Factory Alley was quiet, not being accessible easily by cars or readily by rickshaw pullers, who were reluctant to enter the realm of the fox spirits at night.

The Snows' was easily the most impressive courtyard house on the street, but it looked to be under siege. Its walls were spiked with broken glass to prevent intruders. Outside the main gate stood four tough-looking young Chinese, probably from Shantung, the province that had provided the backbone of China's armies for centuries. A brazier lit up the entrance and the quartet of men, who were equipped with large broadswords tied in sashes at their sides. They stood stiff-backed with their arms crossed, their faces implacable.

Helen Foster Snow appeared, wearing black velvet trousers and an oversize black turtleneck pullover. Her hair was pulled back off her face, and she wore no makeup. Shivering in the courtyard, she looked frail and nervous, her thin lips forcing a smile at the guards to indicate that she was expecting Dennis. They relaxed and let him enter.

'Ed hired them to make me feel safer,' she told Dennis. 'He thinks I'm being silly to worry, but they reassure me.'

The interior of the courtyard house was everything Dennis expected of two youngish and adventurous Americans who were rich in China with American dollars. They had all the accoutrements of the China sojourner—the carved mahogany ashtrays, the Ning-po lacquerware, the Qing-style blackwood furniture. There were noticeably more silk-covered cushions and silk drapes on the sofa than the Chinese would have used, and a display of *chinoiserie* and knickknacks—thumb rings, fingernail protectors, carved Buddhas, an ornate opium pipe on a stand. Gilt idols had been turned into standard lamps. There were also shelves of books, piles of magazines, a large wireless, a gramophone, records.

The whole place was warm and inviting, modern but lived-in—very American to Dennis's English eye. It couldn't have been in greater contrast to Werner's austere courtyard down the alley, where only the presence of a telephone indicated that it was 1937.

Dennis lit a cigarette. Helen handed him an ashtray decorated with the logo of the Dollar Line, no doubt fashionably stolen from the cabin of one of their steamships. In the comfort of the Snows' house, Dennis felt exhaustion ripple through him. His bones craved rest and warmth; his back ached from the lumpy mattress at the Wagons Lits, which held the dents of a thousand prior occupants. The bed itself wasn't long enough for his lanky frame, and the steam heating in the room dried out his throat, already raspy from too many cigarettes smoked down to his fingertips. He had a cold he couldn't shake, and his joints were sore.

Helen later recalled that Dennis had been pale, green-faced and shivering that night—and 'not only from the cold,' she noted. She offered him a glass of brandy to take the chill off. He accepted and felt momentarily revived. Edgar Snow wasn't at home, and Dennis and Helen settled in for a chat. What had she meant when she'd said that Pamela's death was a warning? he asked her.

It was a question with a long backstory. Helen and Edgar Snow enjoyed both sides of two very different Pekings, spending time with the Communists in their remote cave hideouts and starting a radical journal called *Democracy*, but also becoming regulars at the Grand Hôtel de Pékin, where they danced cheek-to-cheek in the ballroom that imitated the Hall of Mirrors at the Palace of Versailles. At their salons and garden parties in the courtyard on Armour Factory Alley, they mixed with revolutionaries and intellectuals, both Chinese and foreign.

That month, Edgar was working on the final manuscript of *Red Star Over China,* his account of the time he'd spent with the Chinese Red Army in the summer and autumn of 1936. It contained interviews with the enigmatic Communist leader Mao Tse-tung, and everyone was whispering that it was going to be an explosive book. It accused Chiang Kai-shek and the Kuomintang of corruption, and contrasted this with what Edgar believed were the glowing prospects and revolutionary purity of the Communists. He wanted to see a united front against Japan and against fascism, Asian or European.

He also wanted Chiang to stop his Red-baiting, a policy that went back to 1927 and the slaughter in Shanghai of the Communists and others on the left. Chiang had been cleaning house, beheading troublesome union leaders along with Communist agents, and at least three thousand were left dead on the streets. The International Settlement, Frenchtown and Chinese Shanghai had run with blood for days while the foreign powers sat back and watched. A disgusted Edgar Snow reported on it.

The fabled old China hands of Peking had failed to take Mao's band of Communists seriously. They'd seen them smashed in Shanghai, then routed from their ad hoc Kiangse Soviet, a hastily conceived Communist-controlled territory, and forced into a long march to Shaanxi with Chiang's army nipping at their heels. The Communists marched for 370 days, over a distance of eight thousand miles, enduring fatigue, hunger, cold, sickness, desertion and death. Only 7,000 of the 100,000 who set out made it to the Yan'an caves in Shaanxi, where they holed up beyond Chiang's reach and plotted their comeback. Edgar had travelled to Yan'an to meet and interview them, and he sent back dispatches praising them. The foreign establishment now firmly distrusted him; Chiang and the Kuomintang hated him.

Those whom Chiang disliked were added to a list. This was compiled by the Spirit Encouragement Society, known commonly as the Blue Shirts, an openly fascistic secret police, a paramilitary force intent on removing enemies of the Kuomintang. The list included every Communist in China, along with anyone, Chinese or foreign, who supported them. Helen believed it included Edgar, since details of his manuscript had leaked out, as well as herself.

Within the Blue Shirts was a yet more secretive, yet more deadly group, simply named the Military Statistical Bureau. This was run by a shadowy figure called Tai Li, who was known even then as the 'Himmler of China,' and its organization was modeled on the Gestapo. Tai Li was the most feared man in China, the generalissimo's 'eyes, ears, and dagger,' the spymaster general. He was known to despise foreigners, particularly the British, whose intelligence services he thought were far too meddlesome in China. Major General Tai was a remover of problems for the Kuomintang, an eliminator of enemies, a dispatcher of assassins. It was said that to be on the wrong side of Tai was to be on the wrong side of life. There were constant rumours about who was behind the assassinations and political killings in Peking that winter, and Tai's name was whispered in every one.

Tai Li and the Blue Shirts, Helen told Dennis, were out of control.

They were running amok, settling scores. They were everywhere in Peking, underground and sometimes overt. Young aspirant Blue Shirt thugs met nightly on top of the Tartar Wall near the Fox Tower, within spitting distance of Armour Factory Alley. Her tailor claimed to be a member. They revered Tai as omnipotent, they practiced tai chi and swordplay, they remembered and honoured the Boxers of 1900, they believed in magic and in organ medicine. They cut hearts out, or so they claimed.

The Blue Shirts wanted Edgar dead, claimed Helen. They wanted *Red Star Over China* buried. Since they were assassinating enemies of Chiang and Tai all over Peking, what was to stop them assassinating foreigners too? Helen believed she may have been the real target on the night of 7 January. The Blue Shirts had wanted to kill her as a warning to her husband, but they got Pamela by mistake.

Dennis had to concede that the theory made sense. In fact, it was the only theory so far that made sense. It supplied motive. He appeared willing to consider it.

Helen Snow was scared. She had hoped a Scotland Yard detective would tell her to stop being silly, to get a grip, to put these foolish ideas out of her head. Her husband refused to take them seriously. He felt himself to be 'the favoured child of providence'; he believed that 'foreigners were still sacrosanct in China.' But if that had ever been true, the mutilation of Pamela Werner showed it wasn't any longer. There was nothing sacrosanct about being murdered and having your heart ripped out.

On the night of 7 January, Edgar and Helen had been at a party with fellow Americans Harry Price, an economics professor at Peking's Yenching University, and his wife Betty. The two couples socialised regularly with each other, and spent the summer together on the beaches of Peitaiho, discussing the deteriorating world situation and the great ideological hope of Marxism. That Thursday night, the Snows had caught a taxi home to Armour Factory Alley around ten o'clock, and when Helen heard the news of the murder, she realised they couldn't have been far away at the time of the killing.

Helen had of course heard all the rumours surrounding the case, those concerning Werner, and Pinfold and Prentice. She knew of the nudist colony in the Western Hills, and caught the servants' gossip about fox spirits. But why kill a young girl home from school for the holidays? she wondered. There had to be another reason. The thought that it was a case of mistaken identity chilled her to the bone.

The Snows' address was hardly difficult to discover, especially given their social calendar and Tai Li's reach. Anyone could quickly find out that Helen regularly walked or bicycled along the Tartar Wall to Armour Factory Alley. Like Pamela, she always took that route home from the Legation Quarter: it was unlit at night, but it avoided the confusing warren of *hutong* that formed the Badlands.

Helen Foster Snow dressed smartly—high heels, long skirts, fur stoles. Her style was radical politics with chic couture. Put Pamela in her glamour shot next to Helen, and in the dark, in a rush, they could be mistaken. Especially by an unknown assailant such as Helen was suggesting. The two women were about the same height and had the same colouring; both were fair-haired and slim. Helen wore her hair pulled tight to her head, sometimes parted to the side, sometimes down the centre—just like Pamela. They lived virtually next door, they both rode their bicycles around the area. The cover of night would easily remove the ten-year age difference between them.

Dennis didn't know what to say to Helen. Sitting by her fire, he looked out at Armour Factory Alley, listening to the howling of the *huang gou* carried on the wind from the Fox Tower. He was amazed that Edgar had gone out and left his wife alone in this state. Dennis had always found Armour Factory Alley ghoulish at night, but this seemed to be the reason Edgar and Helen liked it. They knew it was supposed to be haunted by fox spirits living in the Fox Tower, but she was, she laughed, living 'alone' with fifteen servants, four of them tough men armed with swords.

'Don't you realise,' Dennis asked her, 'that the murderer has to be hiding somewhere, probably nearby?'

The DCI was at the end of his tether. He found himself slipping out of character. No longer the detached copper, he was taking the case too personally. Helen Snow's brandy had left a bad taste in his mouth, or perhaps the virus he had was messing with his sense of taste. He needed rest; he needed to go home to Tientsin. He felt sick and useless.

'There are no lights anywhere,' he said to Helen. 'Anything could happen way out here in the dark.' He implored her to pack up, move out, get away from Armour Factory Alley. It was cursed. DCI Dennis sensed he was losing out to panic—he needed to get a grip. He was the one who ought to get out of Peking.

Brutal though Tai Li and the Blue Shirts were, their assassinations tended to be fast, decisive—a shot to the head, and then they moved on to their next enemy. Tai was fond of the term *liquidation*. His methods didn't square with what had been done to Pamela. Anyway, Dennis was a realist—it would be impossible to ever confirm or rule out Tai's involvement. Nobody—not Han, not his bosses at Ch'ienmen— would ever dare approach Tai about the matter.

However plausible Helen Snow's theory about mistaken identity might be, it could never go anywhere. There were some questions that would just never get asked, some men in China so powerful they could get away with murder. Tai Li was one such. He was the dead end of all dead ends.

The Element of Fire

$\mathcal{T}$he Year of the Ox began at midnight on Wednesday 11 February. Han and Dennis were at Morrison Street, where the station was like a ghost town. Even though both men were expecting it, they still jumped when the sound of a hundred thousand firecrackers burst over the city.

Peking had shut down a few days beforehand for the Spring Festival holiday, but the days leading up to that were a flurry of activity. Outside on Morrison Street the thoroughfare had been busier than ever, louder than usual, as rich Chinese piled their purchases into their chauffeured cars and stubborn foreigners braced themselves against the cold, holding their hats to their heads as they headed for tiffins at the Grand Hôtel de Pékin.

For commercial Peking, the end of the old lunar year and the start of the new was the time for settling accounts. Merchants and banks tallied up the year's business on abacuses with flying fingers and sent their messengers scurrying around the city to collect outstanding bills. Chits that had been issued were redeemed, China's unique credit system of trust and face invoked. Unless by special arrangement, no new accounts would be opened until the new year began. People hurried to make the last trading day for Peking's markets—wheat and bean cake, flour, cotton, stocks and shares—which was on the Saturday, although the gold-bar market always stayed open.

The poor of the city and the newcomers from the countryside walked along Morrison Street gazing at the modern stores and the gleaming black cars. Rickshaw pullers did good business, swarming around anyone with a parcel. Bank messengers darted in and out of rickshaws, the sparking trolleybuses and the lines of cars. Here and there shopkeepers emerged with bags of cash, flanked by bodyguards who escorted them to the bank.

For several days Peking's banks and countinghouses had extended their opening hours as queues formed to settle debts. China now had a paper currency, its own dollar, backed by the national bank in Shanghai, but jittery Peking didn't trust it—in this city, cash might have been king, but silver was God.

As the New Year approached, all Han's black-jacketed constables were out on street patrol, truncheons drawn, whistles blowing, to manage the crowds that gathered at the temple fairs and on the food streets, or to watch the impromptu performances of acrobats and opera singers. Crowds were good cover for pickpockets and other criminals, and plainclothes police were also on duty, mingling with the throng to watch for signs of trouble.

Patrols had been doubled at major intersections to prevent stampedes caused by delays and anger. Han predicted that marauding bandits would disrupt the roads and train lines out of the city. Thomas, Pearson and their small band of constables were also increasing the guards on the entrances and exits to the Legation Quarter. The Peking police bicycle squad was monitoring the temples and parks, while the thousand-strong Peace Preservation Brigade, volunteers with armbands, had been called out to assist the regular constables in patrolling the major commercial districts over the holidays. A celebrating crowd could easily turn into panic and frenzy, and this year

the mood was heightened. Who knew what would be left to celebrate, next New Year? Peking was living while it could.

The receding Year of the Rat was characterized by opportunity
and good prospects, but with the possibility of bleak years to follow.
The incoming ox symbolized problems that appeared never-ending,
and those years were times for discipline and sacrifice. The ox's element was fire: ox and fire combined to make a beast motivated by
combat.

Sitting in the Morrison Street station, Han and Dennis were
thinking not of oxen or rats but foxes, not of fire but blood. Where
was Pamela's blood? It was a question they'd never been able to answer. Those photographs, looked at a thousand times, had given up
nothing.

Pamela herself had been born in the Year of the Sheep, the most
feminine of symbols. People born in those years were considered to
be readily overwhelmed by emotions, negativity and gloom; they had
a tendency to be hopelessly romantic, were easily manipulated and
needed to be cared for. The sheep was a little self-centred but had a
kind heart. Pamela Werner had been more like a lamb to the slaughter.

Exploding fireworks were lighting up the sky across the city and
over the Fox Tower. Firecrackers sounded along Armour Factory
Alley, rockets were launched from the top of the Tartar Wall. Crowds
surged through Soochow Hutong, where sweetmeat hawkers were
doing a roaring trade. The Legation Quarter was alive with parties;
the bars at the Wagons Lits, the Hôtel du Nord and the Grand Hôtel
de Pékin were all packed, maybe for the last time. Champagne,
whisky and gin flowed like rivers among the incessant chatter and
gossip: the Durham Light Infantry had arrived in Shanghai to bolster
defences, it was said, and more American marines were coming. Peking's Hopei-Chahar Political Council was impotent now, and General Sung was expected to flee at any minute.

In the Badlands, too, the bars were having their best night of the
year, or at least since the Russian Christmas. The Kavkaz, the Olympia

Cabaret, the White Palace Dance Hall, and all the other dive bars and seedy cabarets were packed. The Korean-run, Japanese-supplied dope dens were booming, despite the crackdown and the executions. The junction of the Chuanpan and Hougou *hutong* thronged with pimps and heroin dealers.

At 27 Chuanpan Hutong, the Oparinas passed drinks across the bar at a furious rate to the transient, the displaced and the stateless, who were drinking Armenian brandy and cheap Ukrainian wine to try to forget where they were and why they were there. Next door at number 28, the brothel had reopened and the girls were busier than ever. All across the Badlands, drunken bravado, émigré despair and homesickness was boosting the coffers in the bars. The whole place was spiralling out of control. It had always been morally bankrupt, ever corrupting, but now it was succumbing to Bacchus, one last fling before the lights went out, for that was surely coming soon.

On Armour Factory Alley, which for once was not deserted at night—fox spirits shy away from loud bangs—children were running up and down as firecrackers bounced off the walls, ricocheting like rifle shots, welcoming in the good spirits and scaring away the bad. But one house remained in darkness.

And out past Armour Factory Alley, beyond the Legation Quarter and the end of the Tartar Wall, the British Cemetery was as quiet as its graves. By one of them—a grave that held two bodies, beloved wife, beloved daughter, together in death six feet under the recently churned earth—an old man was standing, looking down, remembering.

Back at Morrison Street, the two detectives sat welcoming in the Year of the Ox, the year of fire. Somewhere out there in the crush was a man or men with blood on their hands, killers who needed bringing to justice.

It seemed that all accounts had been settled across Peking except one.

A few days later, Detective Chief Inspector Dennis returned to Tientsin permanently. He left the way he'd arrived, by train, from

Peking Central Railway Station. As the train pulled out, he looked to the left and saw the Fox Tower looming over the Tartar City. He was leaving behind the fox spirits, the dead, the bereaved and the killers. DCI Dennis never returned to Peking. Colonel Han was assigned other cases, other duties, and life in the city moved shakily on.

狐 狸 精

Not until late June was the final session of the inquest held. Once more E. T. C. Werner sat in the British Legation while Consul Fitzmaurice presided as coroner. There were decidedly fewer journalists than for the previous session back in January. Not only was Pamela no longer front-page news, but the case, with nothing new to report on it, had been virtually absent from the papers for months.

These days it was the ever-tightening Japanese encirclement of Peking that grabbed the headlines. Or, from the wider world that June, the wedding of the abdicated Duke of Windsor and his former Shanghai-flapper divorcée, Wallis Simpson: theirs was still the celebrity story of the decade so far. The aviatrix Amelia Earhart was capturing hearts and headlines with her solo flight around the globe; two hundred thousand people had walked across San Francisco's new Golden Gate Bridge; Hitler's *Hindenburg* airship, the pride of the Nazis, had gone down in flames in seconds. And all the while the Great Depression and the Japanese rolled relentlessly on.

Just a few stringers were in court now, hoping for a couple of lines worthy of their pay cheque. It was Saturday 26 June, and spring had given way to summer and the rainy season. This year had been the rainiest in recent years, and the windows of the legation were curtained with raindrops now, rather than snow. Once the rain departed, the serious humidity of the blistering hot months would kick in.

Foreign Peking had continued to dwindle in number. On Armour Factory Alley, where the courtyard cherry trees had finished providing their annual spring carpet of fallen blossoms and their wonderful perfume, many of Werner's neighbours were gone. Edgar and

Helen Snow had returned to the Communist-held cave city of Yan'an. Werner himself stayed stubbornly on, but remained mostly indoors and was rarely seen.

The third and final session of Pamela's inquest was brief. Colonel Han, having nothing new to report and being busy with his other cases, sent a deputy. No new witnesses were called, no new evidence was submitted, and Fitzmaurice was quick to declare his decision.

'The evidence is inconclusive as regards the identity of the murderer,' he announced. 'Verdict: Murder by a person or persons unknown.'

Werner appealed to Fitzmaurice for the investigation to be continued, but the consul was curt. The case was not to be an ongoing one.

Fitzmaurice left China the following week for his traditional extended summer holiday in England, while Werner remained at Armour Factory Alley alone.

The Rising Sun That Chills

*A*nd then it was all over. Peking fell to the Japanese troops on 29 July. The Chinese portions of Tientsin succumbed a day later. All that month, as the summer heated up, Peking had grown edgier and edgier. It started to sweat. The ice-cold terror of winter had given way to a pervasive humid fear as the days grew longer and the city's time grew shorter.

In June, bubonic plague had broken out in eastern China—a bad omen, and right on Peking's doorstep. People ducked involuntarily at the sound of doors banging, a rickshaw tyre blowing out, a taxi backfiring. The sudden sharp screech of the ungreased wheels of the trolleybuses on Morrison Street sent shudders through people, where before it had gone barely noticed. What had once been just the frenetic cacophony of Peking life now rang alarm bells in the city's subconscious. Were they here? Had they finally come? At times the tension of waiting seemed worse than the inevitable attack; at times it seemed it would never happen.

In early July the Japanese provocations at the Marco Polo Bridge intensified to firefights and skirmishes, and eventually the Japanese moved to open confrontation. When Peking finally fell, the city was declared the seat of the Provisional Government of the Republic of China—a collaborationist puppet institution that would have been laughable if it wasn't so brutal.

The wait was over, and the ancient city was occupied. The lights of Peking went out, food queues lengthened, inflation spiralled, arrests and disappearances intensified. Day after day, the Japanese military poured into the city along Front Gate Avenue—tanks first, followed by infantry marching in columns of four. They took over the hotels, as well as large houses and courtyard residences abandoned by Peking's intellectual class and foreigners, who had mostly fled. Outside the city, the Japanese policy of the 'Three Alls'—kill all, burn all, destroy all—amounted to a scorched-earth policy for a hundred miles in all directions from Peking. To the victors the spoils.

Barbarism came to China with a vengeance, accompanied by the flag of the Land of the Rising Sun. Peking and Tientsin were just the start. In August the Japanese moved to swallow Shanghai, leaving the foreign sections of the city a solitary island surrounded by outright war. The heavily populated Chinese district of Chapei burned. Europeans in the International Settlement and Frenchtown took time out from their dinner parties at the Cathay Hotel on the Bund, or their whisky sodas at the American Club and aperitifs at the Cercle Sportif Français, to stand on balconies and pass round binoculars as the flames licked across the northern portions of the city.

The South Railway Station in Shanghai was destroyed, and a trainload of civilians seeking sanctuary in Hangchow was machine-gunned. Refugees flooded into Shanghai's International Settlement as the Imperial Japanese Army swarmed up the Yangtze River.

In December it was Nanking's turn. Chiang Kai-shek was forced to retreat inland to Hankow as the Japanese army descended on Nanking and indulged themselves in a six-week orgy of violence, unseen on such a scale in modern times. In what quickly became known as the Rape of Nanking, some three hundred thousand Chinese civilians were raped, tortured, mutilated or killed by an out-of-control

Japanese military. By the end of 1937, it was clear that China was in a fight for its very survival.

狐 狸 精

Amid such unprecedented horror, the first anniversary of Pamela Werner's murder passed unnoticed, and went unremarked upon in the Peking press. Who was left to remember her? Martial law was firmly in place by then. All the gates of the city, except Ch'ienmen, were closed. Sandbags were piled at the corners of every major thoroughfare, and Japanese machine guns watched over the Chinese populace. All but the most essential commerce was at a virtual standstill, and the crowds that had once thronged Jade Street, Lantern Street, Silver Street and Embroidery Street were now gone. Shops were shuttered, the curio market was closed, food was rationed.

Wealthy Pekingers had packed up and left. The weekend bungalows at Paomachang, where foreigners had once raced their stout Mongolian ponies, were now empty, as was the Pa Pao Shan golf course. Residents no longer weekended in the temples nestling among the Western Hills—all these places were off-limits by official order.

The city was icy cold once again. Chinese New Year had come early, on 31 January, but firecrackers were banned; they sounded too much like gunshots. Out went the Year of the Ox and its great sacrifice, and in came the tiger, fearless, courageous, determined. China desperately needed the attributes of the tiger in 1938.

What was left of foreign Peking felt eerily empty. The wives and families of diplomats had been repatriated, along with the U.S. Marines who had guarded the American Legation. European and American government officials warned foreigners living outside the Legation Quarter that their safety could no longer be guaranteed, and urged them to move inside the Quarter. The few remaining foreigners who could still afford the inflationary prices moved into the Quarter's hotels, which all overflowed but managed to continue to provide heating, food and hot water.

Poorer foreigners lived in canvas tents hastily erected on their legation's grounds, where they ended up stewing through the summer and freezing in the winter. Some ignored the orders sent out by officials and hunkered down in their homes across Chinese Peking, hoping to ride out the storm. Some, like the White Russians and the Jewish refugees, had no choice—they had no papers and no legation, and most of them had no money.

But even with the departures, the overall population of Peking swelled. Tokyo's Three Alls forced yet more peasants to seek sanctuary in the city. The number flooding in more than outweighed those leaving, and many of the newcomers were desperate and close to starving. Crime soared.

The Chinese rumour mill was taken up with new topics. It was said that the Imperial Halls were being refurbished and prepared for the return of the last emperor, Pu Yi. Communist agents were planning to blow up the Forbidden City. Chiang Kai-shek, still in Hankow, would either move the government to the fortress city of Chungking, at the head of the Yangtze, where he would fight to the death, or he would sue for peace with Tokyo and fold before spring ended.

狐 狸 精

Even the occupation of Peking could not shift Werner's thoughts from the murder of his daughter. When Consul Fitzmaurice had slammed down his official gavel the previous June and declared the investigation closed, Werner was a broken man. His heart had been weakened, and his doctor ordered him to rest. With the diplomats, the police and the press all giving up on the case, he sank even lower into despondency.

The summer of 1937 had been Peking's most humid in living memory, and to escape the terrible clammy damp—what the Chinese called *fu-tien*—Werner retreated to his beach house at Peitaiho. There he took the sea air and tried to restore his energy. He also took with him all the material he could gather on the case—newspaper articles, the records of the inquest, the autopsy report—along with the numerous letters sent him by sympathetic people. These he studied as closely as he had previously pored over his ancient Chinese scrolls.

Throughout the autumn and the start of winter that year, he appealed repeatedly to the British authorities in China—to the British legations in Peking and Shanghai—for his daughter's case not to be abandoned. 'I shall not let the matter rest as long as I have breath in my body,' he wrote.

He also wrote letters to the newspapers—the *North-China Daily News*, the *Tientsin and Peking Times*, the *North China Star*. He self-published a pamphlet calling for the case to be reopened, starting with an open letter to Pamela's murderer to come forward. He appealed to DCI Dennis in Tientsin, he appealed to the Chinese police at Ch'ienmen. He appealed from his heart, as a father:

The sight of my child's kind little face, half cut away and bleeding, as her mutilated body lay on the ground that terrible morning, seemed to drag my eyes out of my head, and the shock has permanently injured my heart. During every minute of every day that vision has beat upon my brain.

All his letters were either ignored or turned down. By January 1938, he had accepted that his appeals were falling on deaf ears and stopped making them. Instead he took matters into his own hands.

Werner threw himself into what would become the single quest of his remaining life—a private investigation into the murder of his daughter. He was determined to see justice done for her, and stubbornly refused to walk away from the case. Over the years, many people had found Werner an odd man, and in his own words he stood 'apart from the herd,' but the very same characteristics that infuriated others—his steely determination to see things through to the end, his strength of will that refused to be diverted from a cause, his abundant intelligence—now drove him to learn the truth about Pamela's murder.

He set out to dig through the dirt of the case himself, embarking on a journey that took him deep into the city's underworld, all the way to its sordid, putrid bottom. Wealthy white Peking might have been vastly depleted in number, but the stateless White Russians had nowhere to go, and the criminal class did not want to leave—they believed they could survive and thrive, under Japanese rule. It was with these groups that Werner dealt. He paid informers: nightclub and dive-bar habitués, Russian women who'd worked the Badlands brothels frequented by the gang, people who knew Prentice, Pinfold and their 'sex cult.'

He also hired people to uncover facts, including Chinese ex-detectives—good men who were deemed politically unreliable by the Japanese and had been ousted from the Peking force. They tracked down Chinese witnesses scattered across northern China. He had his agents distribute leaflets across the city, in Chinese this time, appealing for witnesses and offering financial rewards. He took advantage of Peking's collapsed economy. Unemployment had soared, food prices had quadrupled, the number of pawnshops had escalated. People were more and more desperate for money.

He slowly emptied his bank account, but people talked. It might not just have been about the cold, hard cash; perhaps it was guilt, the burden of knowing too much and not speaking out. Werner dedicated five years to the task, and what he uncovered was ultimately far worse, far more evil, than anything Peking's numerous armchair detectives could have imagined.

Meanwhile, it was back to the start he had to go, however painful that might be, sifting through the half-truths and the lies to discover the daughter he thought he had known.

Journey to the Underworld

E. T. C. Werner, former consular judge, barrister-at-law of Middle Temple, knew that the key to the murder was the *locus delicti*, the scene of the crime, the killing floor that Dennis and Han had never found. The detectives were right in their assumptions, Werner believed, that if they could find the blood, they would find the killer.

By the time Werner began his investigation, Colonel Han had been ordered by Peking police headquarters at Ch'ienmen not to talk about the case. The incident room at Morrison Street had long been dismantled, the crime-scene photos taken down and filed away. DCI Dennis, now back in Tientsin, had also been officially warned off any further communication with Werner. Enough muck had been raked for the taste of Consul Affleck at Gordon Hall.

As for Consul Fitzmaurice, Werner's old adversary, he had never returned to Peking from his summer leave in England, instead retiring at the age of fifty-six. The rumour was that London had little faith in their man and had sidelined him. A new consul, Allan Archer, had been installed in September 1937.

But while he had hit an official wall of silence and obfuscation

from his compatriots, Werner did have some friends in the wider diplomatic corps—at the American and Japanese legations in Peking and
at the French Legation in Shanghai. He found allies among former
Peking policemen, who'd been in the force during the investigation
and were now persona non grata with the Japanese occupiers. On the
record and off, many people sought to help him. Some tipped him off
anonymously.

Others made suggestions. They told him to talk to the Gurevitch
girl again, Pamela's skating companion on the night of her murder.
They told him to find Sun Te-hsing, the rickshaw puller who'd been
arrested soon after the murder. Both these people knew more than
they'd said. And most particularly, they told him to focus on Wentworth Prentice and his associates. The dentist was at the heart of it, the
central cog. His nudist colony in the hills, closed down by the Japanese
in the summer of 1937, had been guarded by known Badlands thugs.
And the parties he held in his flat were reportedly debauched.

Werner's informers told him that shortly after the murder, Prentice
had sent his trusted friend and fellow American Joe Knauf to Tientsin,
to secure a reliable lawyer to represent him in case he was arrested. At
the same time Pinfold, who had been lying low in the Badlands, had
been overheard asking his associates whether the police 'had got the
American yet?' The dentist was a man with secrets. And, as Werner
already knew, he was a man who had lied outright to the police.

If Detective Chief Inspector Dennis had not been barred from
talking to Werner, he too would have learnt of the lie. Werner had
proof of it, handwritten evidence in the form of a professional note he
had received. It was dated 1 December 1936.

*This is to confirm my statement that the sum of (Dollars Fifty) $50,
will not be exceeded for the whole course of treatment for Pamela.
This, of course, refers to the regulation of the upper left cuspid, and
to no other teeth that may need treatment at a later date.*

    Sincerely yours,

    WB Prentice

Prentice had been Pamela's dentist. In the treatment to which his note referred, he had simply straightened her upper left canine tooth slightly, a procedure which wouldn't necessarily have been noticed as recent by the doctors who performed the autopsy. And in fact they had missed it entirely. But more important, Prentice had denied repeatedly to the police that he'd ever even seen Pamela. Why was that?

Werner went to see Ethel Gurevitch, who he knew was also one of Prentice's patients. She was still living with her family on Hong Kong Bank Road. Being stateless and without passports, only their useless tsarist documents, they had nowhere to go.

Ethel was frightened. The year since Pamela's death had weighed heavily on her, and she was extremely nervous talking to Werner. He pressed her about the evenings on which the girls had been at the skating rink, and eventually Ethel revealed that she'd seen Pamela speaking with a certain man that first night, Wednesday 6 January. But she either could not or would not name him. Ethel and her friend Lilian Marinovski had said nothing about this to the police. They were afraid of getting into trouble, Ethel told Werner; they didn't want to be involved in a murder case.

Werner thought the man had to be Prentice, and that Ethel was clearly afraid of him. He couldn't help noting that the dentist's flat was almost directly opposite the skating rink, and within a stone's throw of the Badlands.

But while Ethel wouldn't give Werner Prentice's name, she did give him another one. When she'd run into Pamela that Wednesday night, Pamela was in the company of the Gorman family, whose teenage children she knew. She had been to their house for tea, then gone skating with the family.

George Gorman—the pro-Tokyo hack who'd now ingratiated himself completely with the occupying power and was editing the Japanese-controlled *Peking Chronicle* for them, daily spouting their propaganda; who'd always been a gun for hire; who'd attacked the police investigation for alluding to Prentice and his group; who'd accused Dennis and Han of targeting upstanding members of Peking's

foreign community, namely Wentworth Prentice and Joe Knauf—
had backed up the dentist's alibi on the evening of Pamela's murder,
stating that he was at a cinema.

Werner hadn't known that his daughter had gone skating with
the Gormans that final week. George Gorman and Prentice were
close friends. Gorman had been part of the nudist colony, had reportedly also attended Prentice's 'nude dances,' along with Pinfold and
Knauf. Werner had never given any thought to the man until he saw
his newspaper articles during the investigation, but he had come
across the name again recently.

After the case had been closed, Werner had had to appeal repeatedly to the police to have Pamela's belongings returned to him—her
clothes and personal items, along with the things Inspector Botham
and Sergeant Binetsky had taken from her room. Eventually a policeman delivered them, wrapped in brown paper tied with greasy string.
Her clothes were still bloodstained, although the blood had turned a
dark brown, like dried gravy. In one parcel were Pamela's silk chemise, her torn tartan skirt, woolen cardigan, shoes, navy blue overcoat and belt. Another package contained her platinum wristwatch,
the small silver casket from her bedroom, a jade comb, a hair clasp and
her diary. Werner reread the diary.

And there it was, in an entry for the summer of 1936, the year
before she died. Pamela had gone on a picnic with a group of families
to Patachu, an ancient temple a dozen or so miles outside Peking, and
a favourite escape from the sweltering city. In the Western Hills conventions were relaxed somewhat—cool white linen replaced formal
wear.

Werner had as usual been wrapped up in his research and writing,
so Pamela had accepted an invitation and gone along unaccompanied.
George Gorman, a married man and the father of two children, had
'made love' to her, she wrote—meaning that he had flirted with her,
perhaps propositioned her. Pamela's diary recorded that she had rebuffed him, and had laughed at the silliness of it all.

Not having been able to discuss the case with Dennis, Werner had no way of knowing what the DCI had made of this entry. He didn't even know whether Dennis was aware of George Gorman's friendship with Prentice at the time he'd read it. And if Dennis hadn't been aware of that, it was possible he'd interpreted the episode as nothing more than a harmless flirtation with a family friend who'd let the wine and heat go to his head and then acted indiscreetly. Or maybe Dennis had thought it was a case of a young woman reading the signals wrong. But now it meant everything—it linked Gorman to Pamela, and Gorman was linked to Prentice.

Werner came to the conclusion that Gorman had held a grudge against his daughter after her rejection of him that summer day in the Western Hills. What she had taken as a tipsy but innocent flirtation, he had meant seriously. He had identified her as a target for Prentice and his pals, put Pamela in Prentice's mind. The trip to the skating rink that fateful week proved that he knew she was back in Peking.

Werner went back over the long newspaper piece in which Gorman had defended Prentice, and then he trawled through copies of the Peking papers for 7 January 1937. At the two cinemas that showed foreign films, at Dashala and at Ch'ienmen, there had been no screenings that night after five thirty. Prentice claimed he'd gone to an eight o'clock screening on Morrison Street, but that was an impossibility. Gorman had lied for Prentice.

Perhaps George Gorman had told Prentice he'd be at the skating rink with Pamela on the Wednesday night, and Prentice had gone there too. Or maybe he'd been watching the arc-lit rink from his flat opposite. At any rate, it seemed he had approached Pamela there.

Werner went to the British Legation with his evidence. He appealed to the new consul, Allan Archer, to instruct the police that anything Gorman had said or written in defence of Prentice was irrelevant and out of order, but Archer refused, telling Werner curtly, 'You are on the wrong track.'

But Werner knew he wasn't on the wrong track. Before Prentice had been first questioned, Dennis had been ordered to stay away from Werner, and so the detectives had failed to connect Prentice to

Pamela. They didn't know about Gorman, about the summer picnic the previous year, or that he'd been at the skating rink the night before Pamela was murdered. DCI Dennis hadn't known the cinema times in Peking, and clearly he hadn't checked.

Werner now knew his daughter had sat in Prentice's dental chair just a few months after Gorman's clumsy advance to her in the Western Hills, and both men had lied about their connection to her.

狐 狸 精

And then, a chance encounter. In September 1938 Werner was walking along Eight Treasures Alley near Ch'ienmen when he passed a foreign girl walking with a European man. He turned the corner onto Jiao Min Hutong and heard his name being called. Turning, he saw that the girl, alone now, was running towards him.

'Are you Mr Werner?' she asked when she reached him.

She was White Russian but spoke flawless English. She told Werner that she'd come looking for him once before, on Armour Factory Alley, but he'd been away at Peitaiho. Now she was engaged, and was leaving Peking the next day to get married in Tientsin. Her fiancé was waiting around the corner, and she had only a few moments before she must return to him. She'd told him that Werner was an old teacher of hers, and she wanted to say hello. But in fact there was something she wanted to tell Werner, if he would assure her it would remain anonymous.

Hurriedly she explained that she'd lived in Tientsin for seventeen years and had known his daughter a little. She'd been a couple of years behind her at Tientsin Grammar School and, like everyone, had been shocked to hear of her death. Six months before the murder, the girl had had an appointment at Wentworth Prentice's dental surgery, and was surprised when he charged her next to nothing for the treatment. He had then behaved in an improper manner towards her, begging her to 'make a date' with him, adding that he would take her to supper and 'make it worth her while.' She had been scared and rebuffed him. A few weeks later he'd seen her walking along Legation

Street, and had tried to get her to stop and talk to him, jumping out of his rickshaw and running after her.

She knew of other girls, English and Russian, who'd been approached by Prentice, invited to 'parties' with him and his pals. Some had accepted, and they were taken to a place in the Badlands, on Chuanpan Hutong, but none of them would ever speak about what happened there, and most had now left China.

This girl thought it was pretty clear what had happened at those 'parties' in the Badlands—the girls were forced to have sex with Prentice and his friends. And afterwards they remained silent because they knew Prentice would deny all of it. Everyone else involved would deny it too. Any accusations would only tarnish the girls' own reputations. In an unforgiving society, it was they who would be blamed.

The White Russian girl couldn't understand why Prentice and his gang hadn't been arrested. Rumours about him had been rife ever since his wife had left him, taking their three children back to America. The dentist had lured some of his victims with promises of marriage—the White Russian had heard that one of them had committed suicide when she found out he was deceiving her.

Werner's worst fears were beginning to crystallise. Following his meeting with the White Russian girl, he had his private detectives return to the Wagons Lits to seek out Chao Hsi-men, the hotel concierge who'd reported seeing Pamela at the reception desk on the afternoon of her murder. From Chao they got the name of the employee manning reception that day and tracked him down. With an offer of money, they got what they wanted, although the receptionist was too scared to go on the record.

A foreign man answering Prentice's description had left a note to be collected by Pamela on Thursday 7 January. He had tipped heavily and told the receptionist to say nothing, should anyone ever ask about it. The receptionist knew a secret assignation between two foreigners when he saw one. Discretion about any affairs the guests might be conducting was expected from the hotel staff.

Pamela had come in on the afternoon of the same day and picked up the note, thanked him and left. The receptionist had no idea what it said—it was none of his business, just a quick bit of easy cash. He admitted he had kept out of the way when the police came asking questions, and said that his colleague Chao Hsi-men had known nothing of the note.

Werner and his detectives went back to Armour Factory Alley with descriptions of Pinfold, Knauf and Prentice. The police had never circulated any of the men's descriptions, had never released them to the press. Nobody in the alleyway had been asked about them. The foreigners had mostly all left and closed up their houses, leaving them in the care of their Chinese staff. Pamela had been popular with the servants who worked in the courtyards along the street, and they were only too keen to help, now that they were being asked. They remembered seeing Pinfold lurking on Armour Factory Alley on 6 January. Werner's street was narrow and close-knit, and a strange foreigner stood out.

Werner worked through the likely sequence of events. Pinfold, a procurer for Prentice, had been informed by Gorman that Pamela was back in Peking from Tientsin. Hanging around Armour Factory Alley, he had let Pamela know that a note from Prentice had been left for her at the Wagons Lits, and she should pick it up. There was to be a party, the details of which were in the note. Werner saw all the links, and thanks to the chance encounter with the White Russian girl, he now had a better idea of what Prentice's scheme was.

The dentist and his gang identified likely young foreign girls, followed them, hounded them, invited them to suppers and parties that ended up in the Badlands. There they forced themselves upon the girls, afterwards insisting they remain silent, threatening them if they should not. The girls' reputations were on the line. It was their word against everyone else's, and they would be accusing men of good standing, professional men. Nobody would believe them.

This was the game. The men had done it before, and then they'd done it to his daughter. But it had somehow gone very wrong.

Chuanpan Hutong

*T*he Badlands appeared untouched by the Japanese occupation. It was perhaps the one place in Peking where things were pretty much business as usual. In a city now filled to bursting with Japanese soldiers who'd been living for months in rough conditions in northern China, the services that the Badlands specialized in were in high demand.

The area was no longer a place where curious wealthy foreigners went 'slumming it' of a weekend, or where the occasional Chinese ventured to seek illicit pleasures. Now the former had fled and the latter stayed at home in fear. The Badlands had become the playground of the Japanese and the largely collaborationist Peking underworld.

Werner knew that the Chuanpan Hutong angle had gone nowhere in the police investigation. He'd heard from his agents that people had been warned at the time to keep quiet. He'd also confirmed the rumours that Dennis's colleague Inspector Botham was a drunk, who after the night of the roust at number 27 had returned to the Olympia Cabaret and accepted more drinks from the manager, Joe Knauf. And Botham had used his position to spread gossip at the bars of the Legation Quarter. Threats, drunken rages—add these to the existing fear of authority and a desire to avoid being implicated or framed, and no wonder so many people had remained silent. DCI Dennis hadn't known Peking well enough to push the matter of 27 Chuanpan Hutong. Pinfold, Knauf and Prentice were all connected as hunting friends, but not through Pamela—that connection had been just out of reach, since no one had been able to place her in the Badlands that night.

Around the same time that Werner had run into the White Russian girl on the street, his agents managed to get in contact with Sun Te-hsing, the rickshaw puller who was seen washing blood from his cushions on the night of the murder. Sun claimed that he'd been shocked by the false detail given about him in the Chinese newspapers, and the false statements attributed to him. They reported that he'd been arrested, but he never had, just questioned. They reported that the blood on his cushions had come from a drunken American marine who'd been in a fight, and that this man was subsequently tracked down and had given confirmation—that was the first Sun had heard of the story.

At the time he was questioned, the rickshaw puller had told Colonel Han what happened that night, and then he'd been kicked out of the station and told to disappear. He'd never spoken out about the lies in the newspapers because he'd been scared. Like plenty of other Peking rickshaw pullers, he smoked a little opium to give him the strength to work, to keep out the cold, and he knew Han was actively looking for dopers. More than a few were ending up at the Tien Chiao execution grounds.

Sun Te-hsing had gone back to pulling his rickshaw. But now, with the Japanese occupation, times were even harder. Fares were scarce, inflation was rampant, and he was a poor man. Werner's agents had told him they were looking for information about the murder, and Sun was prepared to talk for money—he would set the record straight. And so he told Werner what he'd apparently told Han the day after the murder.

He had been touting for business on the night of 7 January on Chuanpan Hutong. Everyone knew that number 27 was a dive bar, where fares staggered out regularly, and that number 28 was a busy brothel—you didn't have to wait long there either. The Badlands had been busy that night, it was a foreign holiday.

Some time after ten o'clock, Sun had seen a car arrive from the direction of the Legation Quarter. It pulled up outside number 28, and four people got out. From the front seat, beside the Chinese chauffeur, came a short man. Sun couldn't say who he was, but he did remember that the man had a particularly large nose, even for a foreigner. From the back seat came a man whom Sun identified from photographs as Prentice, then a younger half-European, half-Chinese man, and finally a white girl with yellow hair. They all entered number 28, through the small gateway that led into the courtyard. The girl was walking between the two white men, each of whom was supporting one of her arms.

The chauffeur turned the car around and drove back in the direction of the Legation Quarter. Sun was unable to identify the man, beyond his being Chinese and dressed in the typical black uniform and cap of all Peking's chauffeurs. The car was also black, with a brown roof, but as to its make, Sun had no idea. He'd decided at the time that since the car hadn't been told to wait, there was a good chance that one or more of the people who'd just entered number 28 would require his services to get home. So he squatted down on his haunches by the carbide lamp on his rickshaw and bided his time.

Sun Te-hsing was then just nineteen years old. He was fitter and more persistent than most pullers in Peking, and he patiently waited outside number 28 until after midnight. Eventually he got his fare. A Russian woman he knew to be the madam of the brothel appeared at the doorway with a Chinese man and beckoned him over. The two white men then carried a foreign girl out through the door in the wall surrounding the building and into the street, supporting her under the arms—'frog walking' was how Sun described it. They put her in his rickshaw, where she didn't move.

The two men sat either side of her, cramped into the long seat. The girl was scantily clad, despite the cold night, wearing only a long blouse, a cardigan and a short skirt. Her face was partially covered with a white cloth. Sun assumed she was drunk. He was used to passengers from the Badlands being the worse for booze, sometimes semicomatose.

Once running, of course, he wasn't able to see her, and the men had pulled down the canvas overhang that offered passengers some protection from the cold and the rain. But Sun could hear the girl's laboured breathing.

He had also noticed that the hooks at the side of the girl's skirt were torn, and the garment itself looked to have been ripped from the bottom almost to the top.

Sun had been instructed by the brothel's madam to take the men and the girl southeast along Chuanpan Hutong to the Wall Road and the small access point through the Tartar Wall known as the Stone Bridge. Sun wondered why they were going to such a remote location on such a cold and windy night, away from any houses or bars. But he pulled the trio to the southern edge of the Badlands as instructed, and was duly paid. He waited expectantly for a tip, but one of the men told him to clear off, and when the puller lingered a little longer in the desperate hope of some extra coppers, the shorter of the two men pulled out a knife and waved it at him.

Sun needed no further hint and went swiftly on his way, heading back towards Hatamen Street. On his way home, sometime in the early hours of the morning, he stopped at the entrance to the French hospital on the edge of the Legation Quarter, near Morrison Street. There he chatted with the gatekeepers, telling them of his weird experience. When Werner's agents later contacted the gatekeepers, they confirmed Sun's story.

Later that same morning, Sun noticed the blood on the cushions of his rickshaw and went to the canal by the Fox Tower to wash them out. He was worried: the white girl with the golden hair had been his last fare of the night, and the blood must have been hers. Then he had found himself grabbed by two constables and taken to the Morrison Street station, where he was questioned by one man only, Colonel Han Shih-ching.

Colonel Han, Werner well knew, was the man who'd told DCI Dennis that the blood on the rickshaw cushions had come from an American marine. Han had claimed he'd checked the marine out and the story was solid, and so Sun had been released. Dennis subsequently had no cause to think of Sun Te-hsing again. And yet now Sun was saying there'd been no marine, no fight. He had told Colonel Han about the yellow-haired girl on Chuanpan Hutong; he had told him about the rickshaw ride to the Tartar Wall on the night of the Russian Christmas. Sun had just wanted to get out of Morrison Street and back to work.

Werner showed Sun the clothes Pamela had been wearing the night she was murdered, the clothes she had been found in at the Fox Tower. Sun agreed they were similar to those worn by the yellow-haired girl who'd been put in his rickshaw on Chuanpan Hutong.

Werner was left with much to think about. If Sun Te-hsing was telling the truth—and Werner could think of no reason why the man would lie, nor how he would otherwise be able to confirm so many details about that night—then Colonel Han had not only covered up vital evidence but had deliberately laid a false trail. He too had lied. Was this because Han, like DCI Dennis, had been officially directed how to proceed with the case? Had he been ordered to keep the investigation away from number 28? Or had the owners of the brothel paid him off, so as to minimize any disruption to business? Had Han perhaps been in their pay all along, in the way of these things? Werner knew how the policing of Peking worked. For people who owned or ran brothels, it was nothing out of the ordinary to buy official protection. Plenty of policeman were on the take; they didn't necessarily have to be wholly corrupt. It was even feasible that Han had believed the lie he was telling was a small one—it might have struck him as impossible that such a girl as Pamela could have been inside a Badlands brothel.

Then there was the meeting Werner had had with Han after the British Legation had ordered Dennis away from the case. It was the only meeting Werner had been able to secure with the colonel, and the old man now suspected that the British Legation had used their influence with Peking police headquarters to force Han to break contact with him as well. At that meeting, Werner made mention of a place on Chuanpan Hutong that he knew Pinfold frequented. Han was momentarily fazed, and Werner realized that the colonel must have thought he was referring to number 28. When Werner named the Oparinas' bar at number 27, Han had visibly relaxed. It was a detail whose significance had not been apparent to Werner at the time. Now he was certain that 28 Chuanpan Hutong held the secret to that night's events.

In late September of 1938, Werner went back again to Consul Archer at the British Legation and presented Sun Te-hsing's evidence. He was determined that this time the man should listen. And at first Archer did, conceding that this new evidence 'impressed him as being true.' Werner demanded that Archer contact the British ambassador and have the case reopened. Archer said he would see what he could do, and ushered Werner out of his office.

The next day, a note was delivered to Werner's house stating that the new testimony had been 'ruled out on entirely insufficient grounds.' Sun's evidence, Archer now claimed, was 'fantastic,' 'valueless' and 'cannot be true.' He pointed out that the rickshaw puller was contradicting the evidence he'd given to Colonel Han in January, and that the man was an opium addict, and therefore by default a hopeless liar who would say anything to get another fix. Archer then repeated Consul Fitzmaurice's earlier warning to Werner that he should leave the case alone.

To Werner this was incredible. The 'case,' as these people called it, was his daughter, whose horrific slaughter no one seemed to think important enough to properly investigate. He returned to the British Legation with Sun Te-hsing, who repeated his story directly to Archer, but the consul would not budge an inch. He wasn't going to do anything. He refused to discuss the matter of why Colonel Han had given DCI Dennis a false story about a brawling American marine, when Sun had told him something altogether different.

Archer's message was clear—the case was closed, Werner should drop it. It was equally clear that the consul did not consider a Chinese rickshaw puller to be a reliable witness. White face was at issue here, and Sun's story was an embarrassment that Archer and the British establishment in China did not want.

Werner did not yield to them. Other new witnesses came forward. A mechanic called Wang Shih-ming, who worked in a nearby auto-repair garage, contacted Werner's agents after reading one of the leaflets. Wang had seen a lamplight by the Fox Tower in the early hours of 8 January, near where Pamela's body had been found. Another man, an old Chinese coal merchant, also made contact to report seeing a lamplight at the same time. He had been going to Hatamen Street to sell his coal, and when he returned a few hours later, going back past the Fox Tower as dawn was breaking, the lamplight was gone. A third man, a White Russian called Kurochkin, told Werner that he too had seen the light by the Fox Tower when he'd driven home along the City Road.

Neither the mechanic nor the coal merchant had come forward previously because they couldn't read English, the only language the reward leaflets distributed by the police were printed in. The White Russian Kurochkin had left Peking on an extended business trip to Manchuria the day after Pamela's murder, and he hadn't heard of it until now.

The presence of a lamplight by the Fox Tower in the early hours of 8 January answered a question that, as far as Werner could tell, hadn't really been asked before. When a lamp was found in a ditch at the base of the Fox Tower, after Pamela's body was discovered, it was recorded as evidence, but nobody knew whether it was connected to the murder or had been left there previously. The evidence of the mechanic, the coal merchant and the White Russian motorist suggested the lamp had been left by the killers. Presumably, whoever had dumped Pamela's body at the Fox Tower would have needed some sort of light.

And so once more Werner returned to the British Legation, to appeal yet again to Consul Archer. He prepared himself to restate all the additional testimony that he, Werner, with his own resources, had accumulated that the police investigation had not—Ethel Gurevitch's new story; the note left at the Wagons Lits for Pamela; the witnesses to Pinfold being on Armour Factory Alley on 6 January; the note from Prentice to Werner regarding dental treatment for Pamela, which linked the dentist directly to his daughter and caught him out in the lie he'd told about never having met her. Then there was the matter of Gorman being with Pamela at the skating rink, having previously made improper advances to her; the impossibility of Prentice being at the cinema on the night of the murder; Sun Te-hsing's strange trip to the Stone Bridge with a comatose girl matching Pamela's description; and now the lamplight seen by three separate men at the Fox Tower in the early hours of 8 January.

Surely, Werner believed, all this was enough to reopen the case. At the very least it warranted investigation of 28 Chuanpan Hutong. The brothel had in fact never been part of the police enquiry.

And most important of all, it appeared that Colonel Han had deliberately meddled with the evidence of the case, had fabricated the rickshaw puller's testimony. Whatever his reasons for acting this way, the fact was that the real evidence remained uninvestigated.

This time Archer refused to even see him. The British establishment was showing Werner its collective back in no uncertain terms— he was no longer welcome at his own country's legation.

But Werner persisted. Through the long-serving Chief Chen at Ch'ienmen headquarters, head of police for all Peking, Werner arranged for the lamp found at the Fox Tower to be tested for fingerprints. He was surprised that this hadn't been done before, and now the results came back negative. Too many people had handled the lamp, and all the prints on it were smudged. It seemed that Sergeant

Binetsky had not secured the evidence properly, thereby corrupting it beyond recovery.

More remarkably, Werner discovered from the records that none of the items recovered at the murder scene had been tested for fingerprints—not Pamela's clothing, not her shoes, her belt, her diary, nor her membership card for the French Club skating rink. He was simply dumbfounded at this. He requested that all the items be tested now, but the results were the same—all had been contaminated, all had been handled by too many people. No definite prints could be obtained.

Werner remembered the day he'd been interviewed at Armour Factory Alley by DCI Dennis. Botham and Binestky had walked around the house picking up Pamela's personal belongings and placing them haphazardly in their overcoat pockets, never even providing an official receipt for what they had taken. That the evidence had then been useless surprised him not a jot. The attitude of the police towards Pamela's belongings had been slapdash at best. Werner had had to repeatedly request Morrison Street to return Pamela's belongings, including her valuable platinum and diamond wristwatch, which he wanted as a memento of his daughter. The silver casket that had been taken from her room was returned broken.

Werner now attempted to go over the British consul's head. He had come to despise fifty-year-old Allan Archer, whom he saw as incompetent. Archer had entered the diplomatic service through the back door, having failed his entrance exams in 1911 and using his connections to get a posting. He had no formal training in the law, yet he was allowed to sit in judgement over others.

Earlier in 1938, the British crown advocate, the United Kingdom's highest legal representative in China, had visited Peking, and Werner had attempted to see him. Archer blocked the meeting. As Werner was now barred from the legation compound, he appealed directly to the new British ambassador, Sir Archibald Clark Kerr, temporarily based in Shanghai since the fall of Nanking, prompting Archer himself to write to Clark Kerr:

This particular line of enquiry, as Mr. Werner well knows, was fully investigated by British and Chinese police officials at the time the crime was committed, but unfortunately without any result at all. . . . the fullest investigations have been made into all the other lines of enquiry without the authorities being able to put their hands on the criminals—all possible lines of enquiry have now been exhausted without any success and every possible avenue explored.

Clark Kerr, only recently installed in the job and previously unaware of either Werner or the murder of his daughter, backed his man in Peking. And then, in a move suggested by Archer, Clark Kerr offered Werner an inducement to cease his investigation of the case—a prestigious Sinology professorship in London. Werner could return home and sink into quiet academic obscurity.

Outraged, Werner wrote back to Clark Kerr: 'Very flattering, but—nothing doing! Shirking or slinking away is not my idea of how to solve the mystery of the brutal murder of a weak child.'

Putting his anger aside, he appealed repeatedly to the ambassador for help, but Clark Kerr insisted that any decision regarding further action was to be taken by Archer, whose 'exhausted lines of enquiry' and 'fullest investigation' Werner had proved to be anything but.

Eventually, in December 1938 Werner wrote to the Foreign Office in London, enclosing a copy of a report of his investigations, a second copy of which he sent to Ambassador Clark Kerr. Receipt of his report by the Foreign Office was acknowledged in February 1939, and a memo to that effect placed on file. The memo noted:

It is not necessary to read through all the enclosures in Mr. Werner's letter; it is sufficient to glance at his conclusions on pp. 27/28 and his renewed attack on Messers. Fitzmaurice & Archer on pp. 33/35.

The information in Werner's report represented some eighteen months' work, by him and the people he'd paid to assist him. Now it was being dismissed virtually unread, except for those portions the Foreign Office considered to be direct attacks upon them and their officials.

Still Werner did not let up. He paid his two remaining Chinese agents to stake out 28 Chuanpan Hutong, instructing them to approach the staff discreetly and offer money for information. He found out plenty—details that DCI Dennis had never known, and that Han, if he'd known, had never revealed.

The madam of number 28 in January 1937 had been a fat half-Korean, half–White Russian woman called Madam Leschinsky, who lived with—and was possibly married to—a man called Michael Consiglio. This man, an ex–U.S. Marine of Italian and Filipino heritage, had served in Peking and Tientsin before leaving the army to become a full-time brothel manager with Leschinsky.

Werner still had friends at the American Legation, and they searched their files for Consiglio. According to the records, he held neither a Filipino nor an American passport. He was a local hire, having joined the marines in China and served only in China. This was not an uncommon practice for the U.S. Army in China, and as the Philippines were under American control, Consiglio's Filipino heritage was enough for him to join up.

The third secretary at the American Legation, the veteran China hand Arthur Ringwalt, had kept a file on Consiglio since his discharge from the marines. As the operator of a brothel, he was a 'person of interest,' and was described by Ringwalt as being 'of a most ferocious and cruel countenance.' Consiglio had not served with distinction in the marines. He had in fact been thrown out.

Madam Leschinsky and Michael Consiglio had closed down the brothel the day after Pamela's murder. They sold their informal lease on the place soon after—for $4,000 in silver dollars less than they'd paid for it, a brothel that was reputedly earning them $100 in silver dollars a day in profit—and fled to Tientsin. From there they went to Shanghai and the anonymity of the city's Frenchtown, allegedly using hastily gained provisional Chinese passports.

Werner hadn't been able to find out who owned the building at number 28, but it seemed that whoever it was had encouraged Leschinsky and Consiglio to make haste out of Peking, and away from northern China altogether. He heard that the pair had been paid $1,000 in silver dollars by the owners to assist their escape. All the working girls who'd been at the brothel at the time had since been cleared out too, and who knew where they'd gone? Everyone had been told to keep their mouths shut if anyone asked about the place, and especially if anyone asked about the night of 7 January 1937. Most of the Chinese staff were also said to have moved on, or had fled Peking following the Japanese occupation.

Why sell a highly profitable business at a loss and skip town if you were innocent of any crime? And why, if not to prevent the building at number 28 being revealed as a crime scene and therefore closed for longer, had the mysterious owners paid off Leschinsky and Consiglio? Werner was becoming more and more convinced that the owners had also been paying protection money to the Peking police, perhaps to Colonel Han directly. That was why Han had avoided rousting the place, and why he had been so nervous when Werner mentioned it.

But Leschinsky and Consiglio and the owners would have known that no amount of protection money would help them once the daughter of a former British consul was murdered on the premises. They had no option but to shut up shop until things cooled.

Now number 28 was back in business, under new management. It had a new madam, new girls, new clients. The latter were overwhelmingly Japanese these days, but the Badlands was adaptable. If the occupiers wanted sake instead of wine, no problem, and the White Russian prostitutes learned to switch from asking 'Business?' to 'Want to play?' Different words, same game, although things were much tougher now—there was more competition.

The Japanese had set up more than two thousand new businesses in Peking since occupying the city, of which five hundred were brothels and a thousand were dope dens. Number 28 was hanging on as a curiosity. It was one of the last White Russian whorehouses in the Badlands, as most Russian refugees packed their bags and sought greater protection in the foreign-controlled concessions of Shanghai and Tientsin, which hadn't succumbed to the invaders. The remaining white working girls were a novel attraction for the Imperial Japanese Army.

It took Werner a long time to track down the new operator of number 28. She turned out to be a veteran White Russian madam from Tientsin, who had run very profitable brothels on the British Concession's Bruce Road for years, close to the American barracks. She was now calling herself Brana Shazker and was staying at the Hôtel de la Paix, commonly known as the Telegraph Hotel, an otherwise fairly respectable establishment in a traditional courtyard on Da Yuan Fu Hutong, just behind the Grand Hôtel de Pékin. Shazker was apparently making even more money from number 28 than Leschinsky and Consiglio had, as the Japanese soldiers queued to try the Russian girls.

Werner left a note for Madam Shazker in March 1939, saying he wanted to talk to her about a matter of business. When he met her at the Hôtel de la Paix, she was all smiles, until she realised who Werner was and what he wanted. Then she flew into a rage and began screaming and yelling. She had not been on Chuanpan Hutong that night, she said. She hadn't even been in Peking—she was in Tientsin managing her brothel on Bruce Road at the time, and she could prove it. She had bought the lease on the brothel at number 28 fair and square from the owners, and she knew nothing at all about anything that might have happened there in January 1937.

Madam Shazker threw Werner out of her hotel room and refused point-blank to meet or communicate with him in the future.

Werner was left more convinced than ever that number 28 was the place he sought. There were other ways to get to it. Among his friends in Peking was a certain Mr Dolbetchef, head of a White Russian group in the city that hated the Soviet Union and issued a steady stream of anti-Stalin propaganda. Dolbetchef's group was one of several organised White Russian outfits dedicated to bringing down

Stalin and the Bolsheviks, and all of them had some support among the White Russians in China. They were also spied upon by Stalin's secret police and by Tai Li's Blue Shirts. As a result they were all paranoid, and spent most of their time trying to discredit each other's groups as the rightful leaders of the Russian anti-Communist movement in China.

Dolbetchef's group was highly compromised in the eyes of some, since it operated with encouragement from the Japanese authorities, receiving their protection and possibly their funding. Still, Dolbetchef had deep connections in the White Russian community and he told Werner that a woman who made donations to his cause was now the madam of 28 Chuanpan Hutong, which she ran for Brana Shazker.

Her name was Rosie Gerbert, and Dolbetchef had learned about her new job from a Russian Jew called Kan who had lodgings on Yang I Hutong in the Tartar City. Many semi-destitute White Russians and Jewish refugees lived in run-down boardinghouses there. Dolbetchef introduced Werner to Kan, who claimed to have had dealings with Gerbert when she was running a brothel in Newchwang, a small treaty port on the Gulf of Pechili, northeast of Peking.

Rosie Gerbert had fled Newchwang quickly after one of the girls in her brothel was found dead. Eight thousand silver dollars worth of jewellery and $7,000 in cash, believed to be the victim's, were found stashed under Gerbert's house. The authorities had given her twenty-four hours to leave town, and she had reappeared in Peking in the same old business, this time at 28 Chuanpan Hutong.

Dolbetchef, who knew that Brana Shazker had been uncooperative with Werner, thought Gerbert might be more helpful. He set up a meeting between the Werner and Rosie Gerbert in his office. But Gerbert, while she agreed to the meeting, was anything but helpful.

'You heard of the murder of Pamela Werner?' Werner began.

'Murder? I heard of no murder.'

She claimed not to have been in Peking in January 1937. Dolbetchef said he knew for a fact that she'd been in the city, whereupon the woman flew into a rage, attacking Dolbetchef and claiming that she wasn't Russian anyway, but Polish. She cursed Werner, insisting she wasn't the madam of number 28.

Werner appealed to her, tried to reassure her. 'I only wanted to ask you if you could help me,' he pleaded, but she made no reply, swearing at Dolbetchef in Russian before storming out of his office.

It seemed that Brana Shazker had got to Rosie Gerbert before Werner had.

So he looked elsewhere, for people who had been at number 28 on the night of the 1937 Russian Christmas. His agents had established that several of the staff working there that night—houseboys Wang Chen-yu and Liu Pao-chung, and the cook Chen Ching-chun—were still living in Peking. But they were being uncooperative, despite cash inducements.

Then Werner found an unlikely ally in the Japanese. Hisanga Shimadzu, the Japanese Legation's first secretary, offered to help. Exactly why wasn't clear, though discrediting former British consul Nicholas Fitzmaurice might have been high on the list. In 1936 a Japanese man had been killed in Peking by a drunken British soldier, and the incident, to Tokyo's eyes, had been hushed up by Fitzmaurice. The affair still rankled with the Japanese, who were keen to have British justice and British officials revealed as corrupt and incompetent.

For his part, Werner was prepared to take help wherever he could get it. He met with Shimadzu several times at the Japanese Legation on rue Meu, where another man, who refused to shake hands or exchange cards, noted everything that was discussed. He appeared to be influential but said little, and simply called himself Mr Matsuo.

Shimadzu appealed to the Japanese-controlled North China Political Affairs Commission, now the ruling council of Peking. The commission ordered the Japanese Military Police in Peking, the much-feared Kempeitai, who had commandeered a building close to the Forbidden City, to find and hand over to Werner the houseboys and cook from number 28. Displaying their legendary efficiency and reach, the Kempeitai had the houseboy Wang Chen-yu delivered to Werner within days.

With money on the table and the Kempeitai commanding him to cooperate, Wang brought in Liu Pao-chung, the second houseboy. Liu told Werner that on the night of the murder he'd heard two or more screams and the sound of furniture being smashed at number 28. Though his title was houseboy, Liu's job at the brothel had been more like the head of the Chinese staff, overseeing and controlling them, and telling them to shut up when necessary. He'd provided the muscle on the entry gate, and had been with Madam Leschinsky when she beckoned Sun Te-hsing and his rickshaw over. Clearly he knew secrets, but Werner was wary of people saying anything just to please him and take his money. He tested the man.

'Did the stout Russian woman Leschinsky kill the girl?' he asked.

'*Pu shih ta sha ti,*' replied the boy instantly, which translated as 'It was not she who killed her.'

Then who? But Liu was afraid to say. He felt he'd said enough already, though he did mention that he believed Madam Leschinsky had kept a piece of the bloodstained cloth used to cover Pamela's face, in case she was ever made to give evidence at a trial. She would produce the cloth in the hope of clearing herself and incriminating others.

Werner asked Liu where the murder had occurred.

'In the Korean house,' said Liu, perhaps referring to the other half of Madam Leschinsky's ancestry.

Werner asked for the names of the men who had been there with Pamela that night, but Liu claimed he didn't know. One had gone regularly to number 28 before, but all Liu would say was that he was an 'American tooth doctor.'

Werner went back to the Kempeitai and requested they find and formally question Wang and Liu as witnesses, and continue to look for the cook, Chen Ching-chun. Wary of creating yet more bad feeling in a city they occupied, the Kempeitai suggested that Chief Chen at Ch'ienmen headquarters should be the man to do the questioning.

Werner thought they were prevaricating. He knew his timing was bad: it was June 1939, six weeks after the manager of the Japanese-owned Federal Reserve Bank of North China had been assassinated by Chinese Nationalists at Tientsin's Grand Theatre, in the British Concession. The killers were known to be hiding out in the concession, and when the British authorities refused to hand them over, the Japanese had blockaded the area, in what would become known as the Tientsin Incident.

Anglo-Japanese relations, already strained, were now decidedly sour. And the man in Tientsin who was resisting Japanese pressure to hand over the accused killers was the city's head of the British Municipal Police—DCI Richard Dennis.

As long as the British refused to cooperate in Tientsin, Werner was no longer welcome on rue Meu. The Japanese Legation turned its back on him just as the British Legation had. Werner established that the mysterious, publicity-shy Mr Matsuo was in fact the head of Japanese intelligence at the legation, and a high-ranking member of the ultranationalist Kokuryukai, the Black Dragon Society, which was based right inside the Japanese Legation.

Eventually, in August, Britain's ambassador in Tokyo, Sir Robert Craigie, ordered DCI Dennis to hand over the Chinese men wanted by the Japanese. Dennis had no choice, and the men were all executed the same day.

For a brief moment it seemed that the Peking police were going to help Werner. Perhaps in response to the British defying Japanese demands to hand over Chinese citizens to certain death in Tientsin, or perhaps as a last gesture of independence from Tokyo's occupation of Peking, Chief Chen detailed two of his deputy commissioners to work with Werner, who was told that his daughter's case would be reopened. The shadowy Cheng Chi Tui, known in English as the Spy and Investigations Department, was brought in. Werner was assured that Wang and Liu would be arrested and questioned, as would the former cook at number 28, once he'd been located.

But none of it ever happened. The Peking police suddenly broke off all relations with Werner. He was unable to discover exactly who had given the order, although he guessed at the mysterious Mr Matsuo.

In the meantime, Wang Chen-yu and Liu Pao-chung had vanished from Peking, doubtless spooked by the thought of being hauled in once more by the dreaded Kempeitai. With no way of finding them again, Werner grew increasingly desperate. His feeling of hopelessness reached such a depth that he appealed yet again to Archer and the British Legation. Part of his letter declared, 'This is surely a crime of the underworld. Its solution is to be sought in the haunts of the sadist sexualists of the Peking foreign underworld clique.'

Again his plea for help was rebuffed.

Despondent, he pressed on. He heard repeatedly that Madam Leschinsky and Michael Consiglio were lying low in a brothel in Shanghai's Frenchtown, living under assumed names. Madam Leschinsky was now calling herself Shura, he was told, but he got conflicting reports of possible Shuras that seemed to fit the profile. There were different incarnations: a White Russian hermaphrodite in Peking, a beautiful White Russian dance hostess in one or more of the Badlands cabarets, a man who worked as the cashier at the White Russian Kavkaz Bar and sold wine on the side to supplement his income, a Korean woman who had nearly married a Chinese warlord.

Werner gathered all the information and put in a request to the French consul in Shanghai, Marcel Baudez, for the detention and arrest of Shura. Baudez, who knew Werner of old, was sympathetic, but protocol demanded that such a request come from the British authorities, rather than an individual. He assured Werner that if the British ambassador in Shanghai were to make a formal request, Baudez would instruct the French Concession Police to search out anyone matching the description and make an arrest.

Werner passed on to the Shanghai Municipal Police a description of the Shura, possibly spelt 'Shira,' that he was seeking: between five-eight and five-ten in height, rather heavily built but not stout, with light-coloured hair but not blond, and a pallid complexion. This person was probably in his or her forties, was of Korean descent but had rather indiscriminate racial features, and was said to be a hermaphrodite.

The French Consulate in Shanghai thought that locating such a person would be easy enough, given the close watch the French police kept on the underworld in Shanghai. But Baudez never issued an order for the arrest of Shura, because Ambassador Clark Kerr never made a formal request. Werner was persona non grata in Shanghai now too.

So he sent his agents to Shanghai's Frenchtown to see if they could find Leschinsky and Consiglio, the latter of whom was perhaps now calling himself Giraldi and/or Sodnitsky. But it seemed the couple had got wind of his search and moved on. The Shanghai underworld gossip said they had gone to Tsingtao, a Japanese-controlled city where Werner had no influence and where his agents could not easily follow them.

As it turned out, there was more than one Shura in the Russian community, and Werner had been on the trail of the wrong one. The Shura who'd reportedly been a manager of number 28 was not the White Russian hermaphrodite Werner had been told about and had described to the French. That Shura had not fled to Shanghai but was still in Peking.

This Shura knew everyone and everything about the Badlands. He was a local legend, and most importantly, he knew who had been at number 28 on the night of 7 January 1937. It was ultimately a most serendipitous case of mistaken identity.

Alexander Mikhailovitch Sosnitsky, aka Ivan, Vania, Vanushka or, to the habitués of the Peking Badlands, usually just Shura (a common short form of Alexander in Russia), sometimes also confusingly called himself Giraldi. Born in Tomsk, Siberia, the child of a tsarist official who was murdered by the Bolsheviks, Shura had fled with a party of refugees who wandered northern China before eventually settling in Peking.

Shura was of indeterminate sex, and while no one was sure, the story had it that he had been raised as a girl. Due to a mixed heritage, he could pass as a man or a woman, as European or Asian. Depending on mood, Shura was one day a humble wine dealer, another the male cashier of the Kavkaz (though most assumed he was in reality the owner of the bar), and the next a cabaret star for whose attentions wealthy Chinese male patrons vied. He was well known at many cabarets and private parties of the rich across Peking, where he would appear to introduce his dancing troupe, six beautiful White Russian girls in elaborate costumes, accompanied by a Russian guitarist. For those who needed seclusion and a discreet hideaway, Shura ran a "resort" in the Patachu Hills outside Peking.

And Shura the woman was beautiful—jet-black hair, pert breasts, almond-shaped eyes, perfectly formed and brilliantly white teeth. Rumour had it that a Chinese warlord had once begged Shura to marry him, and on discovering Shura's twin sex had fled to another city to avoid the shame.

When passing as a man, Shura bound his small breasts tightly and wore a sharp tailored suit; when she was a woman, she wore startlingly coloured robes, both Chinese-style cheongsams and Western dresses, and let her raven hair flow loose.

Werner first went looking for Shura at the Kavkaz, which had once been the centre of Russian émigré nightlife but was now, with so many White Russians having headed to Shanghai, rather down-at-heel. The place was barely half full, and it was depressing, with its overweight and overpainted Russian prostitutes and a clientele slowly drowning their sorrows in cheap Crimean brandy, able only to leer at the girls, they were so broke.

Werner left a note for Shura, saying he wanted to meet. He got a reply with an address, a Japanese-owned boardinghouse in the White Russian and Jewish enclave of Yang I Hutong, in the Tartar City.

Shura was dressed as a man that day. Werner found him pleasant enough, and sympathetic. Shura knew of the Korean-Russian Madam Leschinsky who sometimes called herself Shura. He also knew about Prentice and his gang; he'd seen them around the Badlands and had heard about their activities. He knew that Prentice and Joe Knauf hunted together, and that both men regularly carried knives. He knew they propositioned young foreign women. He knew all about the parties they organised, the nude dances, and the nudist colony in the Western Hills.

Shura told Werner that Prentice was a man who liked to threaten women with his knife, to manipulate them, scare them. He kept Pinfold as a sidekick, a bit of muscle, and threw him scraps so he remained just shy of destitute. As Werner already knew, Prentice was also friends with Joe Knauf, who'd been a brothel keeper in partnership with the Oparinas before becoming the manager of the Olympia Cabaret. Apparently Knauf and Madam Oparina had fallen out badly over something and now hated each other. According to Shura, Knauf was these days mostly involved with heroin dealing in the Badlands.

Shura advised Werner to look for two White Russian prostitutes called Marie and Peggy, who'd been working in number 28 around the time of Pamela's murder. He also advised him to find a Badlands pimp called Saxsen, who wasted his evenings in the cafés and restaurants along Chuanpan, Soochow, and Hougou Hutong. Track down Saxsen, and most probably he'd find the two women, if they were still in Peking and still alive; but Shura warned Werner that they were veteran Badlands whores—their life expectancy was not to be envied.

Shura claimed that he'd spoken with Peggy shortly after Pamela's murder. Peggy was one of the girls who'd been rousted in number 27 by Han and his men. She'd been taken to Morrison Street, stuck in a cell for the night, and questioned by Inspector Botham in the small hours. The British policeman was drunk and aggressive, Peggy said; he had groped her and leered at her. Scared, she had clammed up.

On her release she returned to number 28, where the brothel was shuttered and closed for business. But the girls were still inside; they were being detained there because Madam Leschinsky was worried they would talk about what they'd seen or heard. Peggy had since fled Peking, but to where Shura had no idea.

It was an unlikely alliance, to say the least—the upright former diplomat scholar Sinologist and the hermaphrodite White Russian nightlife habitué.

But through Shura's network, Werner did find Saxsen. This man was something different altogether from anyone Werner had met. A near-destitute White Russian pimp and small-time heroin dealer with a criminal record that stretched back to tsarist Russia, he was well known to the Legation Quarter police. Saxsen supplied White Russian girls not just to number 28 but also to other brothels in the Badlands, and he handily lived next door, in a seedy lodging house at number 29. He sold dope as well as sex to keep his girls close by. He made sure they were hooked, and he made sure he was their exclusive supplier.

Saxsen spent his waking hours, which were almost exclusively at night, in the dive bars and seedy cafés of Chuanpan Hutong. His world was small and sordid. Through Shura he'd learned that Werner was offering rewards for witnesses to his daughter's murder, and he arrived at Armour Factory Alley with Marie in tow, a 'fairly good-looking, healthy-looking woman of about thirty years of age, who spoke English fluently,' as Werner later described her.

Marie was willing to talk. She told Werner that she knew Prentice, that he had an extremely sadistic nature. She'd seen him flash his knife around in number 28 a bunch of times. The girls were afraid of him, and of his friend Knauf, who was also fond of flashing knives around—as he did regularly at a restaurant opposite number 28 called Fu Sheng, which was where the prostitutes met their pimps. Marie told Werner that Prentice often rented a room for his parties at number 28, always the downstairs bedroom, which was rarely used by the regular working girls, who stayed upstairs. The room was booked in advance and by phone. The going rate was twenty-five Chinese dollars, in cash.

Marie had been hired to dance naked at Prentice's apartment for him and his friends: they paid, but they expected their pound of flesh. She named Pinfold, Knauf, John O'Brian and another man she knew only as Jack as regulars at Prentice's flat, and frequently with him at number 28—these were the men referred to as Prentice's 'pals.'

Prentice, Marie said, was one of the men in that room at number 28 with Pamela on the night she died. Marie and Peggy had been working upstairs with the other girls, and the place was busy. A group of off-duty Italian Marine Guards were availing themselves of the services at

Madam Leschinsky's and also drinking next door at the Oparinas' bar. Security had been tight—number 28 was officially out of bounds for foreign soldiers, so their presence there needed to be kept quiet.

From an upstairs window Marie had seen a car arrive. Three men and a girl got out, all of them foreign, and entered the courtyard. The car turned around and drove back in the direction of the Legation Quarter. A short time later Marie heard two screams from the floor below, followed by one very loud piercing scream, and then a 'terrific thud' that sounded like furniture being kicked over.

She had later talked about the incident with Peggy, who was working in the next bedroom. She too had heard the screams and thud, and had earlier seen Prentice arrive with Joe Knauf and a 'half-caste' man, who she thought called himself John O'Brian. Both girls knew and feared the men. Marie had also seen the doctor to the Italian Marine Guards, a man called Capuzzo, talking with Prentice in the courtyard just after the car arrived.

Marie now said to Werner, 'Prentice killed her.'

At that she was ordered to shut up by Saxsen, who told Werner she'd given him enough to get paid. And Marie, completely under the control of her pimp, who was himself perhaps afraid of being implicated in Pamela's murder, obeyed. She would say no more, and despite Werner's pleas, the two of them left the house.

A few weeks later, when Werner was able to see Shura again, he begged the Russian to appeal to Marie to talk to him once more, this time without Saxsen. But things had changed quickly in those weeks, and Shura now claimed that Marie was a hopeless case. She was a heroin addict like all Saxsen's girls, and Shura had seen her slumped in dive bars with her eyes rolling and her head lolling from side to side, too doped up to work anymore. Saxsen had dumped her.

Werner suggested Marie be taken somewhere to cure her of her addiction. Shura believed that without the drug she would be insane in a day and dead within a week. Werner said he was willing to appeal to her family for help, if he could find them. Shura informed him bluntly that Marie's father was in Peking, but he was a hopeless drunk.

It was he who'd sold her into prostitution in the first place, and he'd done so in return for a share of the profits she brought Saxsen. Those profits had dried up now—her father certainly would not help her.

Werner went searching for Marie himself, through the bars and brothels of the Badlands, but she seemed to have disappeared without a trace.

That left Peggy. Werner had heard she was still in northern China somewhere, and he sent his agents to look for her. They found her in Harbin, a city full of Russian émigrés in Japanese-occupied Manchuria. She agreed to talk, but off the record. She refused to make an affidavit—she was too fearful of revenge, and she had been treated roughly by a drunk Inspector Botham at Morrison Street on the night of the roust. But she confirmed the presence of Prentice, O'Brian, Leschinsky, Consiglio, the Italian doctor Capuzzo and the Italian Marine Guards at number 28 on the night in question. She told Werner's agents that Capuzzo and Prentice were old friends, and they'd been at number 28 together on several occasions.

Peggy too was sinking into a pit of heroin addiction. She was broke and living in appalling conditions in freezing-cold Harbin. No longer able to work, she could not pay her dealers. Werner considered bringing her to Peking for treatment, but before he could arrange it, she disappeared again, this time for good.

Werner seethed. If the detectives had handled the questioning of the prostitutes better at the time, they would have been able to place Pamela in Chuanpan Hutong, and they would have had a link to Prentice, and to John O'Brian, whom Werner had met and disliked. O'Brian had been one of Pamela's most persistent suitors, and it now transpired that he was also one of Prentice's pals. If Pamela had been invited to a party O'Brian was attending, she would not have suspected anything was amiss.

Werner could only wonder how long the gang had been targeting his daughter, and how many men had been involved. It sickened him to think about it. O'Brian, Gorman, Pinfold, Prentice—all of them were connected to Pamela in different ways, and all of them had been at number 28 on that unthinkable night in January 1937.

The Hunters

*I*n that summer of 1939, Werner had also realised he had no choice but to visit 28 Chuanpan Hutong himself, now that he was sure it was the *locus delicti*. He owed it to his daughter to follow the path of her last journey.

He went first to number 27, intending to talk to the Oparinas. He had no doubt they knew exactly what had happened in the premises next door. Werner knew little about the couple except that they were White Russians. Madam Oparina had reputedly been widowed five times over, and had financially benefited from the death of each husband, raising not a few eyebrows over the years. Her son Yashka had been a hunting and drinking pal of Prentice's. And then of course there was the story about Madam Oparina once running a brothel with Joe Knauf, until the two had fallen out.

But when Werner got to the dive bar, he found it shuttered and the Oparinas gone, apparently to Shanghai. Werner was stymied.

Then he recalled a vital piece of information that Shura had given him: that there was only one room inside the compound of number 28 that could have been used for the party with Pamela. It was on the ground floor, on the southern side of the compound, along the wall that adjoined Chuanpan Hutong. This room had a bed in it and was attached to a bathroom. Werner hadn't known of the room previously. He'd heard that the ground floor contained just the reception and a dining room, and that all the bedrooms were upstairs.

He decided to see for himself. He expected the place to be shut and locked up, and that anyone not known or not clearly there on 'business' would be refused admission. He had passed by before at night and noted tough-looking Chinese bouncers on the door. Now he managed to gain access to the roof of a grocery store opposite number 28. The buildings along the *hutong* were only two storeys high at most, but from the roof he could see over the wall of number 28 and ascertain the layout of the brothel.

Once down from the roof, he crossed the road and was surprised to find the street door of number 28 ajar, and no security men present. He went in. Some Chinese servants in the central courtyard asked him what he wanted. Werner ignored them and stepped sharply to the right, walking the few steps to the bedroom that Shura had told him about. An old Russian man stood at the entrance but did not bar Werner's way.

The doorway opened on to a bathroom with a full-size bathtub against one wall and a hand basin on another. Past this anteroom was the bedroom, largish, with a big double bed in the centre. There was also a wardrobe, dressing table and some chairs. Werner noted that the legs on one of the chairs looked to have been broken and then repaired with metal braces.

Back out in the courtyard, he looked around, again ignoring the old Russian and the Chinese servants. Another Chinese man stood leaning on the staircase by the kitchen entrance, watching. Werner approached him, hoping he might be the cook that neither his agents nor the Japanese Kempeitai nor the Chinese Cheng Chi Tui had been able to find.

'Is there anyone here named Chen, Chen Ching-chun?' he asked the man.

'Yes, I am he.'

Werner couldn't believe his luck. He invited the cook to come to Armour Factory Alley, but at that moment Brana Shazker, the new madam of number 28, came down the stairs from the bedrooms above and began to shout and scream at them both. The cook disappeared to his basement kitchen, and Werner was hustled out of the courtyard and onto the street, where the gate was slammed shut and bolted behind him.

For weeks afterward, Werner's agents went regularly to number 28 to try to persuade Chen to talk with Werner, but they could never gain access to the place, or reach the cook. Eventually they learnt that he'd been fired and smuggled out of Peking by Madam Shazker.

狐 狸 精

Apart from the name of the man who'd struck the fatal blow to his daughter—either Prentice, Knauf, O'Brian or Capuzzo—Werner thought he had almost everything now. There was just one other minor detail that had been constantly worrying him: according to the autopsy, Pamela's last meal had been Chinese food. He knew she hadn't eaten Chinese food at the Gurevitches' or at the skating rink, and it seemed unlikely that she'd done so at Prentice's flat or at Chuan-pan Hutong. He finally solved that nagging mystery.

After a long search, Werner's detectives had found several former classmates of the married student Han Shou-ching, whose nose Werner had broken with his cane. The students remembered Han Shou-ching and Pamela being friends, nothing more. He'd been deeply upset by her murder and had told the students that the day before, he had met her by chance outside the American drugstore on Hatamen Street. Pamela felt bad about her father lashing out at him, and he suggested they have dinner the following evening.

And indeed the proprietor of the drugstore, when Werner's agents followed the story up, remembered Pamela talking with a Chinese youth outside the shop on 6 January.

The following night, Han Shou-ching met her at the skating rink and they went to a Chinese restaurant on Tung Tan Pailou Hutong, on the edge of the Legation Quarter. The restaurant was popular with the students at Han's college and not far from Armour Factory Alley. They cycled there, had a quick meal, and then he accompanied Pamela back to the skating rink, just five minutes or so by bike. He knew she lived in the other direction, but assumed she was meeting up with her skating friends again.

So there Werner had it. Pamela's last meal had been eaten just minutes from her home. She would have gotten back to the rink on Legation Street around eight p.m.

He wrote again to the Foreign Office, detailing his visit to the brothel along with the other new evidence, including his own hand-drawn map of the layout of number 28, and a map detailing Chuan-pan Hutong and its proximity to the Fox Tower. He sent copies to Consul Archer and Ambassador Clark Kerr.

In his letter he quoted an old Chinese proverb, 'Shui lo shih chu'— As the water recedes, the rock appears.

At the Foreign Office, the note attached to Werner's latest letter read simply: 'Murder of Pamela Werner. Mr. Werner continues progressive investigation. Further results obtained.'

What Werner wanted now was a confession. As the long and humid summer of 1939 became a blustery and rainy autumn, Werner received an anonymous letter at Armour Factory Alley. The writer of the letter stated that they had heard Pinfold declare on 8 January 1937, 'Prentice killed her.' But Werner wanted to know for sure. He wanted to talk to all the men who'd been in the room at number 28 that night with his daughter—Prentice, Knauf, O'Brian, Pinfold and Capuzzo.

They were a mixed group, from professionals to the destitute, from ostensibly upstanding members of Peking's foreign community to those with lengthy criminal records. They lived in well-appointed apartment buildings or in cheap flophouses; they were American, British, Canadian, Italian. What they had in common was their membership in a gang. They were habitués of the Badlands and, in particular, 28 Chuanpan Hutong.

Werner sought out Pinfold first, but it appeared that the Canadian ex-mercenary had fled Peking shortly after the police released him in January 1937. His whereabouts were unknown. Werner's agents heard that Pinfold had been living in Prentice's flat around the time of the murder, but the two had fallen out after a ferocious argument. The word was that Prentice had paid for Pinfold to get out of Peking and never return.

Prentice himself had refused to discuss the murder or its investigation with anyone since being questioned by the police. In the midst of a whirlwind of half-truths and gossip and speculation, the dentist remained tight-lipped. By March 1937, the talk about him had reached the point where a group of fellow professionals asked him to attend a dinner 'to lay his cards on the table,' as it was described to Werner—to account for himself and the rumours surrounding him. Prentice promised to attend but never showed up.

Shortly after Prentice was questioned by Han and Dennis, an American vice-consul in Tientsin who'd heard the whisperings about the dentist's involvement in Pamela's murder requested a meeting with him. Prentice refused to discuss the case at any length with the man.

With Peking's foreign community being the goldfish bowl it was, Werner had inevitably seen Prentice occasionally on the street, but oddly enough the two had never formally met, even though both were long-term residents of the city, and Prentice had treated Pamela. After her death, any chance encounters between the two men were marked by Prentice's efforts to ingratiate himself. Werner recalled the dentist's 'cringing politeness and exaggerated attempts to express sympathy to me.'

But now Werner had decided to confront Prentice head-on, and he went to his flat on Legation Street.

In this smart, modern building, far from the transient lodgings that most of his associates inhabited, Prentice was still comfortably off; that much was obvious. He was still dressing well, still looking healthy, despite the deprivations of life in occupied Peking. Arthur Ringwalt at the American Legation had intimated to Werner that the

Americans were concerned about Prentice's close relationship to certain Japanese officials. There was a suspicion that he might be receiving access to food supplies, and preferential currency transactions, in return for his support for the occupation. He was, in other words, a collaborator.

Werner knew that when DCI Dennis and Commissioner Thomas had gone to Prentice's flat to bring him in for questioning, Dennis had noted the smell of fresh paint. And here was another thing that had never been followed up on. Nobody had asked the landlord why an entire flat had been repainted in midwinter, when the open windows required to ventilate the fumes would have reduced the place to an icebox. Nobody had sought out the workmen who did the painting to ask what they had painted over.

Prentice talked to Werner in the courtyard of his building, where he expressed sympathy for the loss of Pamela. But wasn't her case closed now? He admitted to having visited 28 Chuanpan Hutong, but only once, and claimed it was a full year before the murder. And yes, he and Joe Knauf had regularly gone hunting together, along with the man known only as Jack. Sometimes they'd been joined by Yashka Oparina, John O'Brian and Dr Capuzzo. Where was the harm in that?

Prentice refused to discuss his now-defunct Western Hills nudist colony, or any so-called nude dances. But he did confirm he'd given some of his pals passkeys to his flat, in case they needed somewhere to stay in difficult times. What were pals for, after all? He then ended the conversation and retreated inside to his flat.

Neither Sun the rickshaw puller nor Marie the prostitute had been able to identify the make and model of the car they saw pull up that night outside number 28, but Sun had sketched the car for Werner, and both his and Marie's description matched the vehicle Prentice had owned at the time: a Ford Black and Tan, with a black body and a tan roof. It was a common enough foreign import in China, but cars in general were not that common.

Werner went looking for Prentice's car, only to find that it had been sold to an unidentified buyer shortly after the murder. He tried to track down the buyer, but too much time had elapsed. Under the occupation, all private cars had been ordered off the road so as to reserve petrol for the Japanese military, a few police cars and diplomatic vehicles. The rest had been sold, mothballed or confiscated, and invariably they'd been repainted and had their plates changed. The Ford proved impossible to trace, as did the Chinese chauffeur who'd been seen driving it. He was another of China's lost millions, people who'd vanished in the wake of the Japanese invasion.

Werner turned his attention to the Italian Marine Guards who were reportedly at number 28 that night, and the marines who'd been seen at the bar next door on the previous evening. He'd heard that the squadron was about to be rotated out of Peking back to Italy, and on contacting Commandant Del Greco, commander of the guard at the Italian Legation, he learnt that he too was being transferred out. The commandant denied that any of his men had been away from their barracks on 6 January 1937. Nor could they have been on Chuanpan Hutong the following night—it was strictly out of bounds.

Werner appealed to Consul Archer to ask the question through official channels. Surprisingly, Archer did, but Del Greco repeated his assertion that none of his men had been on Chuanpan Hutong. Werner suggested Archer have the rickshaw puller Sun Te-hsing taken to the Italian barracks to identify anyone he'd seen that night. And given Del Greco's impending departure, perhaps an order should be issued for his detention? Archer prevaricated, letting crucial time pass, and before he replied to Werner, Del Greco and the marines left Peking for Italy.

Werner knew that the commandant had been covering his hide. If he were to admit knowledge of his men's presence in the off-limits Badlands, he too could be in trouble. So Werner went directly to the one Italian he knew for sure had been there that night, Dr Capuzzo. The doctor was a married man with a large family, but he was said to have been a regular along Chuanpan Hutong, a friend of Michael Consiglio as well as of Prentice. Capuzzo's house, on Viale Italia, near the Italian Legation, was a ten-minute walk from Prentice's flat.

Werner called on the doctor at his surgery in the Italian hospital, close to the Grand Hôtel de Pékin on Morrison Street. Standing in the cramped waiting room, he acted like any other prospective patient waiting to see the doctor. He asked Capuzzo an innocuous question about an Italian family he had connections with. Would Dr Capuzzo know whether they were planning to return to Peking? Capuzzo replied that he thought not, then asked Werner for his name.

On learning who his visitor was, he said at once, 'When your daughter was killed I was in Hong Kong.'

Not wishing to alert Capuzzo to his suspicions, Werner left. On his way out he questioned the gatekeeper at the hospital: Did he know if Signor Capuzzo had ever been to Hong Kong? The gatekeeper said that, as far as he was aware, the doctor had not left Peking for several years.

Werner had the details of a number of Capuzzo's associates, including a Greek businessman who supplied pharmaceuticals to Capuzzo and the Italian hospital, and had done so for years. This man, too, said that Capuzzo hadn't left Peking for many years, something that was confirmed by other associates. Werner's detectives quizzed all the foreign travel agencies in Peking, but none had a record of a Dr Capuzzo leaving Peking for Hong Kong at any time.

Before Werner could approach the next man on his list, he was put in touch with the mysterious 'Jack.' Here Arthur Ringwalt and his voluminous files on American ne'er-do-wells in Peking had once again proved vital.

Jack turned out to be an Italian-born naturalized American who'd taken the name Thomas Jack to hide his ancestry when he'd joined the U.S. Marines. He had enlisted as a local hire in Peking, in the same way Michael Consiglio had, and since his discharge had been hanging around the Legation Quarter working as a mechanic. Arthur Ringwalt had been told by one of his informants that 'there is a marine who knows everything and is willing to talk.' Rumours of a car mechanic being involved in the murder had also reached Werner's Chinese detectives. Ringwalt hadn't been given a name, but he believed the mechanic might be Jack, for whom he had a current address.

When Werner went to see Jack, he thought that whatever the mechanic was calling himself, he couldn't hide his ancestry; his English had a marked Italian accent. He was a short, squat, strong-looking man, and at first he was remarkably open with Werner. He had left his job at the Mina Motor Company, the Legation Quarter's major car dealer, and had branched into the nightclub business. He showed Werner the plans for the new cabaret he was in the process of setting up.

According to Ringwalt's intelligence, Jack had recently got together enough of a stash to buy the Olympia Cabaret, the place that Joe Knauf had once managed and Prentice had frequented. Now Jack was expanding to a second joint, which was to include a large number of bedrooms upstairs, where the real business of the cabaret would no doubt take place.

But when it came to Pamela's murder, he was less open. He claimed to have heard of it only through the newspapers, and said it must have been committed by some low-class Chinese such as a rickshaw puller. He laughed off the suggestion that Prentice might have been involved. He rejected the notion that Knauf was a man of violent tendencies, despite the police records to the contrary.

Werner pushed him. It was impossible for the murder to be the work of a simple rickshaw puller acting alone, he insisted, and moreover a car and foreign men had been seen that night. Jack claimed he'd been to number 28 only once, about a year before the murder, but Werner noted his agitation at the mention of a car being seen there.

Asked if he knew Capuzzo, Jack said he'd often been hunting with him and Knauf, but with that he seemed to think he had said too much, and he hustled Werner out of the flat and slammed the door. If Jack was the marine reported to 'know everything' and be 'willing to talk,' he had since changed his mind.

Next Werner tracked down Joe Knauf. He had been putting off

meeting him due to his reputation for being easily angered and swift to resort to violence. It was said that Knauf wouldn't hesitate to throw his fists or pull his knife out. Werner might have been a determined man but he was also in his mid-seventies, and wary. He had been fairly sure that neither Prentice, a well-known dentist, nor Capuzzo, a physician attached to the Italian Legation, would be physically violent with him, but Knauf was another matter entirely.

Arthur Ringwalt had a large file on Joe Knauf, which included details of the threatening behaviour he'd shown customers in the Olympia Cabaret. The Americans had kept a watch on the Olympia while Knauf was managing it, suspecting him of pimping, selling heroin and dealing in illegal arms and ammunition. There were also reports of his being completely naked in the courtyard of his lodging house, apparently drunk or drugged. The Chinese owners of the building were fearful of him, aware that he'd been kicked out of several other lodging houses, after which he had violently assaulted the landlords.

When Werner went to the run-down house on the edge of the Legation Quarter where Knauf lived, he had just returned from his summer residence in Peitaiho, where he'd been assembling his investigation notes. The train back to Peking was horrendously over-crowded and slow-moving, as were all the trains under the Japanese occupation. He had called at the lodging house earlier in the day and been told by the gateman that Knauf was out. Werner left his calling card, saying he'd come back later.

He returned around five thirty, when it was still light after a sweltering, humid day. The old man with his weak heart was feeling nervous.

As Werner approached the building, he saw Knauf looking out at him through a long tear in the traditional paper windows. Werner later wrote of this moment:

My first impression was that I was looking at an animal instead of a human being. He has a long face, very large eyes, a

pronounced Roman nose (as noticed by the rickshaw coolie
on the night of the murder), and a body (only partly covered
by a kimono as is his custom) evidently thickly covered with
dark hair.

Knauf sent down his houseboy to show Werner to his rooms.
Walking through the maze of corridors, Werner noticed that the
other people in the building, both Chinese and foreigners, were displaying odd behaviour. As they went into rooms they would unlock
the doors and then swiftly lock them behind them. And when leaving
they would close the doors just as quickly and hurriedly lock them
again. He didn't know whether this was because the place was a centre of heroin dealing, as Ringwalt had suggested, and security was
tight, or whether prostitutes were kept there, perhaps against their
will, allowed out only at night, escorted by their pimps.

Knauf's rooms were almost identical to those of Pinfold and of
every other cheap, run-down boardinghouse frequented by Peking's
underworld—cramped, with sparse, worn furnishings, stifling in the
summer heat. The man was seemingly a transient, having no more
possessions than could be put into one suitcase in a hurry.

At first he was hostile to Werner, demanding to know who he was,
although he must surely have known from the card left with the gateman. And he'd been expecting Werner, watching for him at the window. He assumed the old man had come to accuse him of Pamela's
murder; the underworld grapevine was well aware of Werner's investigation. He adopted a loud and aggressive tone, and had to be reas-
sured that Werner had come to seek information, not to point the
finger.

Knauf's story was the same as the other men's, and Werner was
beginning to smell collusion. Knauf had not known Pamela and had
only ever been to number 28 once, a full year before her murder. He
denied being a regular there. He only knew of her killing what he'd
read in the newspapers. Yes, he had often gone hunting with O'Brian,
Capuzzo and Thomas Jack. He also admitted to a close friendship

with Prentice, which had come about through hunting, through the Western Hills nudist group, and in and around the Badlands.

Knauf sought to defend his own reputation. The problems with the Legation Quarter police and the American Legation had been misunderstandings, arising from unavoidable circumstances at the Olympia Cabaret. Knauf was a member of the community; he had umpired games for American boys at a local sports club before the Japanese occupation. (This much was true: Ringwalt had told Werner about it, and had also told him that Knauf was thrown out of the sports club for shouting at the boys and striking a couple of them in a fit of temper.)

Werner challenged him. Why had he gone to Tientsin shortly after the murder? he asked. Was it to procure a lawyer for Prentice in case he was charged?

Not at all, Knauf maintained. He had gone to secure a lawyer to help him recover some money that Prentice owed him.

Werner wasn't buying it—a lawyer to act against Prentice, his good pal?

He continued to dig. He asked Knauf flat out if he was a pimp, and Knauf, far from denying it, defended prostitution, saying that without it the girls would starve. Knauf maintained he only facilitated prostitution, and he didn't use the girls personally, keeping himself to 'one little Korean girl.'

Knauf also fished for information about Werner's investigation, saying unprompted, 'If the murder was committed in Prentice's flat, the Legation Quarter police would certainly have seen the car and have known about it.'

'Not on a night like that,' Werner replied.

Werner hadn't told Knauf of his suspicions about Prentice, and he assumed that Knauf was either trying to protect the dentist or put Werner off the scent.

Then Werner asked if he knew where Madam Oparina could be found, and Knauf's attitude changed. He turned suddenly pale and became hostile once more. Perhaps he assumed it was Madam

Oparina who'd mentioned his name to Werner. For whatever reason, he claimed he didn't know the owner of 27 Chuanpan Hutong.

'Yes, you do,' Werner said; 'you and she ran a bawdy house together, and you had a row with her.'

At this point Knauf exploded and began shouting threats. He called his houseboy and ordered him to show Werner out, telling the boy to make sure the gateman didn't let him back in. And that was that with Joe Knauf.

The last member of Prentice's ring to have been identified at number 28 that night was John O'Brian, the half-Chinese, half-Portuguese youth who had become infatuated with Pamela in Tientsin. Werner's detectives had heard that O'Brian was another person who'd held a passkey to Prentice's flat on Legation Street, and that he too had regularly attended parties there. But they'd had no luck seeking him out. His last known address was a single room in an ex–German Army barracks building at 6 Legation Street, almost next door to Prentice's apartment building. Shortly after 7 January, O'Brian had left for Shanghai, with a loan, according to Werner's sources, from his protector. Werner could only assume that Prentice had been making sure O'Brian was nowhere around to be questioned.

What a disgusting gang they made. A predatory group who not only went hunting together in the Western Hills but also targeted human prey in Peking. They pursued, caught and then gutted their kill.

Together they had hunted Pamela, trapping her in the brothel on Chuanpan Hutong, and together they had killed her.

A fox spirit's most common disguise is to manifest itself as a beautiful woman. A woman with the power to beguile men, capture their hearts, tempt them and lead them astray—away from their wives, their families, their businesses. The fox-woman promises loyalty, swears to be faithful, but will always betray, and leave without warning. Cunning princesses, courtesans, hostesses, the most infamous of Peking's sing-song girls—such women are said to have a touch of the fox in their composition, in their very nature, to perhaps be fox spirits. They can only be overcome by a stronger spirit.

Invitation to a Party

W hen was the moment of realisation? When did the adventure and the flattery cease, the flirtation become something different? When did the night change from being an opportunity for a school-girl to make an entrée into a seemingly glamourous adult world, and instead turn nasty? At what point did Pamela become scared, know-ing that terrible things were about to happen? When did she see the true nature of the men she was with? When had she clenched her fists with her thumbs inside, prepared to fight back? When had she screamed out? When was the moment she knew she was going to die?

Pamela hadn't known she would be taken to a notorious brothel that evening. She thought she was going to a party, or a supper, and why not? It was a last chance for some Peking fun before leaving in a few weeks for England, where she would put the unsavoury events at Tientsin Grammar School behind her. She certainly hadn't been aware that she would be in the company of men who were known to be violent, who preyed on young women and then forced themselves on them. Who would try to rape her in a squalid room in a Badlands whorehouse.

But that's how Prentice and his gang worked. The pretty young white women they invited to their parties and suppers were just realising what life could offer them, but were still unaware of the dangers that lurked. They met in Prentice's surgery, at the French Club skating rink, at Peking's cinemas and department stores, in the tiffin salons and the polite bars of the Legation Quarter hotels. The men sent the girls secret notes, or they 'accidentally' bumped into them on the street and issued invitations to Prentice's flat, the home of a professional man, a family man, safely in the heart of the Quarter.

Prentice had put it about that his family were in America for reasons to do with their health. No rumour had ever leaked out concerning the fears the U.S. authorities held for his daughter's welfare, were she to stay in his presence. But the fact was that Edna Prentice had taken her three young children and left Peking, never to return. Divorce might have been impossible, but Edna made sure that her husband never had contact with his children again.

Prentice had forged a new life for himself in Peking, with two personas. Perhaps it was the life he had always wanted—on the one hand, he was a well-known professional within the upright and proper world of foreign Peking; on the other, a habitué of the Badlands, the host of parties where prostitutes were hired to dance naked for the lowlife of white Peking. But who else was going to these parties? Someone with enough influence to have the investigation into a murder closed down?

And then Prentice had decided to target Pamela. He would have heard she was back in Peking via Gorman or O'Brian, or perhaps others who'd met her over the Christmas holidays. The dentist probably met Pamela at the skating rink the evening before she died. She may also have skated with Thomas Jack—a witness claimed to have seen her skating with a short man that night. And of course Pamela had already met Prentice in his surgery; he was a charming man who lived opposite the rink, who had a family in Los Angeles that he often spoke about, a man of some means and standing in the community. A dapper dresser who knew George Gorman, and Ethel Gurevitch too—they had mutual friends. He had come over to say hello, perhaps to his friend Jack as well; it was nothing more than a pleasant coincidence.

He knew where she lived—he'd sent her father a receipt for her dental work the previous year, and anyway Werner was a well-known figure. He dispatched Pinfold to contact her on Armour Factory Alley the next day, to let her know there was to be a party that night. A note had been left for her at the Wagons Lits reception by way of formal invitation.

The idea of a Legation Quarter party would have appealed to Pamela. Her Christmas holidays had been fun after the confines of Tientsin Grammar School and the unpleasantness of Sydney Yeates. She'd been enjoying her last days in Peking, before the long voyage to England and a new start. Pamela wasn't perfect; she was making the same mistakes many girls do when experimenting with their independence, their newfound power over men. Her tragedy was to encounter the wrong men, at just the wrong moment.

When Pamela left her house on Armour Factory Alley that afternoon, she was dressed in her tartan skirt that fell to just above her knees, silk stockings, an Aertex blouse, a cardigan and black shoes. Over these she put on her blue overcoat, belted at the waist. She had a handkerchief in her purse, some money, her new membership card for the French Club skating rink, and she wore, as she always did, her platinum watch with the diamond settings. Bought with her dead mother's money, the watch reminded Pamela of her.

Lastly she tugged on a black beret and mittens before collecting her ice skates and cycling south out of Armour Factory Alley. She went along the Wall Road and into the Legation Quarter, as far as Canal Road and the Wagons Lits Hotel. This was Pamela's Peking world; she knew it well and loved it.

Pamela was curious about Prentice's party invitation. She was meeting Ethel at the Wagons Lits anyway; it would take only a minute to pick up the note. And so she did. On leaving the hotel, she stopped briefly to read the invitation on the steps of the building. The party was to be a small gathering for the Russian Christmas, and Prentice hoped she could attend. It would start around eight o'clock at his flat—3 Legation Street, just across from the skating rink.

Ethel arrived at the Wagons Lits just after five, as arranged. The two girls rode their bicycles a couple of streets away to the Gurevitches' house on Hong Kong Bank Road, where they took tea with Ethel's parents before going skating. Since Ethel was just fifteen, Pamela didn't tell her about the invitation to the party, in case she might not understand.

After skating happily under the arc lights in the freezing air, the two girls gossiped with their mutual friend Lilian Marinovski, and at seven o'clock Pamela said she had to go. They assumed she meant home, but Pamela had other plans. She wasn't afraid of the dark, but she was bored with being alone. She wanted more from life than school, homework, the dim lights of Armour Factory Alley and her elderly scholar father.

'I've been alone all my life,' she told her friends.

First she met her old friend Han Shou-ching, whom she could see only clandestinely now, after her father's robust treatment of him. He was about the same age as Pamela, a student like her, and they got on well, even though their backgrounds were so very different.

He took her for a quick meal on nearby Tung Tan Pailou Hutong, a street Pamela knew well and where her cook regularly shopped. Afterwards Han cycled with her back to the French Club rink, where he left her.

It was around eight o'clock. Time for the party.

狐 狸 精

In Wentworth Prentice's modern, roomy, high-ceilinged apartment on the main thoroughfare of the smart Legation Quarter, other friends were arriving. If the gathering consisted of Prentice's usual associates, they would have included Thomas Jack, Pinfold, John O'Brian, and Yashka Oparina, the son of Madam Oparina.

Perhaps, too, Peter Liang was there. Liang was an independently wealthy Westernised Chinese who owned a fleet of cars, but he spent most of his time in the bars and cabarets of the Badlands and was regularly seen with Prentice. There would have been other women present, no doubt, and most likely one of them was the notorious Miss Ryan, a secretary with a foreign trading firm in the Legation Quarter. Miss Ryan was reputed to be a nymphomaniac. Rumour had it that soon after Pamela's murder, her fiancé broke off their engagement on the grounds that he believed her to be 'connected with the murder at the Fox Tower.'

But Pamela didn't know any of these people's backgrounds, or anything of the secret and sordid connections that bound them. She would have felt safe in the dentist's prosperous apartment, and grown-up amid these partygoers.

Drinks were poured, jazz records played, mild flirtations indulged in. In the warm and inviting living room, hints ensued, and then suggestions that the night was young; why not head out to a few nightspots, a cabaret, take in the Russian Christmas celebrations? Prentice had a car, a chauffeur, it was easy.

And Pamela, ready for a night of fun with her new friends, who appeared so much more sophisticated and worldly than her boyfriend at Tientsin Grammar, decided to go along. John O'Brian was there, whom she knew, and other men were paying her attention. Perhaps Prentice promised to call her father and tell him she was at a gathering at his flat—it would be all right, the dentist would have assured her, he knew Werner, they'd been in contact before. It was all so flattering, exciting.

But these people were not her friends. Pamela entered number 28 with three men, one of whom was certainly Prentice. The others were probably John O'Brian and Joe Knauf. Dr Capuzzo, it seems, was already in the brothel with the off-duty Italian marines.

Pamela went inside with Prentice on one arm and Knauf on the other. She didn't appear to be going against her will, but with the rickshaw puller the only witness, who could say what state she was in? Perhaps she didn't know exactly where she was, but then again perhaps she did, and was thrilled by the decadence and furtiveness of slumming it in the Badlands.

Once through the narrow gateway into the courtyard, the group entered a side door on the right, which led to the bathroom and bedroom that Werner later saw. It was a distance of only five or six steps—he had measured it to prove that it was possible to get into the room without being seen from the courtyard.

Surely at this point Pamela must have realised there was no party, no cabaret, no Russian Christmas celebration. The room was grim— a dirty floor, a bare harsh lightbulb, sparse furnishings. There were no decorations, nothing to indicate that anyone lived here, but there was a large bed. This bedroom was a place of work.

The mood changed. If Pamela had thought that others from the flat were following behind them, she now knew she was alone with these men, who then tried to force themselves on her.

Did they laugh as they did so? Taunt her, tell her to stop flirting with them? They had done this before, had arranged this sort of scenario many times. Perhaps they told Pamela she should just accept her fate, enjoy it. Perhaps she threatened to report them, but that would have only made them laugh more. Who would she tell, anyway? And who would believe that well-known professional white men, including a dentist, a doctor at the Italian Legation, and a former suitor of hers, had taken her to a White Russian brothel in the Badlands and forced her to have sex with them?

They would all deny it, and if trapped, they would say she offered herself. At worst their reputations would be slightly tarnished, while Pamela's would be destroyed. The Chinese police wouldn't care— this was the Badlands, and bad things happened here.

But Pamela refused to give in. She had an independent streak that now flared up. That would have been the point at which things got decidedly nastier. The shouting started, the yelling. And then the abuse turned to physical violence.

The men cornered her in the room. They yanked at her tartan skirt, ripping it open at the eyelets on the side, right down to the hem. They ripped open her blouse. Her silk stockings got snagged on furniture corners as she tried to edge round the room away from the men. She clenched her fists with her thumbs balled inside to hit them, force them away from her. Impossible to imagine how desperate she must have felt in that bedroom with only one way out, through the bathroom and into the courtyard. And then the gate to the street, where between her and freedom were two or three more large men.

She screamed, a sound that was heard throughout the bedrooms of number 28, heard by the prostitutes Marie and Peggy, who were there that night. She screamed again.

Perhaps her resistance, her refusal to submit as other girls had done before her, angered the men. They were used to having their way. Or perhaps they panicked, and just wanted to shut her up. They grabbed her arms, scratching her as she tried to break free—the pre-mortem scratches on her lower arms identified in the autopsy. That might have also been the point at which they thrust at her with their hunting knives, stabbing her in the face, eliciting the long, piercing final scream heard both within and outside number 28.

Then, to silence her, one of the men hit her hard on the head, just above her right eye. Perhaps with the leg of a chair, which had broken off as a result of the struggle; the autopsy had determined that the fatal blow had come from a wooden instrument of some sort. The blow was so strong it split her skull, causing severe haemorrhaging. Blood poured inside her cranium, drowning her brain. Within two to three minutes Pamela was dead, on the floor of a dirty bedroom in a Badlands whorehouse, a place she should never have been in.

Killing Pamela hadn't been part of the men's plan for the night. The shouting and screaming and smashing of furniture brought Madam Leschinsky and the brothel's security man, Liu Pao-chung, running. Madam Leschinsky took control, perhaps with help from her partner Michael Consiglio. She told the men to get the body out of her brothel and away from Chuanpan Hutong. She told her security man to confine the other girls to their rooms, and to keep the customers there too—the off-duty Italian marines. Dr Capuzzo was on hand to ensure they maintained their silence, in return for not being reported in an off-limits brothel.

Faced with Pamela's dead and bloody body, the men realised they needed to cover up their crime. They considered what to do, and took the decision to mutilate the corpse. They would slash it and stab it and then carve it up beyond recognition. They would dismember it and dump the parts outside the Legation Quarter, shifting any suspicion away from themselves and making the body impossible to identify. It would be seen as the work of a fiendish maniac, most probably Chinese.

Madam Leschinsky and Michael Consiglio would never talk, and they'd make sure their girls didn't either. Dr Capuzzo would ensure that gossip didn't filter out from the Italian marines in the brothel that night. As for the Chinese, one foreigner looked the same as another, and anyway, no Chinese willingly got involved in *laowai* business. Do it right, and the men would be in the clear.

They set to work. They were hunters; they had large, sharp knives that they often carried with them, and they had carved up animal corpses before. The first thing to do was cut the throat and drain the body of blood. They were in luck, because adjoining the bedroom was a bathroom. Dennis had been right in thinking that if he could find the blood, he would find the killers—except that Pamela's blood could never be found, because most of it went down the drain of the bath at number 28.

The bloodletting done, Pamela's body was carried to the courtyard door. One of the brothel's oil lamps was taken for light, and perhaps some additional knives from Chen Ching-chun's kitchen in the basement. Prentice went to the phone, called Pinfold, told him what had happened and that he needed to meet them.

Which of them was it who suggested the Fox Tower as a suitable place to carve up the body? Werner always believed it was Pinfold, who, as the bodyguard of a Chinese warlord, had once regularly patrolled the area. He would have known the legends about fox spirits, he would have known the tower was deserted at night. He certainly knew there were no streetlights there, and that the base of the tower was pitch-black. It was not patrolled by police—in fact, it was the only watchtower in Peking not to be guarded at night—and the nearest manned police box was nearly half a mile away at Hatamen Gate. Moreover it was in Chinese police territory, outside the Legation Quarter. It was the perfect location.

At the door of number 28, Madam Leschinsky called over the only waiting rickshaw puller, Sun Te-hsing. It was a dark night, after midnight, and cold, with a chill wind. Pamela was carried to the rickshaw and propped between Prentice and Knauf, her clothes draped back on and a cloth over her head hiding the damage.

The laboured breathing Sun thought he'd heard would have been caused by the movement of air in Pamela's lungs and throat as her body jolted during the jerky rickshaw ride: Werner had consulted a pathologist about this matter. Given what happened next, Werner could be forgiven for hoping that the end for Pamela had indeed come in that sordid room at number 28.

Sun took his passengers along Chuanpan Hutong to the Wall Road. He went a short distance along that to the small stone bridge that formed a narrow gap in the Tartar Wall and provided access to the Fox Tower, and its desolate grounds on the other side.

When Sun had left, warded off by Knauf's blade, the men carried Pamela across the bridge to the base of the tower. Joined now by Pinfold, they proceeded to mutilate the corpse. They worked by lamplight, the same lamplight seen by the mechanic Wang Shih-ming, the old coal merchant, and the motorist Kurochkin in the early hours of that Friday.

The men cut open Pamela's sternum, cracking the ribs outwards. They worked with their hunter's knowledge of anatomy and at least two different types of knife. There was a control to their work now, after the frenzy of the initial postmortem beating, stabbing and slashing, the repeated blows to the left eye, temples, crown and chin; the wounds about the face and the mutilation of the vagina. By the time Pamela's body was clinically carved up, it was no more to these men than the carcass of an animal killed in the forest for sport.

With the chest cut open and the ribs broken back, they had access to the body cavity. They removed the heart and other organs. They detached the stomach at the oesophagus and the small intestine. If the large gash across her throat was an attempt to cut the head off, then they were unsuccessful. Nor were they able to successfully detach her right arm.

Perhaps it was at this point that the men were interrupted. Perhaps someone heedless of fox spirits had strayed too close, disturbing the gruesome scene. Or perhaps the men were startled by the headlights of the nighttime motorist Kurochkin, coming along the City Road and around the corner of the Fox Tower, above the slope where the carving was taking place. They would not have expected a car at that time of night, and it may not have been apparent to them that they were unobservable down at the base of the tower. Or perhaps they had simply grown exhausted.

Whatever the reason, when they departed the scene, they were careless. They left things behind—the lamp, Pamela's skating rink card, her expensive watch. If these last two items hadn't been found, and if the dismemberment had been completed, identifying the corpse would have been considerably harder.

What happened to Pamela's heart, bladder, kidneys and liver? Perhaps for once the rumours had come close to the truth; perhaps the organs had been eaten by the *huang gou*. Or perhaps they had been thrown into the fetid canal that divided the Fox Tower from the Papermakers' District and Armour Factory Alley.

The men left swiftly, back across the stone bridge to the Wall Road, and from there into the Legation Quarter, to 3 Legation Street. Once they were in Prentice's apartment, they cleaned the blood off themselves. Aware that they could have left traces, the dentist had the whole place painted the following week, just to be on the safe side. Pamela's bicycle and ice skates, left there earlier that Thursday night, were quickly disposed of, perhaps at one of Peking's numerous flea markets, or dumped in the canal by the Fox Tower.

As it turned out, the men had more than a week in which to do all this before the police eventually came knocking at Prentice's door. The details taken care of, the men had nothing to do but wait. They waited knowing that Madam Leschinsky, Michael Consiglio and their working girls would keep their silence, that Capuzzo would ensure the Italian marines never talked, that the bathroom at number 28 had been thoroughly cleaned and any gruesome remains disposed of before the whole place was shuttered and closed down. They waited, knowing that the madam and her husband had left town and the prostitutes had scattered across China, with threats to keep their mouths shut.

Pamela meanwhile had remained on the freezing ground at the Fox Tower, her head to the west and her feet to the east, her watch stopped at a couple of minutes after midnight.

The Wound That Wouldn't Heal

*N*either the outbreak of World War II nor the long years of its duration deterred Werner from sending the evidence he obtained from his investigation to the British authorities. He continued to send this not only to the Foreign Office in Whitehall and to Archer and Clark Kerr in China but to the British foreign secretary, Edward Frederick Lindley Wood, better known as Viscount Halifax. He also copied in the parliamentary undersecretary of state for foreign affairs, Ivor Miles Windsor-Clive, the second Earl of Plymouth.

As for the Chinese authorities, no semblance of an independent police force remained in Peking. Chief Chen had been removed from Ch'ienmen and a puppet Chinese mayor and chief of police installed, a man who studiously ignored Werner's entreaties.

Some of the letters that Werner sent to the Foreign Office appear not to have been received, victims of the disruption of wartime postal services. But finally, in January 1943, someone in Whitehall read one of Werner's reports, and in a file memo noted:

If British administration of justice in China is to recover its good name, a case of this heinous nature cannot be merely pigeon-holed, "dropped" and forgotten. In any event, full unexpurgated detail must be made public in due course.

But being pigeonholed and forgotten was exactly the fate of Werner's evidence. It was shelved deep in the vaults of the Foreign Office, among countless other documents arriving in war-torn and blitzed London. Nobody ever contacted Werner about his correspondence. The case of the murder of his only daughter was never reopened.

And so she slipped from history. Foreign Peking was by now scattered to the four winds, fled to the far corners of the globe, as China and Japan locked horns and the whole world descended into a conflict that swallowed up the people who'd known Pamela.

Pamela's Tientsin boyfriend, Mischa Horjelsky, joined the U.S. Air Force and flew raids over occupied Europe until he was killed in action. His plane was shot down in the massive raids in the summer of 1943 that targeted the Nazi-held Ploesti oil fields in Romania.

Han Shou-ching, with whom Pamela had eaten her last meal, returned to his father's home in Mukden to join the Chinese resistance forces. He was captured by the dreaded Kempeitai in 1940 and executed.

In Tientsin many people continued to believe that Pamela's murderer was Sydney Yeates. When the headmaster and his family were bundled out of China, they hadn't even waited for the next boat to London, but rather sailed for Kobe and then San Francisco, after which they travelled overland to New York. From there they sailed to England. They arrived in Plymouth in March, with no home and no job for Yeates to go to. He never taught again, keeping a low profile as the headmaster's secretary at the City of Oxford Boys School, where he remained until his death in 1955 at the age of sixty-one.

With the Japanese occupation of Peking, Helen and Edgar Snow's radical journal *Democracy* was shut down. Helen later wrote in her memoir that although the Pamela Werner 'mystery was never solved or even reasonably guessed at ... I never really believed the murder was directed against Ed or me, yet there was always a question.' Edgar's *Red Star Over China*, published in 1938, was a worldwide sensation, while Helen's own record of her visits to the Communist bases, *Inside Red China*, was published a year later and became an important historical document.

The Snows' marriage became increasingly strained after the Japanese occupation. Helen returned to America in 1940, and the couple divorced in 1949. She spent the rest of her life in Connecticut, publishing her autobiography in 1984. She died in 1997, aged ninety.

Inspector Botham, accused of drunkenness, consorting with prostitutes and contamination of evidence while in Peking, was dismissed by DCI Dennis soon after returning to Tientsin. He and his wife departed for England. Sergeant Binetsky, whose wife was imprisoned by the Japanese in northern China, made it out of Tientsin to Rangoon, along with a number of other White Russians. There they enlisted in the British army and reputedly showed great courage in battle. It appears that Binetsky died in combat against the Japanese in Burma in October 1943. Meanwhile Commissioner Thomas had died in 1941 at the age of sixty-two, while still secretary of the Legation Quarter's administrative commission.

The fate of Colonel Han is a mystery. He remained at his post at Morrison Street during the early years of the occupation, but it seems he fell foul of the puppet regime installed at Peking police headquarters after being ordered to investigate an assassination attempt on the pro-Tokyo president of China, Wang Kemin, in March 1938. It was widely known that Tai Li had ordered the killing of Wang as an example to other would-be collaborators. When Han failed to uncover any evidence in the case, or bring anyone to trial, the Japanese assumed he was working for the Kuomintang.

Werner had continued to believe that Han was paid to steer the search for Pamela's murderer away from 28 Chuanpan Hutong. And yet Han had always appeared determined to catch the killer, and DCI Dennis for one had believed him to be a capable detective. In Werner's last communication with the colonel, a hurried conversation when they encountered one another on the street in 1938, Han apologised for never having obtained justice for Pamela. The question of the nature of the man's duplicity in the case was one Werner was never able to resolve.

As for DCI Richard Dennis, he was a marked man after the Tientsin Incident of 1939. When Japan attacked Pearl Harbor on 7 December 1941, London declared war in support of the United States, and in the early morning of 8 December, Dennis was arrested at his home by Japanese soldiers and taken to the Victoria Road police station. All across Tientsin his fellow officers were being rounded up and held at Gordon Hall, along with senior British diplomatic and municipal officials and army personnel.

Dennis was placed under house arrest and told to report daily to the Japanese. On 20 December he was formally stripped of his uniform and told that his services had been terminated and he was to remain under house arrest. And so he stayed, shut up in his home on Hong Kong Road, alone. His wife and son had returned to England in 1939, before the situation worsened.

On 4 May 1942 Dennis was arrested once again and this time imprisoned at the Japanese gendarmerie headquarters, a jail that had earned itself a fearsome reputation. He spent the next ninety-four days in solitary confinement, forbidden any communication with his fellow prisoners. The six-foot-plus Dennis was locked in a wooden cage measuring twelve foot by twelve foot. It had no furniture except a rudimentary toilet that he had to use in full view of the other prisoners in cages around him. He was not allowed to wash, or brush his teeth, and was fed only dry bread and water, and these at separate times so as to prevent him using the water to moisten the bread to make it edible. He was permitted just ten minutes' 'exercise' a day.

He was grilled regularly and for long periods, with the same repetitive questions. While he wasn't beaten, as many prisoners were, a bare bulb above his cage was left on day and night, depriving him of sleep. His cage was positioned next to the main interrogation room so that he was able to hear the screams of tortured prisoners at all hours.

During July 1942, temperatures soared to over 100° Fahrenheit for several weeks. Dirty, unshaven and lice-ridden, Dennis was photographed, and his picture published in a book produced by the Japanese entitled *Local Criminals Album*. At one point, he and his long-serving superintendent, Bill Greenslade, were taken from the jail, shackled and filthy, and made to stand on a flatbed truck. They were then driven around Tientsin on display, to reinforce Japanese 'superiority.' Crowds of Chinese stopped to watch in silence as the two well-known men were humiliated.

Dennis was accused of espionage. He protested his innocence. After repeated interrogation sessions in which he refused to admit guilt or betray his former colleagues, along with weeks in his cage with barely any food, he was eventually forced to sign a confession. It was in Japanese and was never translated for him.

In early August, the Swiss consul in Tientsin managed to secure Dennis's release and repatriation. In a greatly weakened state he was taken to Shanghai and put aboard an overcrowded evacuation ship to Lourenço Marques, in Portuguese East Africa. From there he was transferred to another ship bound for London. He was now too weak to stand and had lost thirty-four pounds in weight.

By the time he got back to London, he was unfit for active service and was allocated a desk job with the wartime Ministry of Food. After the war he was assigned to the United Nations War Crimes Commission and sent back to the Far East to work on the trials of senior Japanese military personnel, a list that included those who had imprisoned him in Tientsin. He returned again to England after the tribunals, where he divorced and remarried, and ran a hotel in West London called The Dennis, which had an active bridge club.

He ended up running several pubs in the area, and was regularly seen propping up the bar at the Chepstow Arms near Notting Hill Gate. Dick Dennis died in 1972 at seventy-five years of age.

狐 狸 精

Back in Peking the Badlands, including 28 Chuanpan Hutong, had kept running. Even in the depths of war and deprivation there was still a market for sex and narcotics, and there were those who found a way to flourish and profit. Some in the white underworld were protected by the Japanese, who continued to encourage the sale of narcotics to the Chinese.

Joe Knauf and Thomas Jack seemed to slip away from both the Japanese and from history. Dr Capuzzo, who had left for Italy shortly after Werner questioned him, returned to a country at war with Great Britain. What neither the police nor E. T. C. Werner knew at the time was that Capuzzo's roots into the Badlands and the Peking underworld went much deeper than they had imagined. As well as being a doctor attached to the Italian legation, Capuzzo had also owned a Badlands cabaret called the Roma, close to the Olympia and which was run for him by a half-Chinese, half-English manager who worked at many joints in the Badlands. During the Japanese occupation the Roma was burnt down and destroyed. John O'Brian was never tracked down by Werner or his agents, and was last heard to be living destitute in Shanghai's Frenchtown. The prostitutes Marie and Peggy both died before they could be interned by the Japanese, Marie of a heroin overdose and Peggy in an insane asylum in Harbin.

Madam Leschinsky and Michael Consiglio left Shanghai's Frenchtown for Japanese-controlled Tsingtao, with Leschinsky reportedly near death. George Gorman, the man who published his lies to protect Prentice, remained an overt mouthpiece for Japanese militarism as the editor of the *Peking Chronicle* until 1943, when he was repatriated to England. There he was immediately arrested and imprisoned under Defence Regulation 18B of the Emergency Powers Act, 1939, which allowed for the internment of people suspected of being Nazi sympathisers.

The White Russian hermaphrodite Shura evaded internment and spent much of the war in a Frenchtown brothel in Shanghai under a female identity. Shura was something of a legend in underworld circles. According to the Shanghai Municipal Police, he was a suspect in a major bank robbery in early 1937, and was also thought to be organising the smuggling of drugs from Japanese-occupied China to Shanghai, using gullible white women as mules. He was also believed to be a persistent and daring jewel thief, who in a long career spent only a matter of months in a Peking jail and thereafter was never caught again. Though rumour had it that Shura escaped to Hong Kong with a fortune in stolen gems, it seems he stayed in China and, rendered virtually penniless after the turmoil of the war, ended up in a hotel in Tientsin in the 1950s before leaving for Russia, a country he had not seen since he fled as a teenager. Shura, one of the last White Russians left in China, was eventually swallowed up by the USSR. His fate is unknown, though according to those who knew him in Tientsin in his final days in China, despite impoverishment and losing his figure, he remained a bohemian with a love of life to the end.

狐 狸 精

E. T. C. Werner remained in Armour Factory Alley until the bombing of Pearl Harbor, after which he was forced to move into the British Legation's compound. He was now a refugee in the place he had first come to as a student interpreter, more than half a century earlier.

Then, in March 1943, all Allied nationals remaining in Peking were rounded up by the Japanese for internment, or, as the Japanese officials put it, 'for their safety and comfort.' But the internment camps were neither safe nor comfortable. Along with others, Werner was sent two hundred miles south to Shantung province, to what Tokyo called the Weihsien Civilian Assembly Centre.

He was just one of many foreigners required to assemble at Peking Central Railway Station with no more than a single suitcase. They were a ragtag bunch—British, American, Australian and other nationalities; they were schoolteachers, businesspeople, dope addicts rousted from their garrets. That day they all travelled third class, by order of the Japanese military.

As the foreigners were marched to the waiting train, the Chinese residents of Peking were made to line up and witness the reduced state of Western power and prestige in China. It was too much for some of the internees—one man dropped dead of a heart attack on the spot and was left where he lay. Werner, with his own weak heart, had to leave behind the things that had defined his life—his books, papers, antiques, family heirlooms and mementos. He had to cease his investigation into his daughter's murder and was no longer able to make his pleas to the Foreign Office for the case to be reopened.

The Weihsien Civilian Assembly Centre was a former American Presbyterian mission. It was surrounded by sorghum fields and had an Edwardian-style church close to the huts, guard towers, machine-gun posts and electrified barbed wire. Two thousand foreign nationals were crammed inside with no plumbed toilets, so that a cesspool stench and swarms of flies pervaded. There were long queues for food, and when it rained the camp became a sea of mud, with walls collapsing and roofs leaking. There were pests aplenty, bedbugs and filth. The Shantung winter evenings were bitterly cold, the summer stiflingly humid.

Werner was allocated a bed in Block 47. His room—K—measured nine by twelve feet. Among the room's inmates was a tempestuous American ex-marine given to violent rages, a junkie called Briggs who was forced to go cold turkey in the camp, and, for a while, a young boy from Tientsin who had attended the grammar school and had known Pamela.

Werner was excused from work due to his age. He was also issued a green badge that gave him priority in the food queues. Once he settled in he gave daily lectures as part of the camp's activities program—'Chinese History from a Sociologist's Standpoint' was a lecture that one inmate remembered attending.

The camp was very mixed company—American missionaries, former marines, teachers, a sprinkling of Peking's underworld, now finally rounded up, and at least one former madam of a Badlands brothel, along with several of her daughters who'd worked as prostitutes in her establishment. There were several former managers of Badlands cabarets and nightclubs as well as several women who had been members of Shura's dancing troupe. There were also a number of British policemen from Tientsin who had served under DCI Dennis, and members of the British Municipal Council in Tientsin who had convened to deal with the problem of Sydney Yeates.

Most people in Weihsien knew who Werner was, and they knew about Pamela. One man in particular certainly did—the camp dentist and fellow internee, Wentworth Baldwin Prentice.

Prentice was kept busy. Poor nutrition led to gum disease, and toothpaste for the inmates was dried cuttlefish ground into a powder. Fillings consisted of copper amalgam, although bad teeth were usually just pulled. Prentice spent hours pumping the treadle that powered his drill, or trying to disinfect his equipment.

It's difficult to imagine just how hard it must have been for Werner to be locked up with the man he suspected of murdering his daughter. Some inmates later recalled him pointing at Prentice and calling out, 'You killed her, I know you killed Pamela. You did it.'

At other times he seemed to point to people at random. Some feared for his sanity, but he was forgiven his odd behaviour. His advanced years and tragic past, combined with internment, explained his actions to most.

Prentice himself continued to say nothing at all about the murder. He had perhaps found religion. He certainly gave religious books to several young boys who visited his makeshift surgery. Was it a genuine conversion, or a case of any reading matter in a time of shortage? Or was it evidence of a guilty conscience?

The U.S. authorities were certainly never persuaded of Prentice's moral standing. In August 1942, the newly formed Office of Strategic Services, America's wartime intelligence agency, had opened a file on Prentice to investigate his possible collaboration with the Japanese in Peking. But they never managed to gather any firm evidence. Once again, Prentice had got away with it.

And then, in August 1945, Weihsien was liberated by American forces as the Japanese scuttled out of China in defeat. The internees emerged malnourished and downtrodden. Imprisonment had broken many of the once wealthy and socially important inmates, those who had either been unable to leave China due to their official position or who had simply refused to read the writing on the wall of the Japanese invasion. Ripped from their lives, their grand houses and their elevated status in Peking and Tientsin, they had never adjusted to living in cramped barracks, using fetid toilets, queuing for meagre food rations, and clothing themselves in virtual rags. Many of the older prisoners had succumbed to disease, or simply given up and died.

But not Werner. Despite being in his eighties, he walked out of the camp and took the train home to Peking. He moved back into his old house on Armour Factory Alley, where his loyal staff had stayed on in order to stop squatters taking possession.

He found himself in a China that was irrevocably changed but still fighting a civil war. The Japanese were out of the picture, but the Nationalists and the Communists remained enemies. Peking had forgotten Pamela; the British Legation had forgotten Werner. He made several further enquiries to the Foreign Office and the legation, but they too were ignored. Werner's findings were a potential embarrassment to the British diplomats and officials in China, who'd worked so strenuously to close down his daughter's case and to discredit him. It was a pursuit into which they'd put far more effort than they ever did into solving the crime.

And then he stopped contacting them. Had his tenacity to see Pamela's killers brought to justice finally been exhausted? Or was it because of the death of Prentice, the man Werner believed most directly responsible for his daughter's death?

Prentice too had returned to Peking after Weihsien, and he died at his flat on Legation Street in July 1947, aged fifty-four. His relatively young age was perhaps Werner's one consolation.

Throughout the years of civil war, Werner stayed stubbornly on in Peking as Chiang Kai-shek's Nationalist army began its prolonged retreat. Eventually it crumbled, and the remnants of its forces fled with their generalissimo to the island of Taiwan. In January 1949 Mao

Tse-tung's forces claimed Peking for the Communists, and in October Werner became a resident of the newly proclaimed People's Republic of China. The new regime soon shuttered the brothels and opium dens and gambling joints of the Badlands for good.

By January 1951 Werner was one of just seventy British subjects left in the city, and by October the number had dwindled to thirty. An obstinate, independent man, Werner could find no accommodation with China's Communist rulers, and he finally decided to leave.

He returned to an England he hardly recognised, having not been back there since 1917. He had no family left—his closest relative, his sister Alice, had died in 1935. E.T.C. Werner eventually passed away on 7 February 1954 and was buried at Ramsgate in Kent. It seems that nobody who'd known him was left alive to attend the short service.

He had lived eighty-nine years. He had seen China as a dynasty with an emperor, as a republic with a generalissimo, and finally as a people's republic with a dictator. On 16 February the *Times* of London ran a lengthy and detailed obituary of his life, noting his long diplomatic career, his prolific contribution to the West's understanding of China, and his marriage to Gladys Nina Ravenshaw. Its final comment noted that 'their adopted daughter Pamela was murdered at the age of 20 in Peking.'

Pamela Werner's body now lies somewhere deep under modern Beijing's Second Ring Road, in what was once the British Cemetery. For these past seventy-odd years she has been what she claimed to have always been—alone.

The Fox Tower still looms over Armour Factory Alley, and over what is left of the messy rookery of *hutong* that were the Peking Badlands. It looms over the ancient Tartar Wall, where Pamela was found that freezing morning in January 1937. Only very elderly Pekingers call it the Fox Tower now; only the very old talk of fox spirits. Few, if any, are left who remember the day that the mutilated body of a foreign girl was found at its base.

Chinese mythology has it that when a fox spirit departs this world, its image flickers briefly before disappearing. The spirit's influence is rendered benign, and the world of mortals can finally begin the process of healing. Scars fade and disappear, blemishes and stains gradually recede, until no trace of them is left and life can return to normality. But this is merely illusion, for in reality everything has changed and nothing remains as it was before.

THE WRITING OF *MIDNIGHT IN PEKING*

*J*first read of Pamela Werner in a biography of the American journalist Edgar Snow, whose best-selling *Red Star Over China* introduced
Mao Tse-tung to the world in the late 1930s. A footnote made reference to Edgar's wife Helen feeling nervous after Pamela's mutilated
body was found not far from the Snows' house in Peking. Helen Foster Snow frequently bicycled home that way at night herself. The
footnote also mentioned fox spirits, a 'love cult,' the fact that Pamela's
father had once been a British consul in China, and that the murder
was never solved.

I put the book down and fell asleep, and in the morning the first
thing that came into my mind was the murder of Pamela Werner.
When something casually read remains in the front of your brain the
morning afterwards, it's usually the sign of a great tale.

Unable to get the story out of my head, I began tracking down
newspapers from the time, in archives in Beijing, Shanghai, Hong
Kong and London. I learned that the investigation had been jointly
handled by the Peking police and a British detective working in
China, a unique occurrence and a potentially fascinating collaboration

between a senior Chinese and a European detective. Some papers tantalisingly hinted at official interference in the investigation by the British Legation—a desperate attempt to save face by His Majesty's government in the Far East. The reports of Pamela's autopsy confirmed that this was a particularly nasty murder, one that had set both the Chinese and foreign rumour mills of Peking working overtime, and sparked paroxysms of fear in a city already jittery about an attack by the surrounding Japanese. Pamela's was one murder that seemed to presage thousands; an outrage in a city braced for much worse to follow.

All the details around the murder case were intriguing: an eccentric father with a colourful past, fox spirits running riot at night in the old Tartar City of Peking, the suggestion of illicit sex, a whiff of opium, whispers of scandal, a previously rarely mentioned underclass of criminal and corrupt foreigners in the city, the purposeful obfuscation by pompous British diplomats and the terrible lack of final justice in the case. All taking place against a backdrop of a doomed China slipping inexorably into wholesale war, which was followed by the drawing tight of the bamboo curtain under Mao. Pamela Werner had been forgotten by everyone a long time ago, it seemed.

It was when I came across a photo of her, on a cold morning in the British Library's newspaper archives in north London, that I knew her story had to be told. I started writing. And then, by chance, while tying up the loose ends of some research in Britain's National Archive at Kew, I stumbled across an uncatalogued file in one of several dozen boxes of random correspondence sent from Peking during the years 1941–45. The letters in the file had been recorded, acknowledged, filed and forgotten. There were some 150 pages of close type, with handwriting added by the author in the margins.

It took a while to work out what it all was: the details of the private investigation E. T. C. Werner had conducted after the official one was halted. Peking was by then occupied by the Japanese, yet Werner's search uncovered more than the detectives had found; it answered questions that they had been unable to, settling nagging doubts and bringing more to light than the official inquest ever did. It took these lost letters of Werner's to bring Pamela's murder into focus for me.

In the course of writing this book I travelled to the foreign treaty ports where Werner once served; to the backstreets of Shanghai's Frenchtown, where so many of the accused and guilty fled; and to Tianjin (Tientsin), where Pamela had gone to boarding school and where other scandals dwelt. Naturally I spent time in Beijing attempting to penetrate the increasingly glitzy and modern exterior of the Chinese capital, looking for traces of that prewar, prerevolutionary city—the former Legation Quarter, the once infamous Badlands, the *hutong* of the old Tartar City and the Fox Tower. Remarkably, most of the key locations in Pamela's life and story remain, despite the massive disruption and construction in Beijing in the past three decades. I made contact with the few remaining people around the world who remembered Pamela. I rechecked every false scent and misguided trail, every officious injunction from the British authorities.

I came to agree with Werner's conclusion, and I reconstructed the events of his daughter's final night, in the chapter 'Invitation to a Party,' using his findings. From the start, I thought it important that Pamela Werner not be forgotten, and that some sort of justice, however belated, be awarded her.

—PAUL FRENCH, SHANGHAI, 2011

ACKNOWLEDGEMENTS

*M*y reconstruction of the investigation into Pamela Werner's murder is based on medical records, press reports, Peking police reports, and letters written by officials of Scotland Yard, as well as documents produced by and for the International Military Tribunal for the Far East after the war; these latter are held in Singapore. It also draws on various documents from the British Legation in Peking, the consulate in Tientsin, and the embassy temporarily located at Shanghai, along with the recollections of people who knew Pamela in Peking or at Tientsin Grammar School.

Most helpful were the copious notes sent by E. T. C. Werner to the Foreign Office in London, detailing his private investigation after the case was officially closed in July 1937. I came across these letters in an uncatalogued file in Britain's National Archive at Kew, in one of several dozen boxes of random correspondence sent from Peking during the years 1941–45.

Any number of experts on and former residents of Old Peking and Tientsin offered me help most graciously and enthusiastically, among them Eric Abrahamson, Jacob Avshalomov, Michael Aldrich,

Julia Boyd, Luby Bubeshko, Dora Chun, Ron Dworkin, Robin Farmer, Jim Hoare, Ed Lanfranco, Greg Leck, Desmond Power, R. Stevenson Upton, Joan Ward, Adam Williams and Frances Wood. Much gratitude also to Diana Dennis, the daughter-in-law of Detective Chief Inspector Dennis. Thanks also to Lucy Cavender, Peter Goff and Alexandra Pearson, who offered me a chance to write a shorter version of this story for their collection *Beijing: Portrait of a City*.

Librarians are essential, and I have to thank the helpful staff of the following: the British Library's Chinese Collection, the British Library Newspaper Archives at Colindale, the National Archives at Kew, the Shanghai Library Bibliotheca Zikawei, Hong Kong University Library, the Churchill Archives Centre in Cambridge, and the School of Oriental and African Studies at the University of London.

Grateful thanks to all at Penguin China, especially Jo Lusby, who commissioned this project and then gave up so much of her time and energy to see it to a conclusion, as well as all her staff at Penguin China, especially Abi Howell in Beijing and Mike Tsang in Shanghai. My editor Meredith Rose at Penguin Australia pulled apart and then put together the original manuscript with the skill of a surgeon. Arwen Summers diligently copyedited it and saved me from many potential gaffes. Any remaining errors are entirely the fault of the author. I must also thank Joel Rickett at Penguin in London as well as Stephen Morrison and Emily Murdock Baker at Penguin in New York for taking up Pamela's story so enthusiastically.

Finally, as always, to Lisa (Xu Ni), who was never anything less than totally supportive and who, I hope, will one day finally realise how much her support means to me.

SOURCES

Text

8   'fish in an aquarium': Peter Fleming, *News from Tartary* (London: Jonathan Cape, 1936).

38   all details of Pamela's autopsy: *North-China Daily News*, 30 February 1937; *China Weekly Review*, 13 February 1937.

44   'No comment': Ibid.

47   Desk sergeant: 'What did you do?': Anthony Abbot, *These Are Strange Tales* (Philadelphia: John C. Winston, 1948).

57   'But aren't you afraid': *China Press*, 9 January 1937.

66   'Dig around a bit': *Times* (London), 11 January 1937.

83   'The socially popular man': Abbot, *Strange Tales*.

85   South to the Temple of Heaven: Ibid.

86   'We were to return to England': Ibid.

94 *Unfortunately we have a very:* Lo Hui-min, *The Correspondence of G.E. Morrison,* 2 vols. (Cambridge, U.K.: Cambridge University Press, 1976).

99 *'like a frightened sparrow':* Abbot, *Strange Tales.*

101 *'When you and I beyond the veil':* Ibid.

101 *'inexplicable act of God':* E.T.C. Werner, *Autumn Leaves* (Shanghai: Kelly & Walsh, 1928).

102 *'beneath the trees and flowers':* Ibid.

103 *'The search for the motive':* Jeffrey Bloomfield, 'The Rise and Fall of Basil Thomson, 1861–1939,' *Journal of the Police History Society* 12 (1997): 11–19.

105 *'reluctant to talk':* Times (London), 13 January 1937.

106 *'Optimism prevails':* North-China Daily News, 13 January 1937.

107 *'I will do my best to':* North-China Daily News, 11 January 1937.

108 *'They've got a foreigner with blood':* China Press, 14 January 1937.

112 *'Can you tell us where you were':* Ibid.

113 *HUMAN MUTILATOR OF:* China Press, 11 January 1937.

121 *'Let's talk about the Western Hills':* Abbot, *Strange Tales.*

122 *'dubious background':* North-China Daily News, 14 January 1937.

127 *'dapper':* Jacob Avshalomov and Aaron Avshalomov, *Avshalomov's Winding Way: Composers Out of China—A Chronicle* (Bloomington, Ind.: Xlibris Corporation, 2001).

130 *'not of a placid nature':* China Weekly Review, 20 March 1937.

131 *Mr EC Peters—Chairman* and *In 1927 he became Headmaster:* Peking and Tientsin Times, 23 March 1937.

134 *The old man did it:* Abbot, *Strange Tales.*

140 *'Not in sociology, myths'*: Ibid.

140 *'In view of circumstances'*: Document F3453/1510/10 (Far Eastern), the National Archives, Kew, U.K.

141 *'Remember, you have no powers'*: Ibid.

143 *'Prentice, Miss—Nov. 28'*: U.S. State Department Document 393.1115/14, National Archives and Records Administration, Washington, D.C.

144 *'I have never seen the girl,'* and all details of interview with Prentice: Document F3453/1510/10.

144 *'teeth—healthy—26 present'*: North-China Daily News, 3 February 1937.

145 Gorman's editorial: *Peking Chronicle*, 13 January 1937.

153 *'not the work of an ordinary'*: North-China Herald, 10 February 1937.

154 *'living on the rim of a volcano'*: John B. Powell, *My Twenty-Five Years in China* (New York: Macmillan, 1945).

156 *'It was me they were after'*: All details of Dennis's meeting with Helen Foster Snow are from Snow, *My China Years* (New York: William Morrow & Co., 1984).

168 *'The evidence is inconclusive'*: North-China Herald, 30 June 1937.

173 *'I shall not let the matter rest'*: National Archives, op. cit.

173 *The sight of my child's kind little face* and *'apart from the herd'*: Times (London), 16 February 1954.

176 *This is to confirm my statement*: Document F3453/1510/10.

178 *'made love'*: Document F5480/1510/10 (Far Eastern), National Archives, Kew.

179 *'You are on the wrong track'*: Ibid.

180   *'Are you Mr Werner?'* and details of Werner's meeting with the White Russian girl: Document F3435/1510/10.

185   *'frog walking'*: Doc. F5480/1510/10.

188   *impressed him as being true'*: Ibid.

192   *This particular line of enquiry*: Ibid.

192   *'Very flattering, but'* and *'exhausted lines of enquiry'*: Document F3435/1510/10.

192   *It is not necessary to read*: Ibid.

193   *'person of interest'*: Document F9120/1510/10 (Far Eastern), National Archives, Kew.

196   *'You heard of the murder,'* and details of Werner's interview with Rosie Gerbert: Document F12367/1510/10 (Far Eastern), National Archives, Kew.

198   *'Did the stout Russian,'* and details of Werner's interview with Liu Pao-chung: Ibid.

200   *'This is surely a crime'*: Ibid.

205   *'terrific thud,'* and details about Marie: Document F8038/1510/10 (Far Eastern), National Archives, Kew.

208   *'Is there anyone here'*: Ibid.

210   *'Murder of Pamela Werner'*: Ibid.

210   *'Prentice killed her;* Document F12367/1510/10 (Far Eastern), National Archives, Kew.

211   *'to lay his cards on the table'*: Ibid.

211   *'cringing politeness'*: Ibid.

214   *'When your daughter was killed'*: Ibid.

214   *'there is a marine who knows'*: Ibid.

216   *My first impression was:* Document F9120/1510/10.

218   *'one little Korean girl,'* and all details of Werner's interview with Knauf: Ibid.

227   *'connected with the murder'*: Ibid.

236   *If British administration of justice:* Document F714/714/10 (Far Eastern), National Archives, Kew.

236   *'mystery was never solved'*: Snow, *My China Years*.

241   *'for their safety and comfort'*: Greg Leck, *Captives of Empire: The Japanese Internment of Allied Civilians in China 1941–1945* (Philadelphia: Shandy Press, 2006).

243   *'You killed her'*: Desmond Power, former internee at Weihsien Civilian Assembly Centre, e-mail to the author.

PHOTOGRAPHS

The Badlands

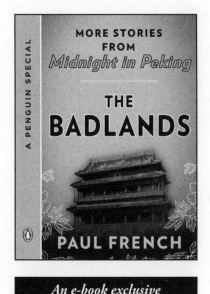

Paul French first discovered the Badlands while researching his bestselling *Midnight in Peking*. As the book was published in China, Australia, America, and the UK, the families and acquaintances of the people he had written about contacted him from around the globe, adding stories, recollections, and photos to his own research. The result is this short but potent portrait of a time and place now lost to history, here vividly brought to life.

An e-book exclusive

ISBN 978-1-101-62500-2

**PENGUIN
BOOKS**